Mastering SaltStack

Second Edition

Take charge of SaltStack to automate and configure your enterprise-grade environments

Joseph Hall

BIRMINGHAM - MUMBAI

Mastering SaltStack

Second Edition

First published: August 2015

Second edition: November 2016

Production reference: 1211116

Published by Packt Publishing Ltd.
Livery Place
35 Livery Street
Birmingham
B3 2PB, UK.
ISBN 978-1-78646-739-3

www.packtpub.com

Credits

Author
Joseph Hall

Reviewer
Peng Yao

Commissioning Editor
Kartikey Pandey

Acquisition Editor
Namrata Patil

Content Development Editor
Amedh Pohad

Technical Editor
Mohit Hassija

Copy Editor
Madhusudan Uchil

Project Coordinator
Judie Jose

Proofreader
Safis Editing

Indexer
Francy Puthiry

Production Coordinator
Shantanu N. Zagade

Foreword

The Mastering SaltStack book is one of my favorite Salt books. This book will get you past the basics of Salt and into what makes it a truly powerful automation framework. Tools like Salt Reactor, Thorium and Salt-SSH allow you to get the most out of Salt. The best ways to take Salt to the next level are revealed in this book, in an easy-to-understand way that will help you solve *your* problems.

Joseph Hall is likely the best person to write this book. He is not only a close friend, but has also been involved with the Salt project from the very beginning, including the early design of the Salt States system. Joseph is the second person to write code for Salt (apart from me). He was the first engineer hired by SaltStack.

Thomas S. Hatch

Founder and CTO, SaltStack

About the Author

Starting as a support technician and progressing to being a web programmer, QA engineer, systems administrator, Linux instructor, and cloud engineer, **Joseph Hall** has touched just about every area of the modern technology world. He is currently a senior cloud and integrations engineer at SaltStack. Joseph enjoys working with some of the best minds in the business with his coworkers and SaltStack's partners. He is also the author of *Extending SaltStack, Packt Publishing*.

You can find him on LinkedIn at `https://www.linkedin.com/in/techhat` and on GitHub at `https://github.com/techhat`.

About the Reviewer

Peng Yao is an operations engineer. He is the founder and coordinator of the China SaltStack User Group. He translated Mastering SaltStack to Chinese.

www.PacktPub.com

For support files and downloads related to your book, please visit www.PacktPub.com.

Did you know that Packt offers eBook versions of every book published, with PDF and ePub files available? You can upgrade to the eBook version at www.PacktPub.com and as a print book customer, you are entitled to a discount on the eBook copy. Get in touch with us at service@packtpub.com for more details.

At www.PacktPub.com, you can also read a collection of free technical articles, sign up for a range of free newsletters and receive exclusive discounts and offers on Packt books and eBooks.

https://www.packtpub.com/mapt

Get the most in-demand software skills with Mapt. Mapt gives you full access to all Packt books and video courses, as well as industry-leading tools to help you plan your personal development and advance your career.

Why subscribe?

- Fully searchable across every book published by Packt
- Copy and paste, print, and bookmark content
- On demand and accessible via a web browser

Table of Contents

Preface

I'm very excited to have been given the chance to put this book together. I've been given the rare opportunity to watch Salt grow from an idea in the brain of Tom Hatch to an award-winning open source project, and onward to the flagship product of an award-winning open source company. Salt has become an incredibly powerful framework, which I wish I'd had access to years ago.

Every day, I learn something new about Salt. This book is a collection of a number of those things, aimed at the advanced user. Don't see it as the last word on any of the topics that it covers. Instead, see it as a guide on your journey to use this tool to its fullest potential.

As you read through this book, I hope that the ideas and examples in it inspire you to update and innovate your infrastructure.

What this book covers

Chapter 1, *Essentials Revisited*, takes a step back to a few of the basics inside of Salt. These concepts are critical to understanding many of the concepts discussed in this book, and many of them will be explored further in later chapters.

Chapter 2, *Diving into Salt Internals*, goes in depth with the management of Salt's own configuration files, how Salt's loader system works, before finally discussing the state compiler.

Chapter 3, *Managing States*, builds upon the state concepts from the previous chapter and goes on to discuss how Salt states can be compiled together to form a more cohesive solution for your organization.

Chapter 4, *Exploring Salt SSH*, will provide you with a basic understanding of Salt's SSH transport layer, before jumping into a more technical overview of the underlying components.

Chapter 5, *Managing Tasks Asynchronously*, explores some of the subsystems in Salt that are designed for handling tasks, which interact with each other to achieve an end goal.

Chapter 6, *Taking Advantage of Salt Information Systems*, looks at some of the subsystems in Salt that are designed entirely for data management. The functionality of these subsystems can be utilized by the master or minion, and sometimes both.

Chapter 7, *Taking Salt Cloud to the Next Level*, brings you an understanding of how Salt interacts with public clouds and how you can extend that interaction to achieve a more cohesive infrastructure definition.

Chapter 8, *Using Salt with REST*, covers using Salt to communicate over HTTP, both as a client and as a server. With these APIs in place, Salt can either be a cog in another system or be the system that manages the cogs.

Chapter 9, *Understanding the RAET and TCP Transports*, follows a very technical discussion of various transport layers, both inside and outside of Salt. If you are looking to move beyond the ZeroMQ transport, this chapter is for you.

Chapter 10, *Strategies for Scaling*, explores a number of subsystems designed to allow Salt to manage large-scale data centers. Even if you are managing a small infrastructure now, I would encourage you to take a look at the options available here: they may just help you rethink your existing infrastructure anyway.

Chapter 11, *Monitoring with Salt*, explores many of the ways that Salt can be used to extend your own monitoring system and even bring its own monitoring tools to the party.

Chapter 12, *Exploring Best Practices*, helps you know how to most effectively use Salt in a way that will not only lead to easy management for you, but also for those who work with or follow you.

Chapter 13, *Troubleshooting Problems*, talks about some of the ways that things can go wrong in Salt and what to do when that happens.

What you need for this book

While this book covers a lot of ground, the focus is on Salt. It is recommended that you use the latest version of Salt available to you, though most of the information is also relevant to older versions.

A number of other products and services are mentioned in this book and its examples. While the examples will be useful with those products and services, they are designed to still be generic enough to demonstrate the intended information without requiring the purchase or installation of or subscription to third-party entities.

Any hardware or platform that can support Salt may be used for the examples in this book that pertain to minion operations. The Salt master is not yet supported in a Windows environment, so any master-oriented examples will require a Linux or Unix environment.

Who this book is for

This book is ideal for IT professionals and ops engineers who already manage groups of servers but would like to expand their knowledge and gain expertise with SaltStack. This book explains the advanced features and concepts of Salt. A basic knowledge of Salt is required in order to get to grips with advanced Salt features.

Conventions

In this book, you will find a number of text styles that distinguish between different kinds of information. Here are some examples of these styles and an explanation of their meaning.

Code words in text, database table names, folder names, filenames, file extensions, pathnames, dummy URLs, user input, and Twitter handles are shown as follows: "Unix distributions will often use the `/usr/local/etc/salt/` directory instead, while Windows uses the `C:\salt\` directory."

A block of code is set as follows:

```
name: apache
os: RedHat, Debian, Ubuntu, Suse, FreeBSD
os_family: RedHat, Debian, Suse, FreeBSD
version: 201607
release: 1
minimum_version: 2015.8
top_level_dir: apache
summary: Formula for installing Apache
description: Formula for installing the Apache web server
optional: mod_perl
recommended: mod_ssl
```

Any command-line input or output is written as follows:

```
# mkdir -p /srv/salt/devenv/
```

New terms and **important words** are shown in bold. Words that you see on the screen, for example, in menus or dialog boxes, appear in the text like this: "On the main screen of the repository, you will see a button titled **Clone or download**."

Warnings or important notes appear in a box like this.

Tips and tricks appear like this.

Reader feedback

Feedback from our readers is always welcome. Let us know what you think about this book-what you liked or disliked. Reader feedback is important for us as it helps us develop titles that you will really get the most out of. To send us general feedback, simply e-mail feedback@packtpub.com, and mention the book's title in the subject of your message. If there is a topic that you have expertise in and you are interested in either writing or contributing to a book, see our author guide at www.packtpub.com/authors.

Customer support

Now that you are the proud owner of a Packt book, we have a number of things to help you to get the most from your purchase.

Errata

Although we have taken every care to ensure the accuracy of our content, mistakes do happen. If you find a mistake in one of our books-maybe a mistake in the text or the code-we would be grateful if you could report this to us. By doing so, you can save other readers from frustration and help us improve subsequent versions of this book. If you find any errata, please report them by visiting http://www.packtpub.com/submit-errata, selecting your book, clicking on the **Errata Submission Form** link, and entering the details of your errata. Once your errata are verified, your submission will be accepted and the errata will be uploaded to our website or added to any list of existing errata under the Errata section of that title.

To view the previously submitted errata, go to https://www.packtpub.com/books/content/support and enter the name of the book in the search field. The required information will appear under the **Errata** section.

Piracy

Piracy of copyrighted material on the Internet is an ongoing problem across all media. At Packt, we take the protection of our copyright and licenses very seriously. If you come across any illegal copies of our works in any form on the Internet, please provide us with the location address or website name immediately so that we can pursue a remedy.

Please contact us at copyright@packtpub.com with a link to the suspected pirated material.

We appreciate your help in protecting our authors and our ability to bring you valuable content.

Questions

If you have a problem with any aspect of this book, you can contact us at questions@packtpub.com, and we will do our best to address the problem.

1
Essentials Revisited

Salt is a very powerful remote automation framework. Before we delve into the more advanced topics that this book covers, it would be wise to go back and review a few essentials. In this chapter, we will cover the following topics:

- Using remote execution
- Basic SLS file tree structure
- Using states for configuration management
- Basics of grains, pillars, and templates

This book assumes that you already have root access on a device with a common distribution of Linux installed. The machine used in the examples in this book is running Ubuntu 14.04, unless stated otherwise. Most examples should run on other major distributions, such as recent versions of Fedora, RHEL 5/6/7, Suse, or Arch Linux.

Executing commands remotely

The underlying architecture of Salt is based on the idea of executing commands remotely. This is not a new concept; all networking is designed around some aspect of remote execution. This could be as simple as asking a remote web server to display a static Web page, or as complex as using a shell session to interactively issue commands against a remote server.

Under the hood, Salt is a more complex example of remote execution. But whereas most Internet users are used to interacting with only one server at a time (so far as they are aware), Salt is designed to allow users to explicitly target and issue commands to multiple machines directly.

Master and minions

Salt is based around the idea of a master, which controls one or more minions. Commands are normally issued from the master to a target group of minions, which then execute the tasks specified in the commands and return any resulting data back to the master.

Targeting minions

The first facet of the `salt` command is targeting. A target must be specified with each execution, which matches one or more minions. By default, the type of target is a *glob*, which is the style of pattern matching used by many command shells. Other types of targeting are also available, by adding a flag. For instance, to target a group of machines inside a particular subnet, the `-S` option is used:

```
# salt -S 192.168.0.0/24 test.ping
```

The following are most of the available target types, along with some basic usage examples. Not all target types are covered here; *Range*, for example, extends beyond the scope of this book. However, the most common types are covered.

Glob

This is the default target type for Salt, so it does not have a command line option. The minion ID of one or more minions can be specified, using shell wildcards if desired.

When the `salt` command is issued from most command shells, wildcard characters must be protected from shell expansion:

```
# salt '*' test.ping
# salt \* test.ping
```

When using Salt from an API or from other user interfaces, quoting and escaping wildcard characters is generally not required.

Perl Compatible Regular Expression (PCRE)

Short Option: `-E`

Long Option: `--pcre`

When more complex pattern matching is required, a **Perl Compatible Regular Expression (PCRE)** can be used. This type of targeting was added to the earliest versions of Salt, and was meant largely to be used inside shell scripts. However, its power can still be realized from the command line:

```
# salt -E '^[m|M]in.[e|o|u]n$' test.ping
```

List

Short Option: `-L`

Long Option: `--list`

This option allows multiple minions to be specified as a comma-separated list. The items in this list do not use pattern matching such as globbing or regular expressions; they must be declared explicitly:

```
# salt -L web1,web2,db1,proxy1 test.ping
```

Subnet

Short Option: `-S`

Long Option: `--ipcidr`

Minions may be targeted based on a specific IPv4 or an IPv4 subnet in CIDR notation:

```
# salt -S 192.168.0.42 test.ping
# salt -S 192.168.0.0/16 test.ping
```

As of Salt version 2016.3, IPv6 addresses cannot be targeted by a specific command line option. However, there are other ways to target IPv6 addresses. One way is to use *grain* matching.

Grain

Short Version: `-G`

Long Version: `--grain`

Salt can target minions based on individual pieces of information that describe the machine. This can range from the OS to CPU architecture to custom information (covered in more detail later in this chapter). Because some network information is also available as grains, IP addresses can also be targeted this way.

Since grains are specified as key/value pairs, both the name of the key and the value must be specified. These are separated by a colon:

```
# salt -G 'os:Ubuntu' test.ping
# salt -G 'os_family:Debian' test.ping
```

Some grains are returned in a multi-level dictionary. These can be accessed by separating each key of the dictionary with a colon:

```
# salt -G 'ip_interfaces:eth0:192.168.11.38'
```

Grains which contain colons may also be specified, though it may look strange. The following will match the local IPv6 address (::1). Note the number of colons used:

```
# salt -G 'ipv6:::1' test.ping
```

Grain PCRE

Short Version: (not available)

Long Version: --grain-pcre

Matching by grains can be powerful, but the ability to match by a more complex pattern is even more so.

```
# salt --grain-pcre 'os:red(hat|flag)' test.ping
```

Pillar

Short Option: -I

Long Option: --pillar

It is also possible to match based on pillar data. Pillars are described in more detail later in the chapter, but for now we can just think of them as variables that look like grains.

```
# salt -I 'my_var:my_val' test.ping
```

Compound

Short Option: -C

Long Option: --compound

Compound targets allow the user to specify multiple target types in a single command. By default, globs are used, but other target types may be specified by preceding the target with the corresponding letter followed by the @ sign:

Letter	Target
G	Grains
E	PCRE minion ID
P	PCRE grains
L	List
I	Pillar
J	Pillar PCRE
S	Subnet/IP address
R	SECO range

The following command will target the minions that are running Ubuntu, have the role pillar set to web, and are in the 192.168.100.0/24 subnet.

```
# salt -C 'G@os:Ubuntu and I@role:web and S@192.168.100.0/24' test.ping
```

Boolean grammar may also be used to join target types, including and, or, and not operators.

```
# salt -C 'min* or *ion' test.ping
# salt -C 'web* or *qa and G@os:Arch' test.ping
```

Nodegroup

Short Option: -N

Long Option: --nodegroup

While nodegroups are used internally in Salt (all targeting ultimately results in the creation of an on-the-fly nodegroup), it is much less common to explicitly use them from the command line. Node groups must be defined as a list of targets (using compound syntax) in the Salt master's configuration before they can be used from the command line. Such a configuration might look like the following:

```
nodegroups:
  webdev: 'I@role:web and G@cluster:dev'  webqa: 'I@role:web and
G@cluster:qa'  webprod: 'I@role:web and G@cluster:prod'
```

Once a nodegroup is defined and the master configuration reloaded, it can be targeted from Salt:

```
# salt -N webdev test.ping
```

Using module functions

After a target is specified, a function must be declared. The preceding examples all use the `test.ping` function but, obviously, other functions are available. Functions are actually defined in two parts, separated by a period:

```
<module> . <function>
```

Inside a Salt command, these follow the `target`, but precede any arguments that might be added for the function:

```
salt <target> <module>.<function> [arguments...]
```

For instance, the following Salt command will ask all minions to return the text, `"Hello world"`:

```
salt '*' test.echo 'Hello world'
```

A number of execution modules ship with the core Salt distribution, and it is possible to add more. Version 2016.3 of Salt ships with around 400 execution modules. Not all modules are available for every platform; in fact, by design, some modules will only be available to the user if they are able to detect the required underlying functionality.

For instance, all functions in the test module are necessarily available on all platforms. These functions are designed to test the basic functionality of Salt and the availability of minions. Functions in the Apache module, however, are only available if the necessary commands are located on the minion in question.

Execution modules are the basic building blocks of Salt; other modules in Salt use them for their heavy lifting. Because execution modules are generally designed to be used from the command line, an argument for a function can usually be passed as a string. However, some arguments are designed to be used from other parts of Salt. To use these arguments from the command line, a Python-like data structure is emulated using a JSON string.

This makes sense, since Salt is traditionally configured using YAML, and all JSON is syntactically-correct YAML. Be sure to surround the JSON with single quotes on the command line to avoid shell expansion, and use double quotes inside the string. The following examples will help.

A list is declared using brackets:

```
'["item1","item2","item3"]'
```

A dictionary is declared using braces (that is, curly brackets):

```
'{"key1":"value1","key2":"value2","key3":"value3"}'
```

A list can include a dictionary, and a dictionary can include a list:

```
'[{"key1":"value1"},{"key2":"value2"}]'
'{"list1":["item1","item2"],"list2":["item3","item4"]}'
```

There are a few modules which can be considered core to Salt, and a handful of functions in each that are widely used.

test.ping

This is the most basic Salt command. Ultimately, it only asks the minion to return *True*. This function is widely used in documentation because of its simplicity, and to check whether a minion is responding. Don't worry if a minion doesn't respond right away; that doesn't necessarily mean it's down. A number of variables could cause a slower-than-usual return. However, successive failed attempts may be cause for concern.

test.echo

This function does little more than the test.ping command; it merely asks the minion to echo back a string that is passed to it. A number of other functions exist that perform similar tasks, including test.arg, test.kwarg, test.arg_type, and test.arg_repr.

test.sleep

A slightly more advanced testing scenario may require a minion to sleep for a number of seconds before returning *True*. This is often used to test or demonstrate the utilities that make use of the jobs system. The `test.rand_sleep` function is also useful for test cases where it is desirable to check the return from a large number of minions, with the return process spread out.

test.version

In a large enough infrastructure, a number of minions are bound to be running in a different version of Salt than others. When troubleshooting issues specific to certain versions of Salt, it helps to be able to take a quick look at the Salt version on each minion. This is the simplest way to check that. Checking the version of other packages that are maintained by the system packaging system can be performed with `pkg.version`.

pkg.install

Every package manager in Salt (as of version 2016.3) supports installing a package. This function can be as simple as asking for a single package name, or as complex as passing through a list of packages, each with a specific version. When using an execution module, you generally do not need to specify more than just a single package name, but inside the state module (covered later) the advanced functionality becomes more important.

pkg.remove

This matches the `pkg.install` function, allowing a certain package to be removed. Because versions are not so important when removing packages, this function doesn't get so complex. But it does allow passing a list of packages to be removed (using the `pkgs` argument) as a Python list. From the command line, this can be done using a JSON string.

file.replace

The `sed` command is one of the oldest members of the Unix administrator's toolkit. It has been the go-to command largely for tasks that involve editing files inline, and performing search and replace tasks. There have been a few attempts over the years to duplicate the functionality of the `sed` command. Initially, the `file.sed` function simply wrapped the Unix `sed` command. The `file.psed` function provided a Python-based replacement. However, `sed` is more than just a find/replace tool; it is a full language that can be problematic when used incorrectly. The `file.replace` function was designed from the ground up to provide the find/replace functionality that most users need, while avoiding the subtle nuances that can be caused by wrapping `sed`.

Other file functions

A number of common Unix commands have been added to the `file` function. The following functions complement the Unix command set for managing files and their metadata: `file.chown`, `file.chgrp`, `file.get_mode`, `file.set_mode`, `file.link`, `file.symlink`, `file.rename`, `file.copy`, `file.move`, `file.remove`, `file.mkdir`, `file.makedirs`, `file.mknod`, and a number of others.

Various user and group functions

The Unix toolset for managing users and groups is also available in Salt and includes `user.add`, `user.delete`, `user.info`, `group.add`, `group.delete`, `group.info`, `user.chuid`, `user.chgid`, `user.chshell`, `user.chhome`, `user.chgroups`, and many, many more.

sys.doc

By design, every public function in every execution module must be self-documenting. The documentation that appears at the top of the function should contain a description just long enough to describe the general use of the function, and must include at least one CLI example demonstrating the usage of that function.

This documentation is available from the minion using the `sys.doc` function. Without any arguments, it will display all the functions available on a particular minion. Adding the name of a module will show only the available functions in that module, and adding the name of a function will show only the documentation for that function, if it is available. This is an extremely valuable tool, both for providing simple reminders of how to use a function and for discovering which modules are available.

SLS file trees

There are a few subsystems in Salt that use an SLS file tree. The most common one of course is `/srv/salt/`, which is used for Salt states. Right after states are pillars (`/srv/pillar/`), which use a different file format but the same directory structure. Let's take a moment to talk about how these directories are put together.

SLS files

SLS stands for Salt State, which was the first type of file inside Salt to use this kind of file structure. While SLS files can be rendered in a number of different formats, by far the widest use is the default, YAML. Various templating engines are also available to help form the YAML (or other data structure) and again, the most popular is the default, Jinja.

Keep in mind that Salt is all about data. YAML is a serialization format that in Python, represents a data structure in a dictionary format. When thinking about how SLS files are designed, remember that they are a key/value pair: each item has a unique key, which is used to refer to a value. The value can in turn contain a single item, a list of items, or another set of key/value pairs.

The key to a stanza in an SLS file is called an ID. If no name inside the stanza is explicitly declared, the ID is copied to the name. Remember that IDs must be globally unique; duplicate IDs will cause errors.

Tying things together with top files

Both the state and the pillar system use a file called `top.sls` to pull the SLS files together and serve them to the appropriate minions, in the appropriate environments.

Each key in a `top.sls` file defines an environment. Typically, a base environment is defined, which includes all the minions in the infrastructure. Then other environments are defined that contain only a subset of the minions. Each environment includes a list of the SLS files that are to be included. Take the following `top.sls` file:

```
base:
  '*':
      - common
      - vim
qa:
  '*_qa':
      - jenkins
web:
  'web_*':
      - apache2
```

With this `top.sls`, three environments have been declared: `base`, `qa`, and `web`. The base environment will execute the `common` and `vim` states across all minions. The `qa` environment will execute the `jenkins` state across all the minions whose ID ends with `_qa`. The web environment will execute the `apache2` state across all the minions whose ID starts with `web_`.

Organizing the SLS directories

SLS files may be named either as an SLS file themselves (that is, `apache2.sls`) or as an `init.sls` file inside a directory with the SLS name (that is, `apache2/init.sls`).

 Note that `apache2.sls` will be searched for first; if it is not there, then `apache2/init.sls` will be used.

SLS files may be hierarchical, and there is no imposed limit on how deep directories may go. When defining deeper directory structures, each level is appended to the SLS name with a period (that is, `apache2/ssl/init.sls` becomes `apache2.ssl`). It is considered best practice by developers to keep a directory more shallow; don't make your users search through your SLS tree to find things.

Using states for configuration management

The files inside the /srv/salt/ directory define the Salt states. This is a configuration management format that enforces the state that a minion will be in: package X needs to be installed, file Y needs to look a certain way, service Z needs to be enabled and running, and so on. For example:

```
apache2:
  pkg:
    - installed
  service:
    - running
  file:
    - name: /etc/apache2/apache2.conf
```

States may be saved in a single SLS file, but it is far better to separate them into multiple files, in a way that makes sense to you and your organization. SLS files can use include blocks that pull in other SLS files.

Using include blocks

In a large SLS tree, it often becomes reasonable to have SLS files include other SLS files. This is done using an include block, which usually appears at the top of an SLS file:

```
include:
  - base
  - emacs
```

In this example, the SLS file in question will replace the include block with the contents of base.sls (or base/init.sls) and emacs.sls (or emacs/init.sls). This imposes some important restrictions on the user. Most importantly, the SLS files that are included may not contain IDs that already exist in the SLS file that includes them.

It is also important to remember that include itself, being a top-level declaration, cannot exist twice in the same file. The following is invalid:

```
include:
  - base
include:
  - emacs
```

Ordering with requisites

State SLS files are unique among configuration management formats in that they are both declarative and imperative. They are imperative, as each state will be evaluated in the order in which it appears in the SLS file. They are also declarative because states may include requisites that change the order in which they are actually executed. For instance:

```
web_service:
  service.running:
    - name: apache2
    - require:
      - pkg: web_package
web_package:
  pkg.installed:
    - name: apache2
```

If a service is declared, which requires a package that appears after it in the SLS file, the `pkg` states will be executed first. However, if no requirements are declared, Salt will attempt to start the service before installing the package, because its codeblock appears before the `pkg` codeblock. The following will require two executions to complete properly:

```
web_service:
  service.running:
    - name: apache2
web_package:
  pkg.installed:
    - name: apache2
```

Requisites point to a list of items elsewhere in the SLS file that affect the behavior of the state. Each item in the list contains two components: the name of the module and the ID of the state being referenced.

The following requisites are available inside Salt states and other areas of Salt that use the state compiler.

require

The `require` requisite is the most basic; it dictates that the state that it is declared in is not executed until every item in the list that has been defined for it has executed successfully. Consider the following example:

```
apache2:
  pkg:
    - installed
    - require
```

```
           - file: apache2
      service:
         - running
         - require:
           - pkg: apache2
      file:
         - managed
         - name: /etc/apache2/apache2.conf
         - source: salt://apache2/apache2.conf
```

In this example, a file will be copied to the minion first, then a package installed, then the service started. Obviously, the service cannot be started until the package that provides it is installed. But Debian-based operating systems such as Ubuntu automatically start services the moment they're installed, which can be problematic if the default configuration files aren't correct. This state will ensure that Apache is properly configured before it is even installed.

watch

In the preceding example, a new minion will be properly configured the first time. However, if the configuration file changes, the `apache2` service will need to be restarted. Adding a `watch` requisite to the service will force that state to perform a specific action when the state that it is watching reports changes.

```
apache2:
   ...SNIP...
   service:
      - running
      - require:
        - pkg: apache2
      - watch:
        - file: apache2
   ...SNIP...
```

The `watch` requisite is not available for every type of state module. This is because it performs a specific action, depending on the type of module. For instance, when a service is triggered with a `watch`, Salt will attempt to start a service that is stopped. If it is already running, it will attempt either a `reload: True`, `service.full_restart`, or `service.restart`, as appropriate.

As of version 2016.3, the following states modules support using the `watch` requisite: `service`, `pkg`, `cmd`, `event`, `module`, `mount`, `supervisord`, `docker`, `dockerng`, `etcd`, `tomcat`, and `test`.

onchanges

The `onchanges` requisite is similar to `watch`, except that it does not require any special support from the state module that is using it. If changes happen, which should only occur when a state completes successfully, then the list of items referred to with `onchanges` will be evaluated.

onfail

In a simple state tree, the `onfail` requisite is less commonly used. However, a more advanced state tree, which is written to attempt alerting the user, or to perform auto-correcting measures, can make use of `onfail`. When a state is evaluated and fails to execute correctly, every item listed under `onfail` will be evaluated. Assuming that the `PagerDuty` service is properly configured via Salt and an `apache_failure` state has been written to use it, the following state can notify the operations team if Apache fails to start:

```
apache2:
  service:
    - running
    - onfail
      - pagerduty: apache_failure
```

use

It is possible to declare default values in one state and then inherit them into another state. This typically occurs when one state file has an `include` statement that refers to another file.

If an item in the state that is being used has been redeclared, it will be overwritten with the new value. Otherwise, the item that is being used will appear unchanged. Requisites will not be inherited with `use`; only non-requisite options will be inherited. Therefore, in the following SLS, the `mysql_conf` state will safely inherit the `user`, `group`, and mode from the `apache2_conf` state, without also triggering Apache restarts:

```
apache2_conf:
  file:
    - managed
    - name: /etc/apache2/apache2.conf
    - user: root
    - group: root
    - mode: 755
    - watch_in:
      - service: apache2
```

```
mysql_conf:
file:
  - managed
    - name: /etc/mysql/my.cnf
    - use:
      - file: apache2_conf
    - watch_in:
      - service: mysql
```

prereq

There are some situations in which a state does not need to run, unless another state is expected to make changes. For example, consider a web application that makes use of Apache. When the codebase on a production server changes, Apache should be turned off, so as to avoid errors with the code that has not yet finished being installed.

The `prereq` requisite was designed exactly for this kind of use. When a state makes use of `prereq`, Salt will first perform a test run of the state to see if the items referred to in the `prereq` are expected to make changes. If so, then Salt will flag the state with the `prereq` as needing to execute.

```
apache2:
  service:
    - running
    - watch:
      - file: codebase
codebase:
  file:
    - recurse
...SNIP...
shutdown_apache:
  service:
    - dead
    - name: apache2
    - prereq:
      - file: codebase
```

In the preceding example, the `shutdown_apache` state will only make changes if the `codebase` state reports that changes need to be made. If they do, then Apache will shutdown, and then the `codebase` state will execute. Once it is finished, it will trigger the `apache2` service state, which will start up Apache again.

Inverting requisites

Each of the aforementioned requisites can be used inversely, by adding _in at the end. For instance, rather than state X requiring state Y, an SLS can be written so that state X declares that it is required by state Y, as follows:

```
apache2:
  pkg:
    - installed
    - require_in:
      - service: apache2
  service:
    - running
```

It may seem silly to add inverses of each of the states but there is in fact a very good use case for doing so: include blocks.

SLS files cannot use requisites that point to a code that does not exist inside them. However, using an include block will cause the contents of other SLS files to appear inside the SLS file. Therefore, generic (but valid) configuration can be defined in one SLS file, included in another, and modified to be more specific with a use_in requisite.

Extending SLS files

In addition to an include block, state SLS files can also contain an extend block that modifies SLS files that appear in the include block. Using an extend block is similar to a use requisite, but there are some important differences.

Whereas a use or use_in requisite will copy defaults to or from another state, the extend block will only modify the state that has been extended.

```
# cat /srv/generic_apache/init.sls
apache2_conf:
  file:
  - managed
    - name: /etc/apache2/apache2.conf
    - source: salt://apache2/apache2.conf
(In django_server/init.sls)
include:
- generic_apache
extend:
  apache2_conf:
    file:
    - source: salt://django/apache2.conf
```

```
(In image_server/init.sls)
include:
  - generic_apache
extend:
  apache2_conf:
    file:
      - source: salt://django/apache2.conf
```

The preceding example makes use of a generic Apache configuration file, which will be overridden as appropriate for either a Django server or a web server that is only serving images.

The basics of grains, pillars, and templates

Grains and pillars provide a means of allowing user-defined variables to be used in conjunction with a minion. Templates can take advantage of those variables to create files on a minion that are specific to that minion.

Before we get into details, let me start off by clarifying a couple of things: grains are defined by the minion which they are specific to, while pillars are defined on the master. Either can be defined statically or dynamically (this book will focus on static), but grains are generally used to provide data that is unlikely to change, at least without restarting the minion, while pillars tend to be more dynamic.

Using grains for minion-specific data

Grains were originally designed to describe the static components of a minion, so that execution modules could detect how to behave appropriately. For instance, minions which contain the *Debian os_family* grain are likely to use the apt suite of tools for package management. Minions which contain the *RedHat os_family* grain are likely to use yum for package management.

A number of grains will automatically be discovered by Salt. Grains such as *os*, *os_family*, *saltversion*, and *pythonversion* are likely to be always available. Grains such as *shell*, *systemd*, and *ps* are not likely to be available on, for instance, Windows minions.

Grains are loaded when the minion process starts up, and then cached in memory. This improves minion performance, because the Salt-minion process doesn't need to rescan the system for every operation. This is critical to Salt, because it is designed to execute tasks immediately, and not wait several seconds on each execution.

To discover which grains are set on a minion, use the `grains.items` function:

```
salt myminion grains.items
```

To look at only a specific grain, pass its name as an argument to `grains.item`:

```
salt myminion grains.item os_family
```

Custom grains can be defined as well. Previously, static grains were defined in the minion configuration file (`/etc/salt/minion` on Linux and some Unix platforms):

```
grains:
  foo: bar
  baz: qux
```

However, while this is still possible, it has fallen out of favor. It is now more common to define static grains in a file called grains (`/etc/salt/grains` on Linux and some Unix platforms). Using this file has some advantages:

- Grains are stored in a central, easy-to-find location
- Grains can be modified by the grains execution module

That second point is important: whereas the minion configuration file is designed to accommodate user comments, the grains file is designed to be rewritten by Salt as necessary. Hand-editing the grains file is fine, but don't expect any comments to be preserved. Other than not including the grains top-level declaration, the grains file looks like the grains configuration in the minion file:

```
foo: bar
baz: qux
```

To add or modify a grain in the grains file, use the `grains.setval` function:

```
salt myminion grains.setval mygrain 'This is the content of mygrain'
```

Grains can contain a number of different types of values. Most grains contain only strings, but lists are also possible:

```
my_items:
  - item1
  - item2
```

In order to add an item to this list, use the `grains.append` function:

```
salt myminion grains.append my_items item3
```

In order to remove a grain from the grains file, use the `grains.delval` function:

```
salt myminion grains.delval my_items
```

Centralizing variables with pillars

In most instances, pillars behave in much the same way as grains, with one important difference: they are defined on the master, typically in a centralized location. By default, this is the `/srv/pillar/` directory on Linux machines. Because one location contains information for multiple minions, there must be a way to target that information to the minions. Because of this, SLS files are used.

The `top.sls` file for pillars is identical in configuration and function to the `top.sls` file for states: first an environment is declared, then a target, then a list of SLS files that will be applied to that target:

```
base:
  '*':
    - bash
```

Pillar SLS files are much simpler than state SLS files, because they serve only as a static data store. They define key/value pairs, which may also be hierarchical.

```
skel_dir: /etc/skel/
role: web
web_content:
  images:
    - jpg
    - png
    - gif
  scripts:
    - css
    - js
```

Like state SLS files, pillar SLS files may also include other pillar SLS files.

```
include:
  - users
```

To view all pillar data, use the `pillar.items` function:

```
salt myminion pillar.items
```

Take note that in older versions of Salt, when running this command, by default the master's configuration data will appear as a pillar item called master. This can cause problems if the master configuration includes sensitive data. To disable this output, add the following line to the master configuration:

```
pillar_opts: False
```

Fortunately, this option defaults to False as of Salt version 2015.5.0. This is also a good time to mention that, outside the master configuration data, pillars are only viewable to the minion or minions to which they are targeted. In other words, no minion is allowed to access another minion's pillar data, at least by default. It is possible to allow a minion to perform master commands using the peer system, but that is outside the scope of this chapter.

Managing files dynamically with templates

Salt is able to use templates, which take advantage of grains and pillars, to make the state system more dynamic. A number of other templating engines are also available, including (as of version 2016.3) the following:

- jinja
- mako
- wempy
- cheetah
- genshi

These are made available via Salt's rendering system. The preceding list only contains renderers that are typically used as templates to create configuration files and the like. Other renderers are available as well, but are designed more to describe data structures:

- yaml
- yamlex
- json
- json5
- msgpack
- py
- pyobjects
- pydsl

Finally, the following Renderer can decrypt GPG data stored on the master, before passing it through another renderer:

- gpg

By default, state SLS files will be sent through the Jinja renderer, and then the yaml renderer. There are two ways to switch an SLS file to another renderer. First, if only one SLS file needs to be rendered differently, the first line of the file can contain a *shabang* line that specifies the renderer:

```
#!py
```

The shabang can also specify multiple Renderers, separated by pipes, in the order in which they are to be used. This is known as a render pipe. To use Mako and JSON instead of Jinja and YAML, use:

```
#!mako|json
```

To change the system default, set the renderer option in the master configuration file. The default is:

```
renderer: yaml_jinja
```

It is also possible to specify the templating engine to be used on a file that created the minion using the `file.managed` state:

```
apache2_conf:
  file:
    - managed
    - name: /etc/apache2/apache2.conf
    - source: salt://apache2/apache2.conf
    - template: jinja
```

A quick Jinja primer

Because Jinja is by far the most commonly-used templating engine in Salt, we will focus on it here. Jinja is not hard to learn, and a few basics will go a long way.

Variables can be referred to by enclosing them in double-braces. Assuming a grain is set called `user`, the following will access it:

```
The user {{ grains['user'] }} is referred to here.
```

Pillars can be accessed in the same way:

```
The user {{ pillar['user'] }} is referred to here.
```

However, if the `user` pillar or grain is not set, the template will not render properly. A safer method is to use the `salt` built-in to cross-call an execution module:

```
The user {{ salt['grains.get']('user', 'larry') }} is referred to here.
The user {{ salt['pillar.get']('user', 'larry') }} is referred to here.
```

In both of these examples, if the `user` has not been set, then `larry` will be used as the default.

We can also make our templates more dynamic by having them search through grains and pillars for us. Using the `config.get` function, Salt will first look inside the minion's configuration. If it does not find the requested variable there, it will check the grains. Then it will search pillar. If it can't find it there, it will look inside the master configuration. If all else fails, it will use the default provided.

```
The user {{ salt['config.get']('user', 'larry') }} is referred to here.
```

Codeblocks are enclosed within braces and percent signs. To set a variable that is local to a template (that is, not available via `config.get`), use the `set` keyword:

```
{% set myvar = 'My Value' %}
```

Because Jinja is based on Python, most Python data types are available. For instance, lists and dictionaries:

```
{% set mylist = ['apples', 'oranges', 'bananas'] %}
{% set mydict = {'favorite pie': 'key lime', 'favorite cake': 'saccher
torte'} %}
```

Jinja also offers logic that can help define which parts of a template are used, and how. Conditionals are performed using `if` blocks. Consider the following example:

```
{% if grains['os_family'] == 'Debian' %}
apache2:
{% elif grains['os_family'] == 'RedHat' %}
httpd:
{% endif %}
  pkg:
    - installed
  service:
    - running
```

The Apache package is called `apache2` on Debian-style systems, and `httpd` on RedHat-style systems. However, everything else in the state is the same. This template will auto-detect the type of system that it is on, install the appropriate package, and start the appropriate service.

Loops can be performed using `for` blocks, as follows:

```
{% set berries = ['blue', 'rasp', 'straw'] %}
{% for berry in berries %}
{{ berry }}berry
{% endfor %}
```

Summary

Salt is designed first and foremost for remote execution. Most tasks in Salt are performed as a type of remote execution. One of the most common types of remote execution in Salt is configuration management, using states. Minion-specific data can be declared in grains and pillars, and used in state files and templates.

With a basic foundation of Salt behind us, let's move on to the good stuff. In the next chapter, we will dive into the internals of Salt, and discuss why and how Salt does what it does.

2
Diving into Salt Internals

Now that we have covered the basic concepts, it's time to start looking at how Salt works under the hood. In this chapter, we will:

- Discover how Salt manages configuration files
- Look at how the renderer system works
- Discuss how the loader system handles modules
- Explore the state compiler, which drives so much of Salt

With a more comprehensive understanding of the internals of Salt, you will be able to craft configurations and states that take advantage of the architectural decisions that inspired the design of Salt.

Understanding the Salt configuration

One of the basic ideas around the Salt configuration is that a configuration management system should require as little configuration as possible. A concerted effort has been made by the developers to assign defaults that will apply to as many deployments as possible while still allowing users to fine-tune the settings to their own needs.

If you are just starting with Salt, you may not need to change anything. In fact, most of the time, the `master` configuration will be exactly what is needed for a small installation, while minions will require almost no changes, if any.

Following the configuration tree

By default, most operating system (primarily Linux-based ones) will store the Salt configuration in the `/etc/salt/`ms (primarily Linux-based ones) will store the Salt configuration in the `/etc/salt/` directory. Unix distributions will often use the `/usr/local/etc/salt/` directory instead, while Windows uses the `C:\salt\` directory. These locations were chosen in order to follow the design most commonly used by the operating system in question while still using a location that was easy to make use of. For the purpose of this book, we will refer to the `/etc/salt/`directory, but you can go ahead and replace it with the correct directory for your operating system.

There are other paths that Salt makes use of as well. Various caches are typically stored in `/var/cache/salt/`, sockets are stored in `/var/run/salt/`, and state trees, pillar trees, and reactor files are stored in `/srv/salt/` and `/srv/pillar/` and `/srv/reactor/`, respectively. However, as we will see later in the *Exploring the SLS directories* section, these are not exactly configuration files.

Looking inside /etc/salt/

Inside the `/etc/salt/` directory, there will generally be one of two files: master and minion (both will appear if you treat your master as a minion). When the documentation refers to **master configuration**, it generally means the `/etc/salt/master` file, and of course, **minion configuration** refers to the `/etc/salt/minion` file. All configuration for these two daemons can technically go into their respective files.

However, many users find reasons to break up their configuration into smaller files. This is often for organizational reasons, but there is a practical reason too: because Salt can manage itself, it is often easier to have it manage smaller, templated files rather than one large, monolithic file.

Because of this, the master can also include any file with a `.conf` extension, found in the `/etc/salt/master.d/` directory (and the minion likewise in the `minion.d/` directory). This is in keeping with the numerous other services that also maintain similar directory structures.

Other subsystems inside Salt also make use of the `.d/` directory structure. Notably, Salt Cloud makes use of a number of these directories. The `/etc/salt/cloud`, `/etc/salt/cloud.providers`, and `/etc/salt/cloud.profiles` files can also be broken up into the `/etc/salt/cloud.d/`, `/etc/salt/cloud.providers.d/`, and `/etc/salt/cloud.profiles.d/` directories, respectively. Additionally, it is recommended to store cloud maps in the `/etc/salt/cloud.maps.d/` directory.

While other configuration formats are available elsewhere in Salt, the format of all of these core configuration files is YAML (except for cloud maps, which will be discussed in Chapter 7, *Taking Salt Cloud to the Next Level*). This is by necessity: Salt needs a stable starting point from which to configure everything else. Likewise, the /etc/salt/ directory is hard-coded as the default starting point to find these files, though that may be overridden using the --config-dir (or -C) option:

```
# salt-master --config-dir=/other/path/to/salt/
```

Managing Salt keys

Inside the /etc/salt/ directory, there is also a pki/ directory, inside which is a master/ or minion/ directory (or both). This is where the public and private keys are stored.

The minion will only have three files inside the /etc/salt/pki/minion directory:

- minion.pem: The minion's private RSA key
- minion.pub: The minion's public RSA key, and
- minion_master.pub: The master's public RSA key

The master will also keep its RSA keys (master.pem and master.pub) in the /etc/salt/pki/master/ directory. However, at least three more directories will also appear in here. The minions.pre/ directory contains the public RSA keys for minions that have contacted the master but have not yet been accepted. The minions/ directory contains the public RSA keys for minions that have been accepted on the master. And the minions_rejected/ directory will contain keys for any minion that has contacted the master but been explicitly rejected.

There is nothing particularly special about these directories. The salt-key command on the master is essentially a convenience tool for the user that moves public key files between directories as requested. If needed, users can set up their own tools to manage the keys on their own, just by moving files around.

Exploring the SLS directories

As mentioned, Salt also makes use of other directory trees on the system. The most important of these are the directories that store SLS files, which are, by default, located in /srv/.

Of the SLS directories, /srv/salt/, is probably the most important. This directory stores the state SLS files and their corresponding top files. It also serves as the default root directory for Salt's built-in file server. There will typically be a top.sls file and several accompanying .sls files and/or directories. The layout of this directory was covered in more detail in Chapter 1, *Essentials Revisited*.

A close second is the /srv/pillar/ directory. This directory maintains a copy of the static pillar definitions, if used. Like the /srv/salt/ directory, there will typically be a top.sls file and several accompanying .sls files and directories. But while the top.sls file matches the format used in /srv/salt/, the accompanying .sls files are merely collections of key/value pairs. While they can use Salt's renderer (discussed later in the *The renderer* section), the resulting data does not need to conform to Salt's state compiler (also discussed later in this chapter, in the *Plunging into the state compiler* section).

Another directory that will hopefully find its way into your arsenal is the /srv/reactor/ directory. Unlike the others, there is no top.sls file in here. That is because the mapping is performed inside the master configuration instead of the top system. However, the files in this directory do have a specific format, which will be discussed in detail in Chapter 5, *Managing Tasks Asynchronously*.

Examining the Salt cache

Salt also maintains a cache directory, usually at /var/cache/salt/ (again, this may differ based on your operating system). As before, both the master and the minion have their own directory for cache data. The master cache directory contains more entries than the minion cache, so we'll jump into that first.

The master job cache

Probably the first cache directory that you'll run across in everyday use is the jobs/ directory. In a default configuration, this contains all the data that the master stores about the jobs that it executes.

This directory uses hashmap-style storage. That means that a piece of identifying information—in this case, a job ID (JID)—has been processed with a hash algorithm, and a directory or directory structure has been created using a part or all of the hash. In this case, a split hash model has been used, where a directory has been created using the first two characters of the hash, and another directory under it has been created with the rest of the hash.

The default hash type for Salt is MD5. This can be modified by changing the `hash_type` value in the master configuration:

```
hash_type: md5
```

Keep in mind that `hash_type` is an important value that should be decided upon when first setting up a new Salt infrastructure if MD5 is not the desired value. If it is changed (say to SHA1) after an infrastructure has been using another value for a while, then any part of Salt that has been making use of it must be cleaned up manually. The rest of this book will assume that MD5 is used.

The JID is easy to interpret: it is a date-and-time stamp. For instance, a job ID of `20141203081456191706` refers to a job that was started on December 3, 2014, at 56 seconds and 191,706 microeconds past 8:14 AM. The MD5 of that JID would be `f716a0e8131ddd6df3ba583fed2c88b7`. Therefore, the data that describes that job would be located at the following path:
`/var/cache/salt/master/jobs/f7/16a0e8131ddd6df3ba583fed2c88b7.`

In that directory, there will be a file called `jid`. This will of course contain the job ID. There will also be a series of files with a `.p` extension. These files are all serialized by `msgpack`.

Looking inside msgpack files:
If you have checked out a copy of Salt from Git, this data is easy to view. Inside the `test/` directory in Salt's Git tree, there is a file called `packdump.py`. This can be used to dump the contents of the `msgpack` files to the console.

First, there is a a file called `.minions.p` (notice the leading dot), which contains a list of minions that were targeted by this job. This will look something like so:

```
[
    "minion1",
    "minion2",
    "minion3"
]
```

The job itself will be described by a file called `.load.p`:

```
{
    "arg": [
        ""
    ],
    "fun": "test.ping",
    "jid": "20141203081456191706",
    "tgt": "*",
```

```
    "tgt_type": "glob",
    "user": "root"
}
```

There will also be one directory for each minion that was targeted by that job and that contains the return information for that job on that minion. Inside that directory will be a file called `return.p`, which contains the return data, serialized by `msgpack`. Assuming that the job in question performed a simple `test.ping` operation, the `return` block will look like this:

```
true
```

The master-side minion cache

Once Salt has started issuing jobs, another cache directory will show up, called `minions/`. This directory will contain one entry per minion, with cached data about that minion. Inside this directory are two files: `data.p` and `mine.p`.

The `data.p` file contains a copy of the grains and pillar data for that minion. A (shortened) `data.p` file may look like the following:

```
{
  "grains": {
    "biosreleasedate": "01/09/2013",
    "biosversion": "G1ET91WW (2.51 )",
    "cpu_model": "Intel(R) Core(TM) i5-3210M CPU @
    2.50GHz",
    "cpuarch": "x86_64",
    "os": "Ubuntu",
    "os_family": "Debian",
  },
  "pillar": {
    "role": "web"
  }
}
```

The `mine.p` file contains mine data. This is not covered in detail in this book, but in short, a minion can be configured to cache the return data from specific commands in the cache directory on the master so that other minions can look it up. For instance, if the output from `test.ping` and `network.ip_addrs` has been configured, the contents of the `mine.p` file will look as follows:

```
{
  "network.ip_addrs": [
    "192.168.2.101"
```

```
    ],
    "test.ping": true
}
```

The external file server cache

In a default installation, Salt wil keep its files in the /srv/salt/ keep its files in the /srv/salt/ directory. However, an external file server, by definition, maintains an external file store. For instance, the gitfs external file server keeps its files on a Git server, such as GitHub. However, it is incredibly inefficient to ask the Salt master to always serve files directly from Git. So, in order to improve efficiency, a copy of the Git tree is stored on the master.

The contents and layout of this tree will vary among the external file server modules. For instance, the gitfs module doesn't store a full directory tree as one might see in a normal Git checkout; it only maintains the information used to create that tree using whatever branches are available. Other external file servers, however, may contain a full copy of the external source, which is updated periodically. The full path to this cache may look like this: /var/cache/salt/master/gitfs/ where gitfs is the name of the file server module.

In order to keep track of the file changes, a directory called hash/ will also exist inside the external file server's cache. Inside hash/, there will be one directory per environment (base, dev, prod, and so on). Each of those will contain what looks like a mirror image of the file tree. However, each actual filename will be suffixed with .hash.md5 (or the appropriate hash name, if different), and the contents will be the value of the checksum for that file.

In addition to the file server cache, there will be another directory called file_lists/ that contains one directory per enabled file server. Inside that directory will be one file per environment, with a .p extension (such as base.p for the base environment). This file will contain a list of files and directories belonging to that environment's directory tree. A shortened version might look like this:

```
{
  "dirs": [
    ".",
    "vim",
    "httpd",
  ],
  "empty_dirs": [
  ],
  "files": [
    "top.sls",
```

```
        "vim/init.sls",
        "httpd/httpd.conf",
        "httpd/init.sls",
    ],
    "links": []
}
```

This file helps Salt with a quick lookup of the directory structure without having to constantly descend into a directory tree.

The minion-side proc/ directory

The minion doesn't maintain nearly as many cache directories as the master, but it does have a couple. The first of these is the `proc/` directory, which maintains the data for active jobs on the minion. It is easy to see this in action. From the master, issue a `sleep` command to a minion:

```
salt myminion test.sleep 300 --async
```

This will kick off a process on the minion that will wait for 300 seconds (5 minutes) before returning `True` to the master. Because the command includes the `--async` flag, Salt will immediately return a JID to the user.

While this process is running, log in to the minion and take a look at the `/var/cache/salt/minion/proc/` directory. There should be a file bearing the name of the JID. The unpacked contents of this file will look like the following:

```
{'arg': [300],
 'fun': 'test.sleep',
 'jid': '20150323233901672076',
 'pid': 4741,
 'ret': '',
 'tgt': 'myminion',
 'tgt_type': 'glob',
 'user': 'root'}
```

This file will exist until the job has been completed on the minion. If you like, you can see the corresponding file on the master. Use the `hashutil.md5_digest` function to find the MD5 value of the JID:

```
# salt myminion hashutil.md5_digest
20150323233901672076
```

External modules

The other directory that you are likely to see on the minion is the `extmods/` directory. If custom modules have been synced to the minion from the master (using the `_modules`, `_states`, or other such directories on the master), they will appear here.

This is also easy to see in action:

1. On the master, create a `_modules/` directory inside `/srv/salt/`.
2. Inside this directory, create a file called `mytest.py`, with the following contents:

```
def ping():
return True
```

3. Then, from the master, use the `saltutil` module to sync your new module to a minion:

```
salt myminion saltutil.sync_modules
```

4. After a moment, Salt will report that it has finished:

```
myminion:
-   modules.mytest
```

5. Log in to the minion and look inside `/var/cache/salt/minion/extmods/modules/`.
6. There will be two files: `mytest.py` and `mytest.pyc`. If you look at the contents of `mytest.py`, you will see the custom module that you created on the master. You will also be able to execute the `mytest.ping` function from the master:

```
# salt myminion mytest.ping
myminion:
True
```

The renderer

While the main master and minion configuration files must necessarily be stored in YAML, other files in Salt can take advantage of the wealth of file formats that the modern world of technology has to offer. This is because of the rendering system built into Salt, which can take files of arbitrary formats and render them into a structure that is usable by Salt.

Rendering SLS files

By default, all SLS files in Salt are rendered twice: first through the Jinja templating engine and then through the **PyYAML** library. This provides some significant advantages:

- **Jinja** provides a fast and powerful templating system is easy to understand and use and follows a Pythonic mindset, comfortable to many administrators. It is particularly well suited for managing YAML files.
- **YAML** has a very shallow learning curve, making it easy to learn and understand. While it does support more complex syntax, such as parentheses, brackets, and braces (JSON is technically syntactically correct YAML), it is not required.

However, it was immediately apparent, even before any renderers were written, that there would be some dissent among users as to which formats were best suited to their own environments:

- A popular alternative to YAML, which was already in common usage in other software, is **JSON**. This format is more strict, making it somewhat harder to read and even more difficult to write correctly. However, because JSON is more strict concerning how data is declared, a properly formatted JSON file is more accurate than YAML and is easier to parse safely.
- **Mako** was also an early addition to the Salt toolkit. While Jinja adds just enough functionality to create a dynamic toolkit, Mako is designed to bring the full power of Python to templates. This is especially popular with a number of users in the DevOps community who are known to mix code with content in a number of innovative ways.

A primary design goal of Salt has always been to provide flexibility, and so the renderer system was designed to be pluggable in the same way as the other components of Salt. While Jinja and YAML have been made the default, either or both can be replaced, and if necessary, even more renderers can be brought into the mix.

If your needs include changing the global renderer from `yaml_jinja`, you can do so in the master configuration file:

```
renderer: json_mako
```

However, you should consider very carefully whether this is better. Keep in mind that community examples, repositories, and formulas are generally kept in YAML, and if any templating needs to be done, Jinja is usually used. This will affect how you deal with the community or act as an enterprise customer on any support issues, and it may confuse any experienced Salt users that your company hires.

That said, even with a standard base of Jinja and YAML, there are times when using a different set of renderers for a small subset of your SLS files is appropriate.

Render pipes

As previously mentioned, SLS files will be rendered using the configured default. However, it is possible to change how a file is rendered by adding a **shebang** (also known as **shabang**) line to the top of the file. A file that is to be rendered only as YAML will begin with the following line:

```
#!yaml
```

However, in the Salt world, this is generally impractical. Adding a templating engine increases the power of an SLS file significantly. In order to use multiple renderers in a specific order, add them to the shabang line in the desired order, separated by pipes:

```
#!jinja|yaml
```

This resembles the Unix method of piping smaller programs together, to create larger, more functional programs. There is no imposed limit on how many renderers are piped together:

```
#!mako|pyobjects|jinja|yaml|json
```

However, this is pretty unrealistic. You will find that, in general, no more than two renderers need to be used. Indeed, too many renderers will create a complexity that is unreadable and unmaintainable. Use as many as are needed and no more.

It is important to note that SLS files will ultimately result in a specific data structure. The most accurate way to say this in simple terms is that the data generated by SLS files must be usable by the `msgpack` serialization package. This is the format used extensively throughout the various subsystems inside Salt (notably, the cache system). A more detailed description of the resulting files will be explored later in the chapter, in the *Plunging into the state compiler* section, as we uncover the mysteries of the state compiler.

Serving templated files

SLS files are not the only files that can take advantage of the renderer. Any file that is served from an SLS file may also be rendered through a templating engine. These files aren't as specific as SLS files because they do not need to return a specific data format; they only need to result in the arbitrary file contents that will be served by Salt.

The most common usage of this is with the `file.managed` state. Adding a `template` argument to this state will cause the file to be rendered accordingly:

```
/etc/httpd/conf/httpd.conf:
  file.managed:
    - source: salt://httpd/httpd.conf
    - template: jinja
```

Because the templated file will not return data, renderers that deal exclusively with data are not available here. But while YAML, JSON, msgpack, and the various Python-based renderers are not available, Jinja, Mako, Cheetah, and the like can be used.

Understanding the loader

The loader system is at the heart of how Salt works. In a nutshell, Salt is a collection of modules tied together with the loader. Even the transport mechanisms, which enable communication between and define the master, minion, and Syndic hierarchies make use of modules that are managed by the loader.

Dynamic modules

Salt's loader system is a bit unconventional. Traditionally, most software has been designed to require all supported components to be installed. This is not the case with every package, of course. The Apache web server is an example of one project that supports a number of components that need not all be installed. Debian-based operating systems manage Apache modules by providing their `modules-available/` and `modules-enabled/` directories. Red Hat-based systems take a different approach: all components that are supported by Apache's `httpd` package are required to be installed with it.

Making such a demand with Salt is beyond unrealistic. So many packages are supported with the default installation of Salt, many of which compete with each other (and some of which compete, in some ways, with Salt itself) that it could be said that to build such a dependency tree into Salt would effectively turn Salt into its own operating system.

However, even this is not entirely accurate. Because Salt supports a number of different Linux distributions in addition to several Unix flavors and even Windows, it would be more accurate to say that installing every package that is supported by Salt would effectively turn Salt into several mutually exclusive operating systems. Obviously, this is just not possible.

Salt is able to handle this using multiple approaches. First, grains (covered in `Chapter 1`, *Essentials Revisited*) provide critical information to Salt to help identify the platform on which it is running. Grains such as `os` and `os_flavor` are used often enough to help Salt know whether to use `yum` or `apt` to manage packages or `systemd` or `upstart` to manage services.

Each module is also able to check other dependencies on the system. The bulk of Salt's Apache module makes use of the `apachectl` command (or `apache2ctl`, as appropriate), so its availability is dependent upon whether or not that command exists on the system.

This set of techniques enables Salt to appropriately detect, as the minion process starts, which modules to make available to the user.

A relatively new feature of Salt's loader system is the ability to load modules on demand. Modules that support the **lazy loader** functionality will not actually load until requested by the user. This streamlines the start process for the minion and makes more effective use of the available resources.

Execution modules

It has often been said that most of the heavy lifting in Salt is performed by the execution modules. This is because Salt was designed originally as a remote execution system, and most module types that have been added to the loader have been designed to extend the functionality of remote execution.

For instance, state modules are designed with one purpose in mind: to enforce the state of a certain aspect of a system. This could be to ensure that a package is installed or that a service is running. The state module itself doesn't install the package or start the service; it calls out to the execution module to do so. A state module's only job is to add **idempotency** to an execution module.

One could say that an important differentiator between runner modules and execution modules is that runners are designed to be used from the master while execution modules are designed to execute remotely on the minion. However, runners were actually designed with something more specific in mind:

System administrators have been using shell scripts for decades. From `csh` in Unix to `bash` in Linux and even batch files in DOS and Windows, this has been the long-running standard.

Runner modules were designed to allow Salt users to apply a scripting language to remote executions. Because so many early Salt users were also Python users, it was not generally difficult for them to use Python as their scripting language. As the Salt user base grew, so too did the number of users who were not fluent in Python, but the number of other options available for them also grew.

Reactor modules (covered in detail in `Chapter 5`, *Managing Tasks Asynchronously*) are a type of module that can pull together execution modules and runner modules and make them available to users with no programming experience. And because Salt states are actually applied using the `state` execution module, even states are available through reactors.

Cloud modules

Cloud modules are not typically thought of by many people as Salt modules, perhaps because Salt Cloud (covered extensively in `Chapter 7`, *Taking Salt Cloud to the Next Level*) started as a project separate from Salt, but they have in fact always used the loader system. They do, however, work a little differently.

Unlike many other modules in Salt, Cloud modules do not make use of execution modules (although there is an execution module that makes use of Salt Cloud). This is in part because Salt Cloud was designed to run on the Salt master. However, it does not make use of runner modules either (though, again, there is a runner module that can make use of Salt Cloud).

Salt Cloud's initial purpose was to create new VMs on various public cloud providers and automatically accept their keys on the Salt master. However, it quickly grew apparent that users wanted to control as many aspects of their cloud providers as possible, not just VM creation.

Now, Salt Cloud is able to perform any action that is available against a cloud provider. Some providers support more functionality than others. In some cases, this is because demand has not been presented, and in other cases, it's because the appropriate developer has not yet had the resources to make the addition. But often it is because the features available on the provider itself may be limited. Whatever the situation, if a feature is available, it can be added and made available via the loader system.

Plunging into the state compiler

Salt was initially designed as a remote execution system to be used for gathering data normally collected by monitoring systems and storing it for later analysis. However, as functionality grew, so too did a need to manage the execution modules that were doing the heavy lifting. Salt states were born from this need and, before long, the engine that managed them had expanded into other areas of Salt.

Imperative versus declarative

A point of contention between various configuration management systems is the concept of declarative versus imperative configurations. Before we discuss Salt's take on the matter, let's take a moment to examine the two.

It may be easiest to think of imperative programming like a script: perform Task A and, when it is finished, perform Task B; once that has finished, perform Task C. This is what many administrators are used to, especially as it more closely resembles the shell scripts that have been their lifelines for so many decades. Chef is an example of a configuration management suite that is imperative in nature.

Declarative definition is a newer concept, and more representative of object oriented programming. The basic idea is that the user declares which tasks need to be performed, and the software performs them in whichever order it sees fit. Generally, dependencies can also be declared that dictate that some tasks are not to be completed until others are. Puppet is a well-known example of a configuration management platform that is declarative in nature.

Salt is unique in that it supports both imperative ordering and declarative execution. If no dependencies are defined, then, by default, Salt will attempt to execute states in the order in which they appear in the SLS files. If a state fails because it requires a task that appears later, then multiple Salt runs will be required to complete all tasks.

However, if dependencies are defined, states will be handled differently. They will still be evaluated in the order in which they appear, but dependencies can cause them to be executed in a different order. Consider the following Salt state:

```
mysql:
  service:
    - running
  pkg:
    - installed
  file:
    - managed
```

```
    - source: salt://mysql/my.cnf
    - name: /etc/mysql/my.cnf
```

In the first several versions of Salt that supported states, this would have been evaluated lexicographically: the file would have been copied into place first, then the package installed, and then the service started, because in the English alphabet, F comes before P, and P comes before S. Happily, this is also the order that is probably desired.

However, the current default ordering system in Salt is imperative, meaning states will be evaluated in the order in which they appear. Salt will attempt to start the `mysql` service, which will fail because the package is not installed. It will then attempt to install the `mysql` package, which will succeed. If this is a Debian-based system, installation of the package will also cause the service to start, in this case without the correct configuration file. Lastly, Salt will copy the `my.cnf` file into place but will make no attempt to restart the service to apply the correct changes. A second state run will report success for all three states (the service is running, the package is installed, and the file is managed as requested), but a manual restart of the `mysql` service will still be required.

Requisites

To accommodate ordering issues caused by such issues, Salt uses requisites. These will affect the order in which states are evaluated and executed. Consider the following changes to the aforementioned Salt state:

```
mysql:
  service:
    - running
    - require:
      - package: mysql
    - watch:
      - file: mysql
  pkg:
    - installed
    - require:
      - file: mysql
  file:
    - managed
    - source: salt://mysql/my.cnf
    - name: /etc/mysql/my.cnf
```

Even though the states have been defined in an order that is not appropriate, they will still be evaluated and executed correctly.

The following will be the order that will be defined:

1. `service: mysql`
2. `pkg: mysql`
3. `file: mysql`

However, the `mysql` service requires that the `mysql` package be executed first. So, before executing the `mysql` service, it will look ahead and evaluate the `mysql` package. But since the `mysql` package requires the `mysql` file to be executed first, it will jump ahead and evaluate the `mysql` file. Because the file state does not require anything else, Salt will execute it. Having completed the list of requirements for the `pkg` state, Salt will go back and execute it. And finally, having completed all the service requirements, Salt will go back and execute the service.

Following successful completion of the service state, it will move onto the next state and see whether it has already been executed. It will continue in this fashion until all states have been evaluated and executed.

It is in this manner that Salt is able to be both imperative (by allowing statements to be evaluated in the order in which they appear) and declarative (by allowing statements to be executed based on requisites).

High and low states

The concept of high states has proven to be one of the most confusing things about Salt. Users understand that the `state.highstate` command performs a state run, but what exactly is a high state? And does the presence of a high state mean that there is a low state as well?

There are two parts of the state system that are in effect. **High data** refers generally to data as it is seen by the user. **Low data** refers generally to data as it is ingested and used by Salt.

High states

If you have worked with state files, you have already seen every aspect of this part of the state system. There are three specific components, each of which builds upon the one before it:

- High data

- SLS file
- High state

Each state represents a piece of high data. If the previous SLS were broken into individual states, those would look like this, respectively (ignoring the fact that duplicate top-level keys would comprise an invalid YAML file):

```
mysql:
  service:
    - running
    - require:
      - pkg: mysql
    - watch:
      - file: mysql

mysql:
  pkg:
    - installed
    - require:
      - file: mysql

mysql:
  file:
    - managed
    - source: salt://mysql/my.cnf
    - name: /etc/mysql/my.cnf
```

When combined with other states, they form an SLS file:

```
iptables:
  service:
    - running

mysql:
  service:
    - running
    - require:
      - package: mysql
    - watch:
      - file: mysql
  package:
    - installed
    - require:
      - file: mysql
  file:
    - managed
    - source: salt://mysql/my.cnf
```

```
    - name: /etc/mysql/my.cnf
```

When these files are tied together using includes and further glued together for use inside an environment using a `top.sls` file, they form a high state, like so:

```
top.sls
base:
  '*':
    - mysql
mysql.sls
include:
  - iptables

mysql:
  service:
    - running
    - require:
      - package: mysql
    - watch:
      - file: mysql
  package:
    - installed
    - require:
      - file: mysql
  file:
    - managed
    - source: salt://mysql/my.cnf
    - name: /etc/mysql/my.cnf
iptables.sls
iptables:
  service:
    - running
```

When the `state.highstate` function is executed, Salt will compile all relevant SLS files inside `top.sls` and any includes into a single definition, called a high state. This can be viewed by using the `state.show_highstate` function:

```
# salt myminion state.show_highstate --out yaml
myminion:
  iptables:
    service:
    - running
    - order: 10000
    __sls__: iptables
    __env__: base
  mysql:
    service:
    - running
```

```
        - require:
          - pkg: mysql
        - watch:
          - file: mysql
        - order: 10001
      pkg:
        - installed
        - require:
          - file: mysql
        - order: 10002
      file:
        - managed
        - source: salt://mysql/my.cnf
        - name: /etc/mysql/my.cnf
        - order: 10003
        __sls__: mysql
        __env__: base
```

Take note of the extra fields that are included in this output. First, an order is declared. This is something that can be explicitly declared by the user in an SLS file using either real numbers or the `first` or `last` keywords. All states that are set to be first will have their order adjusted accordingly. Numerically ordered states will appear next. Salt will then add `10000` to the last defined number (which is `0` by default) and add any states that are not explicitly ordered. Finally, any states set to `last` will be added.

Salt will also add some variables that it uses internally, to know which environment (`__env__`) to execute the state in and which SLS file (`__sls__`) the state declaration came from.

Remember that the order is still no more than a starting point; the actual high state will be executed based first on requisites and then on order.

Low states

Once the final high state has been generated, it will be sent to the state compiler. This will reformat the state data into a format that Salt uses internally to evaluate each declaration and will feed data into each state module (which will in turn call the execution modules as necessary). As with high data, low data can be broken into individual components:

- Low state
- Low chunks
- State module
- One or more execution modules

The low data can be viewed using the `state.show_lowstate` function:

```
# salt myminion state.show_lowstate --out yaml
myminion:
- __env__: base
  __id__: iptables
  __sls__: iptables
  fun: running
  name: iptables
  order: 10000
  state: service
- __env__: base
  __id__: mysql
  __sls__: mysql
  fun: running
  name: mysql
  order: 10001
  require:
  - package: mysql
  state: service
  watch:
  - file: mysql
- __env__: base
  __id__: mysql
  __sls__: mysql
  fun: installed
  name: mysql
  order: 10002
  require:
  - file: mysql
  state: package
- __env__: base
  __id__: mysql
  __sls__: mysql
  fun: managed
  name: /etc/mysql/my.cnf
  order: 10003
  source: salt://mysql/my.cnf
  state: file
```

Together, all this comprises a **low state**. Each individual item is a **low Chunk**. The first low chunk in this list looks like this:

```
- __env__: base
  __id__: iptables
  __sls__: iptables
  fun: running
  name: iptables
```

```
order: 10000
state: service
```

Each low chunk maps to a state module (in this case, `service`) and a function inside that state module (in this case, `running`). An ID is also provided at this level (`__id__`). Salt will map relationships (that is, requisites) between states using a combination of state and `__id__` values. If a name has not been declared by the user, then Salt will automatically use the `__id__` value as the name.

Once a function inside a state module has been called, it will usually map to one or more execution modules, which actually do the work. Let's take a moment to examine what goes down when Salt gets to that point.

Enforcing statefulness

While execution modules are somewhat looser in definition, state modules are necessarily more precise. Certain behaviors can always be expected of a state module:

- A state module will always require a name
- A state module will always return the following data structures:
  - name
  - result
  - changes
  - comment

In the case of monitoring states (covered in `Chapter 11`, *Monitoring with Salt*), a dictionary called `data` will also be returned.

name

The name refers to the specific piece of information that is to be managed by the state module. In the case of a service, it is the service's name, as recognized by that minion's service manager (that is, `apache2`). In the case of a file, it refers to the full path on the minion at which the file is to be located (that is, `/etc/apache2/apache2.conf`).

When the state results are returned to the user, the name will be used to identify the state that was evaluated.

result

There are only three values that will ever be returned as a result: `True`, `False`, and `None`.

A state that returns `True` is declaring that following its execution, Salt believes that the resource to be configured is as desired. This may be because the resource was already properly configured or because the state module successfully performed the steps necessary to enforce the desired configuration.

A state that returns `False` is declaring that following execution, Salt believes that despite its attempts, the resource has not been configured as desired.

In a normal state run, no state will ever return `None`. This value is reserved for state runs that have been executed in test mode. This is also known as a dry run. Here's an example:

```
salt myminion state.highstate test=True
```

When a state run happens in test mode, Salt will not allow changes to occur on the system. If a resource is already configured as expected, it will still return `True`. If Salt detects that changes are required in order to enforce a resource's state, it will return `None` to notify the user.

changes

The `changes` data structure is a list that will never be populated in test mode because it only reflects the changes that have been applied to the system to bring it into compliance with the requested configuration. This will only be populated if the result has been returned as `True`. The contents of this list are dependent on the state module that is executed.

comment

Regardless of whether or not changes were made to a system or whether or not a state was successful, the `comment` field should be populated to inform the user of additional information, in a more human-readable format, that may be helpful to them.

Following any kind of state run, each individual state will return all of these fields. After all the information, a tally of successes and failures will appear, including a tally of how many changes were made. A successful state tree will require no more than one state run. When issues arise, a combination of these fields will be incredibly useful.

Summary

We have discussed how Salt manages its own configuration as well as the loader and renderer systems. We have also gone into significant details about how the state system works.

Now that we have a solid understanding of how Salt works under the hood, we can dive into some of the more powerful components.

Next up, we'll dive even deeper into Salt's state system, and discuss how powerful of a tool it is for managing configuration inside of your infrastructure

3
Managing States

Configuration management is a hot topic, and the state system is what Salt uses to perform it. It's become very powerful over time, and even if you're already well versed in states, I expect there are still a few tricks you haven't learned yet. In this chapter, we'll cover:

- Integrating multiple state files into a cohesive product
- Making state trees span multiple environments
- Understanding the master tops subsystem
- Taking advantage of the `saltstack-formulas` organization on GitHub
- Using SPM, the Salt Package Manager

Handling multiple states

Using single SLS files is pretty powerful as it is, but real power comes from being able to combine them to form a larger orchestration. We touched on some of the basics in `Chapter 1`, *Essentials Revisited*. Let's go ahead and expound upon them.

Including other SLS files

That little `include` code block at the beginning of an SLS file is the start to pulling together SLS files. Let's say that you have a number of formulas that are used to create a development environment for your users. Here are a few examples:

- git
- vim
- emacs
- ack

- pip
- pycharm

Let's go ahead and put together a development environment formula first. Go ahead and create a formula directory called `devenv`:

```
# mkdir -p /srv/salt/devenv/
```

Then, we'll create a file inside that directory called `init.sls` that references those formulas:

```
include:
  - git
  - vim
  - emacs
  - ack
  - pip
  - pycharm
```

Of course, most of your developers will not want both vim and emacs; they'll only want one. Let's give them the ability to choose which one gets installed. We'll add some Jinja code that looks for a configuration value called `dev_editor`. You could set that in a pillar, but this is one time when it is more appropriate to use a grain so that developers can manage the setting on their own systems without having to edit pillars on the master:

```
{% dev_editor = salt['config.get']('dev_editor', 'vim') %}
include:
  - git
{% if dev_editor == 'vim' %}
  - vim
{% elif dev_editor == 'emacs' %}
  - emacs
{% endif %}
  - ack
  - pip
  - pycharm
```

We'll assume that the aforementioned states are pretty generic. For instance, the `vim` state may be no more than the following:

```
vim:
  pkg.installed
vim_tools:
  pkg.installed:
    - names:
      - global_vim_themes
      - global_vim_syntaxes
```

But different types of developers will have different needs. A web developer may need a package that supplies certain extra syntax definitions for Vim (such as language files), and a QA engineer might need a completely different set (such as testing file formats).

The `extend` declaration gives you the ability to take existing definitions and add information to them. If we add a little Jinja code to the mix, we can do something like this:

```
{% dev_editor = salt['config.get']('dev_editor', 'vim')
{% dev_type = salt['config.get']('dev_type', 'web')
include:
  - git
{% if dev_editor == 'vim' %}
  - vim
{% elif dev_editor == 'emacs' %}
  - emacs
{% endif %}
  - ack
  - pip
  - pycharm

extend:
  vim_tools:
    pkg:
      - names:
        - dev_vim_themes
{% if dev_type == 'web' %}
        - web_vim_syntaxes
{% elif dev_type == 'qa' %}
        - qa_vim_syntaxes
{% endif %}
```

When extending SLS files, there are some important rules to remember.

- There is only one `extend` directive. If you have multiple `extend` sections in a single SLS file, you will generate YAML errors regarding multiple key definitions.
- If you extend a value that already exists in the included file, it will be overwritten by the `extend` directive.
- The exception to this are lists such as `require`, `watch`, and `names`. If you extend one of these, then the new information will be appended to the old list.

Spanning multiple environments

The idea behind Salt environments is to allow formulas to be distributed to multiple types of minions while still restricting them from running in areas where they are not appropriate. For instance, if you use LDAP as an authentication mechanism, it probably makes sense to have it available in every environment. However, even if you're using Git for revision control, you probably only want it in your development environment, as other environments are often deployed via some other mechanism.

Using the base environment

By default, all minions will behave as if they are in the base environment, even if you have no environments defined. By convention, most Salt deployments make use of the base environment anyway, so it's not a bad idea to follow suit.

The base environment is designed to provide formulas that will be useful or necessary across all minions. Decide carefully which formulas to add to base: most formulas will have at least one environment that they do not belong in.

Consider the following scenario: your infrastructure includes four environments—dev, qa, stage, and prod. The dev and qa environments are similar, except that the only tools available in the qa environment to manage code should be those that deploy code to the environment for testing. The qa and stage environments are similar, except that the stage environment should look exactly like the prod environment (as appropriate) except that it is not publicly accessible. Deployment in stage must behave exactly the same as in prod so that a production deployment is as predictable as possible.

In this setup, you will likely have a number of developer-centric tools available in the dev environment that are not appropriate for any other environment. However, most of the formulas that are available in production (prod) will also be available in all other environments. The only difference between stage and prod will be the configuration files that maintain the environment and the versions of the packages that are being staged versus the ones that are already in production.

In this setup, you may have a top.sls file that looks something like this:

```
base:
  '*':
    - base_formulas
dev:
  '*-dev':
    - dev_tools
```

```
qa:
  '*-qa':
    - testing_tools
    - testing_configs
stage:
  '*-stage':
    - stage_packages
    - stage_configs
prod:
  '*-prod':
    - prod_packages
    - prod_configs
```

Breaking out environments

Unfortunately, things are rarely that simple. The aforementioned formula may work for a smaller infrastructure in which some servers perform multiple duties. But in a production environment, where each server should only be performing one function, you will probably want to break out into a number of other environments.

Let's say that your infrastructure makes use of web servers, database servers, and load-balancer servers. You may be tempted to set up servers with -web-dev, -db-dev, -lb-dev, and so in in their names. But this can quickly lead to an exponentially large set of environments that are difficult to maintain at best.

Instead, think about setting up environments for web, db, and lb in addition to your dev, qa, stage, and prod environments. Minions may belong to multiple environments, which allows you to combine resources together. For instance, the qa and web sections of top.sls may look like this:

```
qa:
  '*-qa':
    - testing_tools
    - testing_configs
web:
  'web-*':
    - apache
    - mod_ssl
```

With this kind of configuration, a server naming scheme might look like web01-qa, web02-qa, and so on.

There is a potential problem with this scenario, which may be immediately obvious to the experienced admin: how do we specify the version of a package that is appropriate for the qa environment as opposed to stage or prod?

My recommendation relies on a solution both inside and outside of Salt. It is extremely common for infrastructures to rely on public repositories for their packaging needs. But when you do that, you place yourself at the mercy of factors that you cannot control, such as bad package updates or server downtime at the host.

Rather than placing the life of your infrastructure in the hands of somebody else, take control. Set up your own repositories, one for each environment. Repositories for dev will likely be as loose as any other resource in dev, but as code and configuration move up through qa, stage, and prod, you will have the ability to tighten up resources as appropriate.

This will allow you to create formulas that look like this, for instance:

```
apache:
  pkg.latest
```

Because you control what the latest package available is, you will spend less time editing formulas to bring them into compliance.

Understanding master_tops

Up until now, we have referred to the top setup exclusively using the top.sls file. But just as other resources in Salt are modular, so is the top subsystem. By default, Salt will obtain top data from the filesystem, but you can also reach out to external resources. These resources may also be referred to as **master tops**.

Like state files, the only real requirement of a master top is that it return data to Salt in the same format that would be generated by the top.sls file. This format contains a dictionary of environments, each of which has another dictionary containing targets, each of which contains a list of formulas for those targets.

Some of the master tops that ship with Salt are as follows:

- cobbler: An infrastructure deployment tool based around machine images
- mongo: A popular NoSQL database solution

- `reclass_adapter`: A community project that aims to standardize configuration management between multiple disparate projects, including Salt
- `varstack`: A project that allows you to layer together configuration variables

Because Cobbler is both a well-established solution and simple to configure as a master top, let's take a look at its configuration.

First off, master tops are set up in the `master` configuration file using the `master_tops` directive. In this case, we'll add Cobbler to that directive:

```
master_tops:
  cobbler: {}
```

As with external filesystems, master tops expect you to provide configuration on the same line as the configuration key. However, because the Cobbler module uses the same configuration as the Cobbler pillar, we just need to pass in an empty dictionary.

The configuration for Cobbler comes next:

```
cobbler.url: http://cobbler.example.com/cobbler_api
cobbler.user: larry
cobbler.password: 123pass
```

There's not much to this module. It connects to an established Cobbler server and converts the information about that minion to top data that the master can use.

Using Salt Stack Formulas on GitHub

A number of formulas have been built by various engineers and are compiled together on GitHub under the Salt Stack Formulas organization. You can find these formulas at `https://github.com/saltstack-formulas`.

At the time of writing this, there are over 200 formulas hosted under this organization. Some are better maintained than others, but a number of them see frequent maintenance by the community.

Probably the most helpful thing about these formulas is that, outside of rare special cases, each software package that is supported by a formula will only have one formula. This is a vast improvement over similar user repositories, which may include dozens or even hundreds of different examples for the exact same package.

Examining the standard layout

Most formulas adhere to a standard layout, which has been developed and honed over time to help encourage a consistent look and feel. You will generally find the following files and directories:Because Cobbler is both a well-established solution and simple to configure as a master top,

formula name

The `apache-formula` repository has a directory called `apache`, which in turn holds an `init.sls` file and any other supporting files. Likewise, the `mysql-formula` repository has a `mysql` directory with its own `init.sls` and so on.

pillar.example

Anything that can be made a variable inside a formula should be made a variable. Each of those variables, a sane default, and a description of what they do should be contained inside the `pillar.example` file. It is up to you, the user, to implement those variables in your pillar or grain data.

README

`README` is a file containing a description of the formula and any relevant documentation that should be seen immediately. The contents of this file will be displayed on GitHub, below the list of files in the repository.

LICENSE

All projects on GitHub should contain a `LICENSE` file, and this is no different. It is extremely common for Salt-related projects, such as those in Salt Stack Formulas, to contain a copy of the Apache 2 license.

FORMULA

If present, the `FORMULA` file can be used to create SPM packages of this formula. Refer to the *Using the Salt Package Manager* section later in this chapter.

Cloning formulas

It is possible to use the GitFS external filesystem to make a formula available, but I would strongly discourage using it to point directly to GitHub. Not only is it discourteous to GitHub themselves, but it also introduces the possibility of an unexpected commit causing issues in your infrastructure.

No, it is better to clone a repository, test it, and then implement it. As new commits appear upstream, you can fetch, test, and deploy them as you see fit.

Go to `https://github.com/saltstack-formulas/apache-formula`, and you will see this:

On the main screen of the repository, you will see a button titled **Clone or download**. This button will offer you the ability to choose between cloning using HTTPS or SSH. Go ahead and set aside a location on your machine for checkouts:

```
# mkdir -p /src/saltstack-formulas
```

Move into that directory:

```
# cd /src/saltstack-formulas
```

Then, clone the repository:

```
# git clone https://github.com/saltstack-formulas
/apache-formula.git
```

I'm going to assume that you have a basic understanding of Git, but I will give you a couple of pointers. First off, most formulas use a master branch as the default. When you clone a repository from a remote source, that source will be called `origin` by default.

So to fetch new data from a repository, use the following two commands:

```
# git fetch origin
# git pull origin master
```

I'm not going to get into Git any more here, as that's way outside the scope of this chapter. But even if you're not used to Git, this should still be enough to get you going, so long as you don't make any local changes to your clone.

Using the Salt Package Manager

The **Salt Package Manager (SPM)**, was added in version 2015.8 to address a very common problem: the distribution of states and formulas to other systems. You may be tempted to think of SPM only as an extension of Salt Stack Formulas, but that is far from the truth. In fact, there is a much larger need for the distribution of Salt-specific files.

In fact, while Salt Stack Formulas was kept in mind during the development of SPM, the bigger concern were private customers and, in particular, government, military, and other secure organizations that have a need to distribute information in environments that by necessity cannot have a connection to the Internet.

Thinking of SPM as a package manager

Package managers are, in theory, a simple concept. A package is created that contains a set of files to be copied to an individual computer. Older package managers did little more than that, while modern package managers also keep track of file metadata so that installed packages can be queried, monitored, and removed.

Unfortunately, these modern package managers tend to carry quite a bit of complexity in order to offer those features to their users. A well-made package manager coupled with well-made packages hides these complexities from the bulk of the users using those packages.

SPM is a very new package manager and still has plenty of quirks. As with other package managers, it will evolve based on the needs of its users and the communities that they create. Fortunately, its design has borrowed from existing package managers in order to try and cut down on the learning curve.

From a package-management point of view, SPM borrows heavily from Pacman, the package manager of Arch Linux and its derivatives, and a little from RPM Package Manager, favored by Suse and RedHat among others.

SPM uses a tarball that has been processed with the `bzip2` compression format. These decisions were made because both `tar` and `bzip2` are supported by Python 2.6, which is the lowest version of Python supported by Salt.

The tarball contains a handful of metadata files, most notably `FORMULA`, which is analogous to an RPM spec file or a Pacman `PKGBUILD` file. As this is a Salt tool, `FORMULA` files are stored in YAML format. We'll get into the actual layout of this and other files in the *Building packages* section coming up.

The same command (`spm`) is used for all SPM operations. If you have an SPM file locally saved on your computer, you can use the following command to install it:

```
# spm local install /path/to/package.spm
```

All `spm` commands that operate on a locally available package use `local`. For instance, to show the metadata for a package, you'd use this command:

```
# spm local info /path/to/package.spm
```

This one lists the files inside a package:

```
# spm local info /path/to/package.spm
```

Thinking of SPM as a repository manager

The SPM commands in the previous section may look familiar to those of you who are used to the `yum` command that is common on so many Red Hat-based systems. This is by design. Because `yum` commands are (more or less) in plain English, rather than relying on option flags, they tend to be much easier to remember. SPM has taken usage cues from `yum` and tried to utilize plain-English commands as well.

This leads in well to SPM as a repository manager in addition to its function as a package manager. While usage is based on `yum` commands, the concept of building a package manager and a package repository manager into the same program is copied from Pacman.

When package managers were created, the concept of a package repository was still a long way off. By the time Pacman (and of course SPM) came about, the developers were able to take advantage of the existing knowledge of both.

Many of the SPM commands that don't use `local` are designed to be used with a package repository. For instance, the following command will install a package from a repository:

```
# spm install <packagename>
```

Of course, this command assumes that:

- You have one or more SPM repositories configured
- One of those repositories has the requested package available
- You have downloaded the latest metadata from that repository

The second of those should be obvious; let's discuss the others in turn.

Configuring SPM repositories

SPM repositories are configured using the `/etc/salt/spm.repos.d/` directory, which contains one or more file with a `.repo` extension. Users of `yum` will recognize this naming convention. As with other Salt configuration files, these are in YAML format. One or more repositories can be configured in these files, using the following format:

```
<repository name>:
    url: <repository url>
```

At the moment, the only argument available inside a repository definition is `url`. This URL can use one of the following schemes:

- http
- https
- ftp
- file

Here's an example:

```
local_spm_repo:
  url: file:///srv/spm/
remote_spm_repo:
  url: https://repo.example.com/spm/
```

Downloading repository metadata

Once a repository has been configured, you need to download its metadata to be able to use it. You can download the metadata for all repositories at once, like this:

```
spm update_repo
```

Or you can download the metadata for one specific repository:

```
spm update_repo remote_spm_repo
```

Creating SPM repositories

It's all well and good to be able to configure your system to download repository metadata, but how do you create one in the first place? As packages become readily available, this skill will become more important than building the packages in the first place (but don't worry; we'll get to those in the next section).

Once again, if you are familiar with creating yum repositories, these steps will not surprise you. It's up to you what order you want to do these steps in, of course.

Set aside a directory to hold packages

The placement of this directory will likely depend largely on the mechanism that you will use to share the directory. For the purpose of our examples, we'll use /srv/http/spm/:

```
# mkdir -p /srv/http/spm/
```

Share that directory

It doesn't matter what program you use to share the directory as long as it supports one of the necessary schemes. Apache and Nginx are excellent web servers, and vsftpd is an excellent FTP server. For our example, we'll use darkhttpd:

```
# darkhttpd /srv/http/spm
darkhttpd/1.12, copyright (c) 2003-2016 Emil Mikulic.
listening on: http://0.0.0.0:80/
```

Populate the directory

Go ahead and copy all of the SPM files into the directory that you wish to serve to users. As you'll see in the next section, there's a good chance those files live in /srv/spm_build/:

```
cp /srv/spm_build/*spm /srv/http/spm/
```

Create the repository metadata

Once that directory is populated, you can use the spm command to turn it into a repository:

```
spm create_repo /srv/http/spm/
```

This will create a YAML file called SPM-METADATA in that directory. When a user issues the spm update_repo command, this is the file that will be downloaded.

This file describes each SPM package in that directory, including the package name, filename, and package metadata. As of Salt version 2016.3, no other information is included, but future versions are intended to contain a list of files inside the package as well.

Building packages

Before you can put together an SPM repository, you need packages. When SPM packages become more readily available, this won't be so much of a problem. Until then, you will need to build packages on your own.

The package structure is reasonably simple and is based on existing repositories in the Salt Stack Formulas GitHub repository. In fact, the one thing that allows most of those repositories to become an SPM package is the presence of a YAML file called FORMULA.

Let's look at the fields required in all FORMULA files.

version

The version field denotes the version of the formula. By convention, this is usually the year and month that this formula was last updated, in YYYYMM format.

release

The `release` field has the iteration of the formula in a given month. The first release build of the month is 1, the second is 2, and so on. Combined with the version, you will end up with formula versioning that looks like `201607-1`.

summary

The `summary` field has a one-line description of the formula. This should be short, sweet, and to the point.

description

The `description` field has a longer description of the formula. This field can span multiple lines if necessary, but don't go overboard.

There are a number of other fields that can be added as well to provide further information about the formula. Some of these fields are descriptive only; they will not affect the installation in any way. Others will affect how the formula is built.

name

The `name` field denotes the name that will be used to refer to the package, both in the name of the package file and any databases (such a repository or local install metadata) that refer to the package. This field is highly recommended, but if it's not included, then SPM will attempt to discover the package name based on the files present.

os

The `os` field has a comma-separated list of operating systems (as seen in the `os` grain) that the formula explicitly supports. This has no bearing on the machine where the formula is installed, as that machine is likely to only be serving formula files to other machines.

os_family

Like `os`, `os_family` is a comma-separated list of operating system families (as seen in the `os_family` grain) that this formula explicitly supports.

dependencies

The `dependencies` field has a comma-separated list of SPM package names that are required in order for this formula to work. The items in this list are enforced at installation time. That means that if the dependencies are not already installed, SPM will attempt to install them.

This is one of the most useful fields as it allows you to create virtual packages of a sort, which serves only to tie together other disparate packages. For instance, you may create a formula called `wordpress-nginx-mysql` that contains the following line:

```
dependencies: wordpress,nginx,mysql
```

And you might have another formula called `wordpress-apache-mysql`, which contains the following line:

```
dependencies: wordpress,apache,mysql
```

Such formulas would contain few or no files, except possibly configuration files that tie the dependencies together.

optional

The `optional` field is a comma-separated list of SPM packages related to this formula. During the installation of this formula, SPM will display the names of these packages but will not force them to be installed.

recommended

The `recommended` field has a comma-separated list of SPM packages that are not required but are recommended for this package. For instance, an `apache` package may recommend another package called `mod_ssl`.

minimum_version

The `minimum_version` field holds the minimum version of Salt that is required in order for this formula to function properly. This is not currently enforced, but as SPM was introduced in version 2015.8, it is assumed that any SPM package supports at least that version of Salt.

top_level_dir

Normally, a formula directory will contain another directory with the files that belong to the formula. For instance, the `apache` formula contains another directory called `apache`. However, you may wish to use a directory that does not match the name of the formula. For instance, you may have an `apache` formula with a directory inside of it called `apache2`. In this case you would set `top_level_dir` to `apache2`.

license

The `license` field contains the license under which the formula itself (and not any packages managed by the states inside the formula) has been released.

A complete formula file might look like this:

```
name: apache
os: RedHat, Debian, Ubuntu, Suse, FreeBSD
os_family: RedHat, Debian, Suse, FreeBSD
version: 201607
release: 1
minimum_version: 2015.8
top_level_dir: apache
summary: Formula for installing Apache
description: Formula for installing the Apache web server
optional: mod_perl
recommended: mod_ssl
```

Once you have a `FORMULA` file in place, you can issue an `spm build` command on the directory that it lives in, like this, for instance:

```
# spm build /srv/formulas/apache-formula
```

This command assumes that the `FORMULA` file exists inside `/srv/formulas/apache-formula/`. If that file contains the aforementioned `FORMULA` content, then it is also assumed that there is an `apache` folder there as well (that is, `/srv/formulas/apache-formula/apache/`).

In the case of this formula, a file will be created here:

```
/srv/spm_build/apache-201607-1.spm
```

Once it has been created, you may distribute it as you feel appropriate.

Where to use SPM

Because formulas are so commonly used on the master, a common misconception has arisen that SPM may only be run on the master. In fact, SPM can be run on any machine running Salt 2015.8 or greater, whether the master or minion service is running or no active Salt service is running at all.

SPM configuration

It may seem strange to wait until the end to go over SPM configuration, but I did this for two reasons:

- These options don't make a lot of sense without understanding the rest of SPM
- The defaults will work well for most installations.

However, you may have a need to tweak certain settings as your usage of SPM increases. These settings may be set in either the `minion` or `master` configuration file or in the `spm` configuration file. The one exception is `conf_file`, which we'll cover first.

spm_conf_file

Default: `/etc/salt/spm`

The name and location of the SPM configuration file is held in `spm_conf_file`. Obviously, it doesn't make sense to place this inside the SPM configuration file itself.

formula_path

Default: `/srv/spm/salt`

The `formula_file` setting holds the directory where SPM will install formula files. This is intentionally set outside of the standard location for formula files (`/srv/salt/`) as it is common for organizations to keep the files in the standard location inside some sort of revision control.

pillar_path

Default: `/srv/spm/pillar`

As with `formula_path`, `pillar_path` complements the standard pillar path of `/srv/pillar/`. Each formula will normally contain a `pillar.example` file, which will be renamed to match the formula name, and placed in this directory. For example, `pillar.example` in the Apache formula will be installed as `/srv/spm/pillar/apache.sls.orig`.

reactor_path

Default: `/srv/spm/reactor`

When a formula's name ends in `-reactor`, its files will be installed in the directory specified by `reactor_path` rather than in the `formula_path`.

spm_logfile

Default: `/var/log/salt/spm`

The `spm_logfile` setting has the location of SPM's log file.

spm_default_include

Default: `spm.d/*conf`

The `spm_default_include` setting complements `spm_conf_file` by specifying a directory in which other SPM-related configuration files may live. The directory specified here will be located in the same directory as the SPM configuration file.

spm_repos_config

Default: `/etc/salt/spm.repos`

Repository definitions may live entirely inside `spm_default_include` if you wish. However, this file is also used as the base for the `.d` directory, where `.repo` files may live. For instance, a setting of `/etc/salt/spm.repos` will also automatically include `/etc/salt/spm.repos.d/*repo`.

spm_cache_dir

Default: `/var/cache/salt/spm`

Any cache files belonging to SPM will live in `spm_cache_dir`. This includes both copies of any repository metadata and copies of any packages that were downloaded from those repositories to be installed.

spm_build_dir

Default: `/srv/spm_build`

When an SPM package is built, it will be created in the `spm_build_dir` directory.

spm_build_exclude

Default: `['CVS', '.hg', '.git', '.svn']`

When an SPM package is built, files ending in any of these names will be skipped. This helps keep SPM packages clean.

spm_db

Default: `/var/cache/salt/spm/packages.db`

Metadata concerning installed packages is stored inside the `spm_db` file.

Summary

One SLS file is powerful, but combining them together into multiple, connected SLS files can make for an infrastructure definition that is complex but not complicated. The key to combining states together is the `include` directive. Data that is included like this can be augmented using the `extend` directive.

Multiple environments can also be used to merge together state trees, combining multiple types of formulas into a cohesive infrastructure definition. Master tops can be further used to define those environments and the targets that go in them.

There are already a number of formulas available from the community, which are provided by the Salt Stack Formulas organization on GitHub. You can use these or your own formulas to build SPM packages, making the distribution of formulas as easy as using other package managers.

Next up, we'll take a deep dive into the hows, whys, and how-tos about Salt SSH.

4
Exploring Salt SSH

Salt introduced the powerful concept of using message queues as a communication-transport mechanism. There are times when the old tools just make sense. However, there's no reason not to give them a kick in the seat of their pants when necessary. This is why Salt SSH was created. In this chapter, we'll cover the following topics:

- Using rosters
- Building dynamic rosters
- Understanding the salt-thin agent
- Using the raw SSH mode

Grappling with SSH

SSH is in fact based on concepts very different from the primary architecture of Salt. Salt was designed to communicate with large numbers of remote machines at once; SSH was designed to interact with only one at a time. Let's take a few minutes to examine some of the differences between Salt and SSH.

Remote shells

Let's take a step back in time to when the Internet wasn't around yet and the ARPANET was brand new. To accompany this new concept to nationally and globally interconnected networks, a series of new protocols was introduced. Telnet, a communication mechanism to take advantage of them, was also introduced. Internet protocols were based on telnet, including a remote shell.

As security needs grew, so did the need to secure telnet. SSH was born; eventually, the **OpenSSH** project was broadly shipped and supported by a number of Unix-based platforms. While SSH means Secure Shell, it was in fact designed to securely tunnel applications that had traditionally communicated with telnet. The default application was a shell, replacing traditional telnet and its kin, but many, many more possibilities also existed.

With all of this in mind, it makes sense that developers and administrators would be so used to their shell-based remote administration tools. SSH offers security, a reasonably (but not completely) consistent platform between remote systems, and a familiar environment to work in. It was never designed to handle communications between multiple machines.

A number of solutions were available to address this situation. SSH password agents and passwordless SSH keys, along with with the power of shell scripts, comprised the bulk of the solutions for years. One particular tool called **ClusterSSH** allowed multiple login windows to accept input from a single location and relay it across all connections.

Salt SSH was not the first of these. It was released by SaltStack to accommodate the needs of some of their users, who enjoyed the principles behind the Salt framework but had a need to use SSH in an automated fashion to manage some of their systems.

Using rosters

Salt was originally designed to operate without the traditional database that many of its forefathers used to store remote system configuration. As its message bus could retrieve information directly from remote machines, often faster than a database lookup, the need for a database was minimized.

As minions connect to the master and not the other way around, in a traditional Salt infrastructure, the master did not even have a need to store the network and host configuration for the minions. The game changes when dealing with SSH-based connections because the master necessarily connects to its minions via SSH.

Rosters were introduced as a means for Salt SSH to keep track of the host information. The default roster, which uses flat text files, is enough to get the job done. More dynamic rosters add vast depths of power.

The flat roster

As its name suggests, this roster uses a flat file. This is normally stored as
`/etc/salt/roster`, but it can be changed with the `-roster-file` option:

```
# salt-ssh --roster-file=/etc/salt/altroster myminion test.ping
```

At its most basic level, this file needs to contain only two pieces of information: the name of
a minion and a network address (IP or hostname) through which this minion is reached:

(In `/etc/salt/roster`)

```
dufresne: 10.0.0.50
adria: 10.0.19.80
achatz: 10.0.200.5
blumenthal: 10.0.19.95
```

However, more information can be added as required:

(In `/etc/salt/roster`)

```
dufresne:
  host: 10.0.200.3
  user: wd50
adria:
  host: 10.0.19.80
  passwd: bulli
achatz:
  host: 10.0.200.5
  priv: /root/alinea.pem
blumenthal:
  host: 10.0.19.95
  sudo: True
```

The options supported in a flat roster file as of version 2016.3 are discussed in the following
subsections.

host

`host` can be an IP address or a hostname address. It should contain only the address and no
other information, such as protocol, port, and so on.

port

`port` is normally port 22, the SSH default. In nonstandard installations, this value can be changed as appropriate.

user

`user` will default to the user running the `salt-ssh` client, which is normally `root`. As system administration tasks are often carried out using the root user, this is generally okay. If the username differs, add this field.

If there is a need to run different tasks as different users on the same machine, it may be useful to create separate roster entries for each user.

passwd

If using password authentication, then the value in `passwd` is the password to use. This is normally discouraged because this file is plain text and viewable by anyone with appropriate permissions. If passwords are unavoidable in a roster file, then the read permissions on the file should be restricted to the very least.

This option can be avoided by specifying the password from the command line with the `--passwd` option:

```
# salt-ssh --passwd=verybadpass myminion test.ping
```

Alternately, Salt SSH can prompt the user for the password, eliminating the need for a plain text password to ever appear on screen:

```
# salt-ssh --askpass myminion test.ping
```

This should only be required on the first execution. Salt will ask whether or not it should set up its own access key for future commands (see the `priv` option). If allowed, subsequent commands will just use Salt's own SSH key instead of the user password.

sudo

In a situation where a privileged command must be performed by an unprivileged user, the `sudo` option should be set to `True`. The default is `False`. As of version 2016.3, the user specified must be set to not require a password. This can be accomplished by editing the `sudoers` file (normally, `/etc/sudoers` is editable with the `visudo` command) and adding the `NOPASSWD` flag to a user's entry:

```
heston ALL=(ALL) NOPASSWD: ALL
```

priv

In a situation where a private key is required to access a minion, the `priv` option will specify the path to a user-defined private key. If no such key is defined, then Salt will create one. The default location is `/etc/salt/pki/ssh/salt-ssh.rsa`.

timeout

The `timeout` option is the number of seconds to wait for an SSH connection to be established. The default is `60`.

thin_dir

The `thin_dir` option is the directory on the target minion in which Salt's thin agent will be installed. This agent is discussed in more detail later in the chapter, in the *Understanding the salt-thin agent* section.

Other built-in rosters

A number of other rosters ship with Salt, which allows a much more dynamic means of identifying hosts and their connection parameters. To use a different roster than the standard flat file, add the `--roster` option to `salt-ssh`:

```
# salt-ssh --roster=cloud myminion test.ping
```

There are additional rosters available as of version 2016.3, which we will look at now.

scan

The `scan` roster was the first dynamic roster to ship with Salt SSH. It directs the client to attempt to log in to a range of IP addresses in order to issue the requested command. This roster is unique in that it does not make use of a minion ID; the IP address that is generated in the scan is used instead.

The following command will scan a small subnet and return `True` for each IP address that is able to answer:

```
# salt-ssh --roster=scan 10.0.0.0/24 test.ping
```

There are some considerations that should be kept in mind when working with the scan roster. First of all, all the connection information (aside from the IP address) needs to be the same across all hosts. The exception to this is SSH keys that have already been established and stored in an SSH key agent, if applicable.

However, there are security concerns with using preexisting SSH keys. Consider a scenario where you have deployed your public key across your entire infrastructure. Believing your network to be secure, you assume that any machine that is accessible via your key belongs to you and can be trusted. However, your key, public as it is, is acquired by an attacker in your network, who proceeds to set up a bogus minion with it. As you issue what you believe to be secure commands using the scan roster, which may include sensitive data, their minion is busy collecting this data.

This is not an attack vector unique to Salt SSH. This attack was in use long before automated SSH tools hit the market; users have been falling prey to it for years. Rather than using the scan roster to issue sensitive commands, it should be used only for network discovery.

There are two specific options that can be used with the scan roster. The `--scan-ports` option accepts a comma-separated list of ports to attempt to log in to the target minion. The default is `22`. As this may be seen as a form of port scanning in some organizations, be sure to check your security policy before using this option. The `--scan-timeout` option can also specify a timeout for the scanning process. The default is `0.01`, which translates to 10 ms.

cache

While Salt was not initially designed to use a database, some optimizations have since been added that accomplish many of the same goals. In particular, the grains for each minion are cached by default on the master. As IPv4 addresses are among the data stored with the grains, the `cache` roster takes advantage of it to obtain IP addresses for minions that have already been accessed via another transport mechanism, such as Salt's ZMQ-based transport.

This can be useful when troubleshooting a machine on which the `salt-minion` client was previously installed but is now no longer responding. So long as the IP address has not changed, the `cache` roster can look it up with the following command:

```
# salt-ssh --roster=cache myminion service.start salt-minion
```

As of version 2016.3, the limitations of this roster are similar to the `scan` roster. The user will default to whichever user is issuing the `salt-ssh` command. Also, if SSH keys are not established or specified with `--priv`, passwords must be supplied with either `--passwd` or `--askpass`.

The cache roster only supports IPv4 addresses. However, it can differentiate between addresses that are local (`127.0.0.0/8`), private (`10.0.0.0/8`, `172.16.0.0/12` and `192.168.0.0/16`), or public (everything else). It can also be configured to prefer one type over another. This is done with the `roster_order` option in the master configuration. The default is this:

```
roster_order:
  - public
  - private
  - local
```

cloud

The `cloud` roster is similar to the `cache` roster, but there are some differences. As with Salt, Salt Cloud caches information by default about the minions that it creates. The difference is that minions created with Salt Cloud don't need to have a connection established with the Salt master in order to have their IP address cached; since the hostname was required to run the deploy process in the first place, Salt Cloud already knows what it is and caches it.

Keep in mind that if a minion that was created with Salt Cloud reboots, then the IP address will likely change unless it is specifically configured not to. However, issuing a **full query** (covered in Chapter 7, *Taking Salt Cloud to the Next Level*) will refresh this data. Therefore, the cloud roster may be able to obtain the IP information that is otherwise not accessible to the cache roster:

```
# salt-ssh --roster=cloud myminion service.start salt-minion
```

The cloud roster also has the ability to borrow authentication information (SSH keys, passwords, and so on) from the provider or profile configuration that was used to create the minion. So long as this information has not changed, it should not be necessary to specify that information again.

Like the cache roster, the cloud roster supports the roster_order option in the master configuration with the same defaults.

ansible

A notable SSH automation platform is the Ansible product. This program has seen widespread adoption (especially among developers) because of its ease of use and its abundant suite of tools. Many users of Ansible have found a need to use both Salt and SSH to manage their machines. Other users have decided to switch altogether.

Rather than rosters, Ansible uses inventories to maintain the host information. The ansible roster allows Salt SSH to natively use Ansible inventories instead of roster files to obtain the host information.

As a path to an Ansible inventory must be specified, the --roster-file option is used in conjunction with this roster:

```
# salt-ssh --roster=ansible --roster-file=/etc/salt/hosts myminion
test.ping
```

Building dynamic rosters

There is no reason to restrict yourself to the rosters that ship with Salt. As with pillars, any external source that can provide the appropriate data can be used. In the case of rosters, the appropriate data should look like the data that is stored in flat roster files.

Consider the following entry from a flat roster file:

```
myminion:
```

```
host: 10.0.11.38
user: larry
password: 5700g3z43v4r
```

If you have a data source that provides this data, then you can plug the data into it. In fact, if you have a command that outputs this data, for instance in YAML, then you can easily write a roster that wraps this command.

```
import yaml
def targets(tgt, tgt_type='glob', **kwargs):
    return yaml.safe_load(__salt__['cmd.run']('cat /etc/salt/roster'))
```

This is almost identical to the code used in the cmd_yaml external pillar, but it can be adapted for use with rosters. Even if you don't know Python, the preceding code can easily be changed to wrap your own custom commands, even those written in a different language.

Using Salt SSH

We've spent some time discussing how to configure minions using rosters. Let's take a few minutes to discuss some basic usage.

The salt-ssh command is very similar to the salt command in usage. A target is provided, followed by a module and function, which is optionally followed by any arguments for the function. Targets can be specified in the same way as with the salt command, although not as many target types are supported. As of version 2016.3, the following target types are supported by Salt SSH:

- Glob (the default)
- Perl Compatible Regular Expression (-E or --pcre)
- List (-L or --list)
- Nodegroup (-N or --nodegroup)
- Range (-R or --range)

Using a target type is the same as with the salt command:

 # salt-ssh -L minion1,minion2 test.ping

All the outputters available in the salt command are also available and accessed the same way. The command to access the outputters is as follows:

 # salt-ssh myminion grains.items --out json

Other options are unique to Salt SSH. For instance, in order to target by grain, the master needs to have a copy of the minion's grain data in its cache. This can be done using the `--refresh` flag:

```
# salt-ssh --refresh myminion test.ping
```

Using a Saltfile

If a number of options are commonly used with Salt SSH, it can become cumbersome to type all of them. Fortunately, a **Saltfile** can be used to automate adding these options. This is a YAML file that can contain any number of options that are normally passed on the command line. The following is a snippet from a Saltfile:

```
salt-ssh:
  max_procs: 15
  wipe_ssh: True
```

This file is normally called `Saltfile`. If it is present in the current working directory when the `salt-ssh` command is issued, it will be used. The `salt-ssh` command can also point directly to a Saltfile in another directory, as shown in the following code:

```
# salt-ssh --saltfile=/etc/salt/Saltfile myminion test.ping
```

If you have a global Saltfile that you want to use everywhere, you can create a shortcut to it as well with an alias (if your shell supports it):

```
# alias salt-ssh='salt-ssh --saltfile=/etc/salt/Saltfile'
```

You can also set an environment variable called `SALT_SALTFILE`:

```
# export SALT_SALTFILE=/etc/salt/Saltfile
```

The following options and their command-line equivalents are available in a Salt SSH Saltfile:

- `raw_shell` (`-r`, `--raw`, `--raw_shell`)
- `roster` (`--roster`)
- `roster_file` (`--roster-file`)
- `refresh_cache` (`--refresh`, `--refresh-cache`)
- `max_procs` (`--max-procs`)
- `extra_filerefs` (`--extra-filerefs`)
- `wipe_ssh` (`-w`, `--wipe`)
- `ssh_priv` (`--priv`)

- `ignore_host_keys` (`-i`, `--ignore-host-keys`)
- `ssh_user` (`--user`)
- `ssh_passwd` (`--passwd`)
- `ssh_askpass` (`--askpass`)
- `ssh_key_deploy` (`--key-deploy`)
- `ssh_scan_ports` (`--scan-ports`)
- `ssh_scan_timeout` (`--scan-timeout`)

Salt versus Salt SSH

In its default mode, Salt SSH is designed to behave (as far as `user` is concerned) exactly like the `salt` command. Minions can be targeted just like the `salt` command, modules are made available exactly the same way across minions, arguments are specified the same way, and output is displayed in exactly the same way. However, there are some differences.

Architecture

The primary difference between the standard `salt` command and the `salt-ssh` command is how the communication is architected based on the transport mechanism. The `salt` command uses a message queue whereas the `salt-ssh` command uses SSH (of course).

Think of the message queue like a television station. All of your minions are watching the television and waiting for instruction. As tasks are issued, they will be broadcast to the minions along with information on who should perform them. When a minion finishes a task, it will return the result to the master along a similar queue. The transmission from master to minions is a one-to-many communication whereas the transmission back is a many-to-one communication. In fact, since the master makes use of its own group of local workers to receive responses, the transmission back really is more of a many-to-*not-quite as-many* connection.

SSH is more like a telephone line in that it is designed for one-to-one communication. Individual minions listen for their phone to ring, and when a call comes in with a task, they can execute it and return a result immediately. The more minions required to perform tasks, the more phone calls must be made. The master can use local workers to set up multiple concurrent connections, much like a call center, but each task must still be relayed individually.

Performance

Another difference is performance. Salt SSH is very fast, but it has some overhead, some of which is consistent with SSH in general. The following actions are performed in addition to what Salt already does:

- Building and deploying the salt-thin agent
- Building and deploying the states tarball
- Establishing an SSH connection to the target

The last of these will happen with any program that uses SSH under the hood. The others may or may not happen with other frameworks. In a small infrastructure, this may be unnoticeable, but in a larger setup, it may be problematic.

The salt-thin agent (covered in the next section) is not a problem because it will be generated in the first connection. Then, it will be cached until the version of Salt changes on the master.

The state tarball (also covered in the next section) will be generated each time a state run is issued, which does cause some slowdown. However, it will not affect other execution modules.

Establishing SSH connections may be the biggest overhead. One system can only maintain so many connections at once. In fact, with a large enough job, Salt SSH will limit the number of active connections to 25 by default. This can be changed with the `--max-procs` flag:

```
# salt-ssh --max-procs 100 '*' test.ping
```

Exercise caution here: increasing the maximum number of connections to a number that is not supported by the available resources can cause other issues outside Salt.

Understanding the salt-thin agent

As it turns out, automating SSH commands is not as simple as it may look at first. In an environment where every server runs exactly the same version of exactly the same operating system and exactly the same pieces of software, executing remote commands can be greatly simplified. However, very few environments meet this requirement, and Salt was designed to handle multiple environments.

In order to accommodate these disparate configurations, the code that performs the tasks needs to be able to autodetect pieces of its environment and then execute the tasks required by the user. In short, a piece of software that behaves exactly like Salt is necessary. Fortunately, in the Salt environment, that software is already available.

The salt-thin agent was designed to be a lightweight version of Salt that could be quickly copied to a remote system by Salt SSH in order to perform tasks. It doesn't ship with Salt (not as such, at least). It is built as needed by Salt SSH using the Salt version and modules already installed on the master.

Once salt-thin has been packaged, it can be copied to the target system, where it is unpacked and then executed. Let's look at the specifics.

Building the thin package

In its default mode, Salt SSH requires the thin package. The raw mode doesn't require the thin package, but we'll cover this in a bit. However, since the package doesn't ship with Salt in a form that is usable by Salt SSH, it gets built on demand and cached for later use.

The thin package contains just a little more than the bare essentials to run Salt. All the files for this package are collected from various locations on the master. Most of these files exist inside the installation directories for Salt itself, but some belong to other packages that Salt depends on.

Interestingly, not all of Salt's dependencies will be needed. Many of the packages that Salt normally depends on are not necessary. As the communication will happen using SSH instead of ZeroMQ, this will not be included. The encryption libraries that are used to secure this communication transport are also not needed because the connection is secured by SSH itself.

Python will also not be packed in the thin package because a minimum version of Python must already be installed on the target system. Why not include Python in the thin package? There are a number of answers, but the most prominent one is binary compatibility. Python itself is compiled differently across various platforms with different versions of the gcc compiler. A master running Enterprise Linux would not be able to control a target running Ubuntu because the version of Python on the master would not meet the environment requirements on the target. Likewise, a 64-bit master would not be able to control any 32-bit targets.

Once the necessary files have been collected, they are bound to a tarball called `salt-thin.tgz`. This package will contain only files that do not depend on the binary compatibility between the master and minion. This limits the tarball not only to scripts, mostly written in Python, but also to shell scripts (specifically the Bourne shell, also known as `sh`).

The actual construction of the `thin` package is performed by the thin runner. If necessary, for purposes such as testing, the `thin` package can be generated manually using this runner:

```
# salt-run thin.generate
```

The tarball will be saved in the cache directory on the master, usually in the `/var/cache/salt/master/thin/` directory. If the file already exists, you will want to make sure to tell the runner to overwrite it. The command to overwrite the file is as follows:

```
# salt-run thin.generate overwrite=True
```

If you were to unpack the tarball after it was built, you'd find a small file structure with a handful of files in it. Libraries such as Jinja2 and PyYAML will be there along with a directory for Salt.

Including extra modules

By default, the `thin` package will include all the modules that ship with Salt and the dependencies for the core Salt code. However, it will not include the Python modules that are required for noncore modules. For instance, if you are using the `etcd` execution module, which requires the `etcd` Python module, you need to be sure to include it in your `thin` package by adding it to the end of the `thin.generate` command. The command to carry out this action is as follows:

```
# salt-run thin.generate etcd
```

Multiple modules can be specified and separated by commas with the following code:

```
# salt-run thin.generate etcd,MySQLdb
```

Deploying the thin package

After Salt SSH packages this file, it will be copied to the remote system. By default, it will be placed in the `/tmp/` directory in a hidden directory with the name of the user that will be logged in on the target and a unique ID seeded with the hostname of the target system.

For instance, on a system whose FQDN is simply `dufresne`, the directory may be called `/tmp/.root_0338d8__salt/`. This directory will be owned by the user that Salt SSH logged in as (usually root), and the permissions will be set to `0700` so that no other users can read it.

If you would like to see this directory in action, including the unpacked `thin` package, you can do so by executing some introspective Salt commands:

```
# salt-ssh myminion cmd.run 'ls -ls /tmp'
myminion:
    drwxrwxrwt 16 root     root      420 Apr  3 16:51 .
    drwxr-xr-x 20 root     root     4096 Jul 29  2014 ..
    drwx------  8 root     root      260 Apr  3 16:50
    .root_0338d8__salt
# salt-ssh myminion cmd.run 'ls -ls /tmp/.root*'
myminon:
    drwx------  8 root     root      280 Apr  3 17:43 .
    drwxrwxrwt 17 root     root      440 Apr  3 17:46 ..
    drwxr-xr-x  2 root     root      160 Apr  3 16:50
    certifi
    drwxr-xr-x  3 root     root      880 Apr  3 16:50
    jinja2
    drwxr-xr-x  2 root     root      220 Apr  3 16:50
    markupsafe
    drwxr-xr-x  4 root     root       80 Apr  3 16:50
    running_data
    drwxr-xr-x 31 root     root     1300 Apr  3 16:50 salt
    -rw-r--r--  1 root     root       79 Apr  3 16:50
    salt-call
    -rw-r--r--  1 root     root    27591 Dec 13 21:18
    six.py
    -rw-r--r--  1 root     root        8 Apr  3 16:50
    version
    drwxr-xr-x  2 root     root      720 Apr  3 16:50 yaml
```

Executing the thin package

Now that the thin package has been installed on the target, it must be executed. However, there is more work to be done before Salt is actually executed. Python can live in different locations depending on the environment, and Salt SSH needs to find where it is before it can call it.

The Salt SSH shim

A shim is a very tiny shell script whose job is to find the Python interpreter on the target system and then use it to start Salt. It is encoded to a Base64 string on the master, sent to the minion, decoded, and executed.

There are certain conditions that will affect how the shim is executed. If sudo is required on the target system, then the necessary commands will be embedded in the shim. If debug logging is turned on on the master, then the shim will be executed in a debug mode, the output of which will be displayed on the master.

The way the shim is run can also vary. If the target system requires a connection with a tty, then the shim will be copied to the remote system using scp and then piped to /bin/sh; otherwise, it will be executed directly as one large command over SSH.

Preparing for Salt states

To run an execution command, not much is needed. However, executing Salt States does require a little more work. This is because even a traditional minion that runs salt-call in local mode requires a local copy of all the necessary files in the State tree.

When a Salt SSH command is executed using the State system, another tarball called salt_state.tgz will need to be created. This file will be placed in the same hidden thin directory on the target as the salt-thin.tgz package. This tarball contains a copy of the necessary files from the State tree on the master so that the salt-call command will have access to everything that it needs for a State run.

The State tarball will also contain a copy of the State data (this is converted to low chunks) and a copy of any pillar data from the master. These files can also be viewed with a couple of the following introspective Salt commands:

```
# salt-ssh myminion state.single cmd.run name='tar
-tzvf /tmp/.root*/salt_state.tgz'
myminion:
    ----------
          ID: tar -tvf /tmp/.root*/salt_state.tgz
    Function: cmd.run
      Result: True
     Comment: Command "tar -tvf /tmp/.root*
     /salt_state.tgz" run
     Started: 17:53:46.683337
    Duration: 7.335 ms
     Changes:
              ----------
```

```
               pid:
                   26843
               retcode:
                   0
               stderr:
               stdout:
                   -rw-r--r-- root/root     15891 2015-04-03 17:53
pillar.json
                   -rw-r--r-- root/root       128 2015-04-03 17:53
lowstate.json
    Summary
    ------------
    Succeeded: 1 (changed=1)
    Failed:    0
    ------------
    Total states run:      1
    # salt-ssh myminion state.single cmd.run name='tar
    -Ozxvf /tmp/.root*/salt_state.tgz lowstate.json'
    myminion:
    ----------
               ID: tar -Ozxvf /tmp/.root*/salt_state.tgz lowstate.json
         Function: cmd.run
           Result: True
          Comment: Command "tar -Ozxvf /tmp/.root*/salt_state.tgz
lowstate.json" run
          Started: 17:58:35.972658
         Duration: 10.14 ms
          Changes:
                   ----------
                   pid:
                       29014
                   retcode:
                       0
                   stderr:
                       lowstate.json
                   stdout:
                       [{"fun": "run", "state": "cmd", "__id__": "tar -Ozxvf
/tmp/.root*/salt_state.tgz lowstate.json", "name": "tar -Ozxvf
/tmp/.root*/salt_state.tgz lowstate.json"}]
    Summary
    ------------
    Succeeded: 1 (changed=1)
    Failed:    0
    ------------
    Total states run:       1
```

Running Salt

Once the shim has found the Python interpreter and the `salt_state.tgz` tarball is deployed (if necessary), it is able to execute Salt. Unlike a traditional Salt setup, it will not be run as a daemon. Instead, the `salt-call` command will be executed in local mode, just like it would on a minion. The output will then be collected by the Salt SSH client on the master, parsed, and sent to the user. We can see this information by running with the `trace` log level:

```
# salt-ssh myminion test.ping --log-level trace
...SNIP...
SALT_ARGV: ['/usr/bin/python2.7',
'/tmp/.root_0338d8__salt/salt-call', '--local',
'--metadata', '--out', 'json', '-l', 'quiet', '-c',
'/tmp/.root_0338d8__salt', '--', 'test.ping']
_edbc7885e4f9aac9b83b35999b68d015148
caf467b78fa39c05f669c0ff89878
[DEBUG   ] RETCODE localhost: 0
[DEBUG   ] LazyLoaded nested.output
[TRACE   ] data = {'myminion': True}
myminion:
    True
```

It is also possible to take a deeper look at the `salt_state.tgz` tarball, but it will require logging in to the minion for the final command, as shown in the following code:

```
master# cp /etc/services /srv/salt/
master# salt-ssh myminion state.single file.managed /tmp/services
source=salt://services
myminion:
    ----------
            ID: /tmp/services
      Function: file.managed
        Result: True
       Comment: File /tmp/services is in the correct state
       Started: 18:18:28.216961
      Duration: 5.656 ms
       Changes:
Summary
------------
Succeeded: 1
Failed:    0
------------
Total states run:     1
minion# tar -tzvf /tmp/.root_0338d8__salt/salt_state.tgz
-rw-r--r-- root/root     15895 2015-04-03 18:18 pillar.json
-rw-r--r-- root/root       118 2015-04-03 18:18 lowstate.json
```

```
-rw------- root/root    289283 2015-04-03 18:18 base/services
```

It will not be possible to view using two sequential `state.single` commands over Salt SSH because the second command will generate a new `salt_state.tgz tarball`, which will not include the `base/services` file. In order to obtain a truly informative view of the target with a single `salt-ssh` command, a full SLS file with enough States to perform sufficient introspection on the target will be required.

Salt's running data

One more directory that you may have noticed in the temporary directory is the `running_data/` directory. One design goal is to have Salt SSH remain as nonintrusive as possible. This means that the directory structure that Salt normally uses has to live someplace different: the temporary directory. We can take a look at this structure with another Salt SSH command:

```
# salt-ssh myminion cmd.run 'tree /tmp/.root*/running_data'
myminion:
    /tmp/.root_0338d8__salt/running_data
    |-- etc
    |    `-- salt
    |         `-- pki
    |              `-- minion
    `-- var
         |-- cache
         |    `-- salt
         |         `-- minion
         |              `-- proc
         |                   `-- 20150403195105124306
         `-- log
              `-- salt
                   `-- minion
    11 directories, 2 files
```

As you continue to issue commands against this minion, the directory structure will continue to grow and look more like a standard minion directory structure. If you want Salt to completely remove all its traces when finished, including this directory, you can use the --wipe or -w flag:

```
# salt-ssh --wipe myminion test.ping
```

Using the raw SSH mode

Salt SSH is very powerful in its default mode with salt-thin. However, there are some situations where it makes more sense to issue a raw SSH command. This can be accomplished using the `--raw` flag (referred to in its short form as `-r` from here on for brevity).

Using the raw mode will bypass all the overhead of creating and deploying the `thin` package: just log in to the target, issue a command, and log out. The following two commands are functionally identical:

```
# salt-ssh myminion cmd.run date
myminion:
     Fri Apr  3 21:07:43 MDT 2015
# salt-ssh -r myminion date
myminion:
     ----------
     retcode:
         0
     stderr:
     stdout:
         Fri Apr  3 21:07:43 MDT 2015
```

However, the raw command will execute faster because it has less overhead. It will also contain more information, such as STDERR, STDOUT, and the `exit` or `return` code from the command that was issued.

This can be useful if you wrap Salt SSH with another program that depends on the output (especially the `return` code) of the command on the remote machine. Make sure to run the command with an outputter that is consistent and easy to parse, such as JSON:

```
# salt-ssh -r myminion 'ping 256.0.0.0' --out json
{
    "myminion": {
        "retcode": 2,
        "stderr": "ping: unknown host 256.0.0.0\n",
        "stdout": ""
    }
}
```

In this example, there is no output to examine, but the error message can certainly be checked. Also, the `return` code will always be available.

Caching SSH connections

The raw SSH mode makes the execution model of Salt a little clearer. When a command is executed anywhere in Salt–be it the `salt` command, `salt-call`, or the `salt-ssh` mode–it will start a job, issue the command, and return the result. Depending on how it is called, Salt may or may not have a connection already established, but it will behave (so far as the user is concerned) as if it were creating a new connection, executing the job, and tearing down the connection.

This is fine in most instances, but there are some notable exceptions. For instance, configuring a network switch over SSH can be problematic. This is because a number of switches use the following configuration models:

- SSH into the switch
- Switch to a privileged user mode
- Execute commands that change configuration
- Review changes (if necessary)
- Commit changes
- Exit the privileged user mode
- Log out of the switch

Trying to use Salt SSH in raw mode may take it as far as switching to privileged user mode, but then it will log back out, forcing you to start over.

If you want to use OpenSSH on your master, you can take advantage of SSH, caching to maintain a connection to the switch as necessary. This is not something that is built in to Salt SSH, but it can be used nonetheless. It is especially useful when scripting Salt SSH in a bash script, for instance.

First, use the following command to set up the connection:

```
# ssh -fMN -o "ControlPath /tmp/salt_ssh_ctrl" myminion.com
```

This will tell SSH to set up a connection in `myminion.com` but to do nothing with it. However, subsequent commands to that machine will automatically use the connection, which will be cached with a socket stored at `/tmp/salt_ssh_ctrl` on the master.

This trick is useful outside Salt SSH as well, especially if you are regularly issuing one-off SSH commands against a machine. Even Salt SSH in its default and non-raw mode will see a slight performance increase because the overhead of establishing and tearing down each connection disappears.

When you are finished with this host, be sure to tear down the connection, as shown in the following code:

```
# ssh -O exit -o "ControlPath /tmp/salt_ssh_ctrl" myminion.com
```

This will disconnect it from the target and remove the socket file from the master.

Summary

Salt SSH is a powerful tool. It can be very comfortable for users in smaller infrastructures. This tool can also be useful for dealing with devices that allow SSH connections but are not able to have Python installed or cannot allow software (such as Salt) to be installed.

Rosters are used to store information about minions which Salt SSH will connect to. You can use a `Saltfile` to store extra configuration in the current working directory. Salt SSH makes use of a specialized tarball to deploy a thin version of Salt on the remote minion.

Next, we will delve into the asynchronous nature of Salt and start to really explore how Salt can be used as an autonomous management platform.

5
Managing Tasks Asynchronously

Salt is commonly thought of as a configuration management system. This is fine because Salt does an excellent job of managing various aspects of its minions. However, this is only a small part of what Salt can do. One of the biggest components is the event system, which forms the basis of an asynchronous execution framework.

In this chapter, we'll spend some time looking at the following topics:

- Going through the event system in depth
- Understanding the reactor system
- Building more complex reactors
- Using the Thorium engine
- Using the queue system

Looking at the event system

The event system is one of the oldest components of Salt. Yet, it is now used more than almost any other part. Most of its usage is internal to Salt, but don't worry because there are plenty of functionalities that we can take advantage of as users and administrators.

Reviewing the basics

Salt is built based on a message queue. Commands that are issued from the master generate jobs, which are posted to the queue. Minions watch the queue for anything that targets them. When a minion picks up a job, it attempts to perform the work associated with it. Once it has finished, it posts the return data back to another queue; this is the one that the master listens to.

Minions also have the ability to fire information that is not associated with a job that was generated on the master. These pieces of information form the basis of the event bus.

There are in fact two event buses: one for minions to communicate with themselves (but not with other minions) and one for minions to communicate with the master. The minion event bus is currently only used internally by Salt. Minions only use it to fire events to themselves. While it is possible for a user to manually or even programmatically fire messages along the minion event bus, there is nothing built in to Salt for the user to directly take advantage of.

The master event bus is a different story altogether. The ability of a minion to send messages to the master is very powerful, especially with the reactor system in place on the master. However, we'll get to this in just a moment.

The structure of event data

In older versions of Salt, event data was very simple: there was a message and a short tag. Tags served as a short description of the message. This changed in version 0.17.0, when both the message and the tag were expanded.

The tag, which was previously limited to 20 characters, now has no limit imposed on its length. However, there are restrictions on which characters may be used: tags must be ASCII-safe strings, and no Unicode is allowed.

The message was also expanded and is now often referred to as the event data or payload. The most notable change involved moving it from a single string to a dictionary. Depending on which part of Salt fired the event, there are certain pieces of data that can reasonably be expected to appear. One piece of data that should always be expected is a timestamp called _stamp. This stamp will look something similar to the following code:

```
2015-04-18T17:49:52.443449
```

Other event data will vary. For instance, when a minion authenticates with the master, an event will be fired with a tag called `salt/auth`. The payload for this event will include a timestamp (`_stamp`), an action (`act`), the ID of the minion (`id`), and the minion's public key (`pub`).

Watching event data

It is easier to get a sense of what event data looks like by watching events in real time-as they occur. There is a script in the GitHub repository designed for this purpose, called `eventlisten.py`. As this is part of Salt's test suite, it does not ship with any of the packages for individual distributions. However, it can be downloaded and used on any system with Salt installed.

Installing the event listener

If you are only interested in using the event listener, it can be downloaded directly from GitHub:
`https://raw.githubusercontent.com/saltstack/salt/develop/tests/eventlisten.py`

However, there are a number of other tests also available that may be interesting to you. Assuming that you have Git installed, you can clone a copy of the repository and use the event listener directly from there, like this, for instance:

```
# cd /root
# git clone https://github.com/saltstack/salt.git
# cd salt/tests
```

Using the event listener

As the most common usage of the event listener is on a Salt master with the default socket location, it will use these settings by default. Just change to the directory that it resides in, and issue the following command:

```
# python eventlisten.py
```

Note that because of differing Python versions and command names on different systems, you may need to change the command to one that is more appropriate for Python 2 on your system:

```
# python2 eventlisten.py
```

If you are listening to the minion event bus instead of the master, you need to tell the event listener what kind of node you are working on (the default is `master`):

```
# python eventlisten.py -n minion
```

If you have changed the location of Salt's socket directory, you will need to pass that in, as shown in the following code:

```
# python eventlisten.py -s /var/run/salt
```

By default, the event listener assumes that you're using ZeroMQ, the default transport mechanism for Salt. If you have configured it to use RAET instead, you'll need to specify it as the transport, as follows:

```
# python eventlisten.py -t raet
```

Once you have started the event listener, it will show you the name of the socket that it will listen to:

```
ipc:///var/run/salt/master/master_event_pub.ipc
```

It will then wait for events to appear on the bus. You can trigger events by issuing Salt commands. Even a simple `test.ping` will generate a series of events that contain the job data, as shown in the following code:

```
Event fired at Sat Apr 18 12:58:48 2015
*************************
Tag: 20150418125848177748
Data:
{'_stamp': '2015-04-18T18:58:48.177999', 'minions': ['cantu']}
Event fired at Sat Apr 18 12:58:48 2015
*************************
Tag: salt/job/20150418125848177748/new
Data:
{'_stamp': '2015-04-18T18:58:48.178257',
 'arg': [],
 'fun': 'test.ping',
 'jid': '20150418125848177748',
 'minions': ['cantu'],
 'tgt': 'cantu',
 'tgt_type': 'glob',
 'user': 'sudo_homaro'}
Event fired at Sat Apr 18 12:58:48 2015
*************************
Tag: salt/job/20150418125848177748/ret/cantu
Data
{'_stamp': '2015-04-18T18:58:48.227514',
```

```
'cmd': '_return',
'fun': 'test.ping',
'fun_args': [],
'id': 'cantu',
'jid': '20150418125848177748',
'retcode': 0,
'return': True,
'success': True}
```

In this case, there were three events fired. The first two denoted that a new job was created with a job ID of 20150418125848177748. The first was an older style of the event, while the second was a newer style. The event tagged as salt/job/20150418125848177748/new contains information about the job and the user that created it. We can see that it wasn't just created by the root user; it was created by a user named homaro, who issued the command using sudo. The test.ping function was sent directly to the cantu minion (otherwise, the target or tgt would be *), and there were no arguments to it.

The last event, tagged as salt/job/20150418125848177748/ret/cantu, contains the job return data from the minion. Among other things, we can see the function again, the arguments for this function, and the return value from the function (True). We even have an indicator that tells us whether or not the job was completed successfully.

Firing custom data

It is possible to fire custom data from a minion to the master with the salt-call command. Of course, it is also possible to issue a command from the master, which tells the minion to fire a message back, but this is largely only useful for test purposes and little more than an advanced test.echo command.

To fire a custom event to the master, both the message and the tag must be supplied in that order. Doing this from the command line requires that the message be declared in a YAML-parsable form. As it turns out, empty data is valid YAML. Issue the following command from a minion:

```
# salt-call event.fire_master '' myevent
```

Take note of the two quotes between `fire_master` and `myevent`, which will denote an empty string. After issuing this command, look at the output in the event listener:

```
Event fired at Sat Apr 18 13:21:55 2015
*************************
Tag: myevent
Data:
{'_stamp': '2015-04-18T19:21:55.604193',
 'cmd': '_minion_event',
 'data': {},
 'id': 'cantu',
 'pretag': None,
 'tag': 'myevent'}
Event fired at Sat Apr 18 13:21:55 2015
*************************
Tag: salt/job/20150418132155629018/ret/cantu
Data:
{'_stamp': '2015-04-18T19:21:55.629583',
 'arg': ['', 'myevent'],
 'cmd': '_return',
 'fun': 'event.fire_master',
 'fun_args': ['', 'myevent'],
 'id': 'cantu',
 'jid': '20150418132155629018',
 'retcode': 0,
 'return': True,
 'tgt': 'cantu',
 'tgt_type': 'glob'}
```

The first is the custom event that was requested by the command that we issued. We see the `myevent` tag associated with it and the data (which was empty). To make this a little more useful, let's add some actual YAML to our command:

```
# salt-call event.fire_master '{"key1": "val1"}'
myevent
```

Doesn't look like YAML, does it? As JSON is syntactically correct YAML and more accurate than it, it is safest to issue command-line data as a JSON string.

With this event, we sent a dictionary with a single key (`key1`) and its associated value (`val1`). The event listener will show the following data:

```
Event fired at Sat Apr 18 13:23:28 2015
*************************
Tag: myevent
Data:
{'_stamp': '2015-04-18T19:23:28.531952',
```

```
  'cmd': '_minion_event',
  'data': {'key1': 'val1'},
  'id': 'cantu',
  'pretag': None,
  'tag': 'myevent'}
Event fired at Sat Apr 18 13:23:28 2015
*************************
Tag: salt/job/20150418132328556517/ret/cantu
Data:
{'_stamp': '2015-04-18T19:23:28.557056',
  'arg': ['{"key1": "val1"}', 'myevent'],
  'cmd': '_return',
  'fun': 'event.fire_master',
  'fun_args': ['{"key1": "val1"}', 'myevent'],
  'id': 'cantu',
  'jid': '20150418132328556517',
  'retcode': 0,
  'return': True,
  'tgt': 'cantu',
  'tgt_type': 'glob'}
```

Once again, we can see the same kind of data as before, but now, we can see that an actual data structure was returned in the custom event. However, it is still possible to make this event even more useful.

Namespacing events

Part of the redesign of the event system involved making use of namespaced event tags. You can see these by looking at the preceding examples. Consider this tag:

```
salt/job/20150418132328556517/ret/cantu
```

This tag is delimited by forward slashes. Once it's split up, we will see the following components:

- salt: This event was fired by Salt itself
- job: This event pertains to Salt's job system
- 20150418132328556517: This is the ID of the job
- ret: This event contains the return data from the job
- cantu: This specifies the ID of the minion that will return the data

Other components of Salt will use a similar convention to tag their events. For instance, consider the following event from Salt Cloud:

```
Event fired at Sat Apr 18 13:36:48 2015
*************************
Tag: salt/cloud/myminion/creating
Data:
{'_stamp': '2015-04-18T19:36:48.642876',
 'event': 'starting create',
 'name': 'myminion',
 'profile': 'centos65',
 'provider': 'my-ec2-config:ec2'}
```

The tag for this event can be broken down as follows:

- `salt`: This event was fired by Salt itself
- `cloud`: This event pertains to Salt Cloud
- `myminion`: This specifies the name of the VM that is affected
- `creating`: This denotes what will happen to that VM now

When you create custom events for your own application or infrastructure, it may be useful to namespace your own event tags in a similar fashion. Perhaps you have an internal application in your organization that you call `mcgee`, which manages a component that archives the server data. You can make use of a tag similar to the following code:

```
mcgee/archive/incremental/myserver/start
```

To declare that a server called `myserver` is starting an incremental backup process, add a tag like this:

```
mcgee/archive/incremental/myserver/finish
```

This is to declare that the incremental backup has completed.

Namespacing guidelines

Why use slashes to delimit event tags? Most of the examples in this book use minion IDs, which contain single words with punctuation. What if a minion ID contains a fully qualified domain name? Consider the following event tag with periods instead of slashes on a minion called `web01.example.com`:

```
salt.cloud.web01.example.com.creating
```

Which is a part of the tag, and which is a part of the minion ID? We can tell this based on our existing knowledge of the tag and the minion, but the ambiguity makes it very difficult to accurately parse. Using slashes makes it much more obvious:

```
salt/cloud/web01.example.com/creating
```

This is why Salt itself uses slashes to delimit tags. Technically, it is entirely up to you how you namespace your tags as long as you keep your tags ASCII safe. However, you should keep some things in mind:

- Tags are like index markers. They should be reasonably unique and adequately describe the contents of the payload.
- Keep tags as short as possible, but as long as necessary.
- Use tags that are both human readable and machine parsable.
- Forward slashes are standard in Salt; consider whether or not a different delimiter would be confusing to experienced Salt users.

Some common events

There are a handful of events extremely common in Salt. Some are common only to various subcomponents of Salt. Knowing what these events mean and how they work can be very helpful when you build reactors.

salt/auth

Periodically, minions will reauthenticate with the master using this event. The following data is contained in the payload:

- `act`: This specifies the current status of the minion
- `id`: This denotes the ID of the minion
- `pub`: This specifies the public RSA key of the minion
- `result`: This denotes whether or not the request was successful

salt/key

When a minon's key is accepted or rejected on the master, the `key` event will be fired. The following data is contained in the payload:

- `id`: This specifies the ID of the minion
- `act`: This denotes the new status of the minion

salt/minion/minion_id/start

When a `salt-minion`process begins, it has some work to do before it is available to receive commands. Once the process has finished starting up and is ready to perform jobs, it will fire the `start` event. You may also see an event called `minion_start` with the same payload. The `minion_start` event is a remnant of the old tag system and is expected to be removed in a future release. The data contained in the payload is as follows:

- `cmd`: This is another indicator to tell Salt which kind of event this is. In this case, it will be `_minion_event`.
- `data`: This specifies the human-readable information about when the minion was started.
- `id`: This denotes the ID of the minion.
- `pretag`: This is used internally by Salt to generate the namespace.
- `tag`: This is a copy of the event tag.

salt/job/job_id/new

When a new job is created, an event will be fired. This contains metadata about the job. The following data will be contained in the event payload:

- `arg`: This specifies any arguments that were passed to the function.
- `fun`: This indicates the actual function that was called (such as `test.ping`).
- `jid`: This indicates the job ID.
- `minions`: This denotes a list of minions that are affected by this job.
- `tgt`: This specifies the target that was specified for this job (such as `*`).
- `tgt_type`: This denotes the type of target that was specified (such as `glob`).
- `user`: This specifies the user that initiated this job. If the user used `sudo`, then `sudo_` will be prepended to the username.

salt/job/job_id/ret/minion_id

Once a minion finishes a job, it will fire an event with the return data. The following data will be contained in the payload:

- cmd: This is another indicator to tell Salt what kind of event this is. In this case, it will be _return.
- fun: As with salt/job/<job_id>/new, this indicates the actual function that was called (such as test.ping).
- fun_args: Similar to the preceding args, this specifies any arguments that were passed to the function.
- id: This is the ID that is returning the data.
- jid: This specifies the job ID.
- retcode: This indicates the return code from the process that was used for this job.
- return: This is all of the return data from this job. Depending on the function, this could be very short or very long.
- success: This indicates whether or not the job was completed successfully.

salt/presence/present

The present event will only be used when presence_events is set to True in the master configuration. When enabled, this event will periodically be fired with a list of minions that are currently connected to the master. The following data will be contained in the payload:

- present: This specifies the list of minions that are currently connected

salt/presence/change

This event will only be used when presence_events is set to True in the master configuration. When enabled, this event will be fired any time a minion connects to or disconnects from the master. The following data will be contained in the payload:

- new: This specifies a list of minions that have connected since the last presence event
- lost: This denotes a list of minions that have disconnected since the last presence event

Common cloud events

Salt Cloud fires a number of events when you create or destroy machines. Which events are fired and when depends on the cloud provider driver; some even fire events for other tasks, but there are a few events that are generally found in all cloud drivers.

Cloud events are unique in that they don't necessarily refer to an existing ID; they refer to a VM name. By design, the VM name in Salt Cloud matches the minion ID that is used by the master. However, some events refer to a VM that is in the process of creation (and not yet ready to receive commands), whereas others refer to a VM that is in the process of being destroyed or has just been destroyed.

salt/cloud/vm_name/creating

The VM in question is about to be created. At this point, no actual work has been performed. Every cloud driver is required to use the `creating` tag. The following data will be contained in the payload:

- `name`: This contains the name of the VM to be created
- `provider`: This indicates the name of the provider configuration used
- `profile`: This denotes the name of the profile configuration used

salt/cloud/vm_name/requesting

All the information required to create a VM has been gathered, and Salt Cloud is about to make a request to the cloud provider that a VM be created. The following data will be contained in the payload:

- `kwargs`: This specifies all the arguments from the provider, profile, and, if used, cloud map, which will be used to generate this request

salt/cloud/vm_name/querying

The cloud provider has begun the process of creating a VM and has returned an ID, which Salt Cloud can use to refer to it. However, it has not yet returned an IP address that Salt Cloud can use to access the VM. Salt Cloud will now wait for an IP address to become available. The following data will be contained in the payload:

- `instance_id`: This specifies the ID of the VM to be created as the cloud provider knows it. This may not match the actual VM name or the minion ID.

salt/cloud/vm_name/waiting_for_ssh

An IP address has been returned for the VM, but it is not necessarily available. Salt Cloud will now wait for the VM to become available and will be able to respond to SSH connections. The following data will be contained in the payload:

- `ip_address`: This denotes the hostname or IP address that will be used to connect to this VM

salt/cloud/vm_name/deploying

The VM is now available via SSH (or, in the case of a Windows VM, SMB or WinRM). The deploy script (or the Windows installer) and any accompanying files (such as public and private keys and the minion configuration) will now be uploaded. Then, the deploy script (or the Windows installer) will be executed. The following data will be contained in the payload:

- `name`: This specifies the name of the VM that has been created.
- `kwargs`: This denotes all the arguments that will be used to deploy Salt on the target system. This is a very long list, and some of the items (such as the contents of the deploy script) may also be extremely long.

salt/cloud/vm_name/created

The VM has been successfully created. This does not necessarily mean that the `salt-minion` process is able to receive connections. It may still be in its starting phase. There may be firewall issues. Also, something may have caused the deploy script or the Windows installer to fail. If you are waiting for a minion to be available, it is far more reliable to look for the `salt/minion/<minion_id>/start` tag. Every cloud driver is required to use the `salt/cloud/<vm_name>/created` tag. The following data will be contained in the payload:

- `name`: This specifies the name of the VM that has been created.
- `provider`: This denotes the name of the provider configuration used.
- provider: This identifies the name of the profile configuration used.
- `instance_id`: This specifies the ID of the VM as it is known by the cloud provider. This may not be the same as the VM name or the minion ID.

salt/cloud/vm_name/destroying

Salt Cloud is about to make a request that a cloud provider destroy a VM. Every cloud driver is required to use this tag. The following data will be contained in the payload:

- `name`: This specifies the name of the VM to be destroyed

salt/cloud/vm_name/destroyed

Salt Cloud has finished destroying a VM. Every cloud driver is required to use this tag. The following data will be contained in the payload:

- `name`: This denotes the name of the VM that was just destroyed

Salt API events

Salt API is a daemon that ships with Salt, which provides a REST interface to be used to control Salt instead of the command line. A notable feature of the Salt API is its ability to fire custom events from a webhook. We will cover the configuration of the Salt API later on in this chapter.

salt/netapi/url_path

The actual URL path that will be used will depend on how Salt API is configured is configured with `salt/netapi/<url_path>`. Often, it will contain the word `hook` to denote that it is a webhook, followed by a slash and an arbitrary command. The following data will be contained in the payload:

- `data`: This denotes any custom data that was POSTed to the Salt API URL

Building reactors

Now you have seen what events look like, but what can you do with them? One of the most powerful features that distinguishes Salt from similar systems is not only its ability to fire events, but also the ability for the master to initiate new jobs based on the information contained in the event.

This reactor system serves as a platform for users to build systems that are both asynchronous and autonomous, which can range from simple to very complex.

Configuring reactors

Reactors are master-side processes, so none of the configuration needs to happen directly on any minions. In fact, as the reactor system needs to actively listen to an event bus in order for it to function, it doesn't even make sense to attempt to use it in a masterless environment based on the `salt-call` commands.

Before setting up the master, decide which directory will contain reactor files. By convention, this will be `/srv/reactor/`, but this is not a hardcore requirement and is not enforced anywhere in Salt.

Reactors are set up in the master configuration file. The `reactor` block contains a mapping of tags to look for, each of which will contain a list of SLS files that will be used when that tag is found. Consider the following reactor block:

```
reactor:
  - 'salt/minion/*/start':
    - /srv/reactor/highstate.sls
```

This is a very simple reactor that waits for minions to identify that they have started and are ready to accept commands. When they do, it responds by calling the `highstate.sls` file.

There are a couple of things to note here. First of all, the tag in this example doesn't contain a minion ID; it contains a wildcard instead. Event tags are interpreted as globs by the reactor system, allowing it to take advantage of namespaced tags and perform generalized jobs based on events from specific minions.

Secondly, both the tag and the SLS file that follow are part of a list. There is no imposed limit on how many tags may be watched by the reactor or how many SLS files may accompany a tag.

This is important because `reactor` is a top-level declaration; you may not have multiple `reactor` blocks in one master. However, the following single `reactor` block is valid:

```
reactor:
  - 'salt/minion/<minion_id>/start':
    - /srv/reactor/highstate.sls
  - 'salt/netapi/hook/ec2/autoscale':
    - /srv/reactor/ec2-autoscale.sls
  - 'salt/cloud/*/creating':
    - /srv/reactor/cloud-create-alert-pagerduty.sls
    - /srv/reactor/cloud-create-alert-hipchat.sls
```

This block makes use of internal Salt events as well as two subsystems that ship with Salt: the Salt API and Salt Cloud. We can make reasonable guesses as to what each SLS does because they were given names that are somewhat human readable.

However, mapping out relationships between tags and files is only one part of the equation. Let's see what reactor SLS files actually look like.

Writing reactors

As with other parts of Salt, reactors are written in YAML by default. And as with other parts of Salt, reactors can also be written in any other format that is supported by Salt's renderer system. For the moment, we will focus on reactors written in YAML with a little Jinja templating.

Reactor SLS files resemble State SLS files that contain a block of data, which starts with an ID followed by a function and any arguments to the function. The following is an example of the `highstate.sls` file referenced before:

```
highstate_run:
  cmd.state.highstate
    - tgt: {{ data['id'] }}
```

The ID for this `reactor` block is `highstate_run` (not to be confused with `{{ data['id'] }}`, which is a piece of Jinja templating that references the minion ID). The ID for each `reactor` block is entirely arbitrary. Unlike with State SLS files, the ID does not affect any other items in the block. It does need to be unique, but beyond this, you can consider it to be a little more than a reference to you as to what the `reactor` block will do.

There are three different kinds of reactors that can be written: those that call execution modules, those that call runner modules, and those that manage the master via `wheel` modules. The function name for each of these will be preceded by `cmd`, `runner`, and `wheel`, respectively. For instance, a reactor that uses `cmd.run` to execute an arbitrary command on a minion would look like this:

```
local.cmd.run
```

First, let's take a look at the reactors based on execution modules to get a feel of what reactors are like. Runner and wheel reactors are both simpler, so once you understand execution runners, the others will be easy.

Calling execution modules

As execution modules form the basis of Salt itself, it is no surprise that these would be the most common types of reactor. As Salt States are kicked off using execution modules, even State runs can be initiated here.

As execution modules are run on minions, they are targeted as they would be with the `salt` command. The target is referred to as `tgt`. If a target type other than `glob` is to be used, it is declared as `tgt_type`. The target types supported by the reactor system are as follows:

- `glob`
- `pcre`
- `list`
- `grain`
- `grain_pcre`
- `pillar`
- `nodegroup`
- `range`
- `compound`

Most execution modules require a list of arguments. In a reactor, these may be declared in one of two ways: `arg` or `kwarg`.

The `arg` argument contains a list of arguments to be sent to the function in the order in which they are expected to appear. This is directly analogous to the concept of `*args` in Python.

```
kilroy:
  cmd.cmd.run:
    - tgt: {{ data['id'] }}
    - arg:
      - 'touch /tmp/kilroy_was_here'
```

The `kwarg` argument contains a dictionary of argument names and the associated values to be sent to the function. The order is not important here because the arguments are named. This is directly analogous to the concept of `**kwargs` in Python.

```
kilroy:
  cmd.cmd.run:
    - tgt: {{ data['id'] }}
    - kwarg:
      cmd: 'touch /tmp/kilroy_was_here'
```

Calling runner modules

As runner modules are executed on the master, no targeting is necessary. However, both the `arg` and `kwarg` arguments are still valid and behave as they do with execution modules:

```
webhook1:
  runner.http.query:
    - arg:
      - http://example.com/path/to/webhook
webhook2:
  runner.http.query:
    - kwarg:
      url: http://example.com/path/to/other/webhook
```

Calling wheel modules

Wheel modules also do not require targeting because they are designed to manage the master itself. By far, the most common usage of wheel reactors is to either accept or delete minion keys on the master.

```
accept_minion:
  wheel.key.accept:
    - match: {{ data['id'] }}
```

Exercise extreme caution when using wheel reactors, especially those that accept minion keys. You can tell that the preceding reactor was not designed to be kicked off by an event from a minion. How would the minion fire an event if it wasn't yet accepted on the master? So, instead of including the Jinja code to make use of an ID, it instead looks inside the payload of the event for a name.

This particular example does not perform any validation on the event to ensure that it came from a trusted source. When you accept keys via the reactor system, it may be more appropriate to render the reactor SLS in Python rather than YAML. One example of a reactor that uses Python to perform validation is the EC2 Autoscale reactor, which can be found here:
`https://github.com/saltstack-formulas/ec2-autoscale-reactor`.

When you write reactors in Python, try to keep them as simple as possible. Salt will only process one reactor at a time whereas complex reactors will cause others to begin to queue up while waiting for their turn.

Writing more complex reactors

As the number of modules that ship with Salt is vast, there is an enormous number of functionalities that can be harnessed in the reactor system. Let's take a look at a few use cases and ways of how reactors can be used with them.

These examples will make use of various parts of Salt that are not covered in this chapter, but we will try to keep them simple enough to only demonstrate the use case presented.

Sending out alerts

There is a growing number of modules appearing in Salt designed to send notifications to others. Some of these, such as the `smtp` and `http` execution module, are based on the longtime standards that the Internet is based on. Others, such as the `pagerduty` and `hipchat` module, were built for commercial services. Some of them have free components, whereas some require a paid account.

Let's set up a simple monitoring system that checks for disk space on a minion and sends out an alert if the specified disk is too full. First, let's set up a monitoring State to keep an eye on disk space.

Create `/srv/salt/monitor/disks.sls` with the following content:

```
root_device_size:
  disk.status:
    - name: /
    - maximum: '90%'
    - onfail_in:
      - event: alert_admins_disk

alert_admins_disk:
  event.send:
    - name: alert/admins/disk
```

Then, we will map the event tag to the reactor in the master configuration, as follows:

```
reactor:
  - alert/admins/disk:
    - /srv/reactor/disk_alert.sls
```

While we're in the master configuration file, let's also add the configuration to use the `pagerduty` service:

```
my-pagerduty-account:
  pagerduty.subdomain: mysubdomain
  pagerduty.api_key: 1234567890ABCDEF1234
```

Then, we will create `/srv/reactor/disk_alert.sls` in order to create an incident with the `pagerduty` service:

```
new_instance_alert:
  runner.pagerduty.create_event:
    - kwarg:
        description: "Low Disk Space: {{ data['id'] }}"
        details: "Salt has detected low disk space on {{
        data['id'' }}"
        service_key: 01234567890ABCDEF0123456789abcde
        profile: my-pagerduty-account
```

In order to kick off this State and only this State, we can issue the following command:

```
# salt myminion state.sls monitor.disks
```

If Salt detects that the root device is within the specified parameters, the event will not be fired, and the reactor will not be triggered:

```
local:
    ----------
          ID: root_device_size
```

```
     Function: disk.status
         Name: /
       Result: True
      Comment: Disk in acceptable range
      Started: 18:53:54.675835
     Duration: 6.393 ms
      Changes:
----------
           ID: alert_admins
     Function: event.send
         Name: alert/admins/disk
       Result: True
      Comment: State was not run because onfail req did not
      change
      Started:
     Duration:
      Changes:

Summary
------------
Succeeded: 2
Failed:    0
------------
Total states run:       2
```

However, if Salt detects that the root device has grown to more than 90% capacity, we will see a different response:

```
local:
----------
           ID: root_device_size
     Function: disk.status
         Name: /
       Result: False
      Comment: Disk is above maximum of 90 at 93
      Started: 19:07:06.024935
     Duration: 6.315 ms
      Changes:
----------
           ID: alert_admins
     Function: event.send
         Name: alert/admins/disk
       Result: True
      Comment: Event fired
      Started: 19:07:06.033681
     Duration: 28.329 ms
      Changes:
               ----------
```

```
                data:
                    None
                tag:
                    alert/admins/disk

    Summary
    ------------
    Succeeded: 1 (changed=1)
    Failed:    1
    ------------
    Total states run:    2
```

This is what we will see from the command line, but there will be more going on under the hood. We can see it fire the `alert_admins_disk` event. What we won't see is the `disk_alert` reactor getting triggered, which will create an incident in `PagerDuty`. At this point, `PagerDuty` will take over and send alerts to the admins configured in that service.

We can automate this process by using the Salt scheduler. To the minion configuration, add the following block:

```
schedule:
  disk_monitoring:
    function: state.sls
    seconds: 300
    args:
      - monitor.disks
```

After making this change, restart the minion. From the point at which the minion starts up again, it will issue the `monitor_disks` SLS every 5 minutes.

Using webhooks

As mentioned previously, the Salt API provides a REST interface that can be used to accept webhooks on the master. These webhooks are translated into events, which are intercepted by the reactor.

Before we can accept webhooks, we need to configure the Salt API. First, edit the master configuration to tell the Salt API to accept webhooks:

```
rest_cherrypy:
  port: 8080
  host: 0.0.0.0
  ssl_crt: /etc/pki/tls/certs/localhost.crt
  ssl_key: /etc/pki/tls/certs/localhost.key
  webhook_url: /hook
```

```
webhook_disable_auth: True
```

 Instructions to create the `ssl_crt` and `ssl_key` files can be found in `Chapter 8`, *Using Salt with REST*, under the *Creating SSL Certificates* section.

Next, we need to map any events that we are expecting to the corresponding SLS files. Add the following lines to the master configuration:

```
reactor:
  - salt/netapi/hook/customevent:
    - /srv/reactor/webhook.sls
```

Let's assume that the master's hostname is `salt-master` for our purposes. This means that the URL for this webhook is as follows:

```
https://salt-master:8080/hook/customevent
```

With the master configured, restart it. The Salt API is a separate process from the master, so go ahead and start it up too:

```
# systemctl restart salt-master
# systemctl start salt-api
```

We can trigger this event from the command line of another system with cURL:

```
$ curl -k https://salt-master:8080/hook/customevent -H
'Accept: application/json' -d passphrase=soopersekrit
```

If you're watching the event bus with `eventlisten.py`, you will see the following event:

```
Event fired at Sat Apr 18 20:07:30 2015
*************************
Tag: salt/netapi/hook/customevent
Data:
{'_stamp': '2015-04-19T02:07:30.460017',
 'body': '',
 'headers': {'Accept': 'application/json',
             'Content-Length': '23',
             'Content-Type': 'application/x-www-form-urlencoded',
             'Host': 'localhost:8080',
             'Remote-Addr': '127.0.0.1',
             'User-Agent': 'curl/7.41.0'},
 'post': {'passphrase': 'soopersekrit'}}
```

Notice that we've used a passphrase here. HTTPS may protect the data being sent, but it doesn't protect us from any unauthorized usage. It is still up to the user to implement their own authentication scheme.

While reactors are normally written in YAML, we need something that allows you the logic to actually check the passphrase. Fortunately, Jinja does provide enough logic to perform this. Create /srv/reactor/webhook.sls, with the following content:

```
{% set passphrase = data['post'].get('passphrase', '') %}
{% if passphrase == 'soopersekrit' %}
authenticated:
  cmd.cmd.run:
    - tgt: myminion
    - arg:
      - 'touch /tmp/somefile'
{% endif %}
```

Jinja provides just enough logic for a simple authentication scheme. If something more advanced is required, it may make sense to write the reactor in pure Python instead. The following SLS is the Python version of the preceding YAML and Jinja reactor:

```
#!py

def run():
    passphrase = data['post'].get('passphrase', '')
    if passphrase == 'soopersekrit':
        return {
            'authenticated': {
                'cmd.cmd.run': [
                    { 'tgt': 'dufresne' },
                    { 'kwarg': {
                        'cmd': 'touch /tmp/somefile'
                      }
                    }
                ]
            }
        }
```

This example shows two different SLS files. These files give a reasonably simple reaction to the webhook. Let's get a little more advanced.

Reactors calling reactors

Let's set up a new set of reactors. First of all, let's add a couple of new events to the `reactor` block in the master configuration:

```
reactor:
  - 'salt/netapi/hook/gondor':
    - '/srv/reactor/gondor.sls'
  - 'salt/netapi/hook/rohan':
    - '/srv/reactor/rohan.sls'
```

The `salt-master` service will need to be restarted to pick up the new mapping, but the `salt-api` service will not. Go ahead and restart the master with this command:

```
# systemctl restart salt-master
```

Next, create `/srv/reactor/gondor.sls`, with the following content:

```
ask_rohan_for_help:
  runner.http.query:
    - kwarg:
      url: 'http://localhost:8080/hook/rohan'
      method: POST
      data:
        message: 'Rohan, please help!'
```

Then, set up `/srv/reactor/rohan.sls`, with the following content:

```
respond_to_gondor:
  cmd.cmd.run:
    - tgt: gandalf
    - arg:
      - "echo 'Rohan will respond' > /tmp/rohan.txt"
```

Go ahead and get things rolling. As we have one reactor calling another via another webhook, we'll add a slight delay before checking for the response:

```
# curl https://localhost:8080/hook/gondor -H 'Accept:
application/json' -d '{}' ; sleep 3; echo; cat
/tmp/rohan.txt
{"success": true}
Rohan will respond
```

For the purpose of this example, this set of reactors will reside on the same master. However, there is no reason that the URL and the `rohan` reactor couldn't exist on an entirely different Salt infrastructure altogether.

This example also shows that as reactors have the ability to call each other, minions, masters, and even entire infrastructures can be configured to communicate with each other autonomously using a series of asynchronous events.

Using Thorium

The Thorium system is another component of Salt with the ability to watch the event bus and react based on what it sees there. But the ideas behind it are much different than with the reactor.

A word on engines

Thorium is one of the engines that started shipping with Salt in version 2016.3. Engines are a type of long-running process that can be written to work with the master or minion. Like other module types, they have access to the Salt configuration and certain Salt subsystems.

Engines are separate processes that are managed by Salt. The event reactor runs inside the Salt processes themselves, which means that long-running reactor operations can affect the rest of Salt. Because Thorium is an engine, it does not suffer from this limitation.

Looking at Thorium basics

Like the reactor, Thorium watches the event bus. But unlike the reactor, which is configured entirely via SLS files, Thorium uses its own subsystem of modules (which are written in Python) and SLS files. Because these modules and SLS files use the state compiler, much of the functionality has been carried over.

In order to use Thorium, there are a few steps that you must complete. These steps work together to form the basis of your Thorium setup, so be careful not to skip any.

Enabling Thorium

First, as an engine, you need to enable Thorium in the `master` configuration file using the `engines` directive:

```
engines:
  - thorium: {}
```

Because Thorium is so heavily configured using its own files, no configuration needs to be passed in at this point. However, engines do need a dictionary of some sort passed in, so we pass in an empty one.

Setting up the Thorium directory tree

With Thorium configured, we need to create a directory to store Thorium SLS files in. By default, this is `/srv/thorium/`. Go ahead and create that:

```
# mkdir /srv/thorium/
```

If you'd like to change this directory, you may do so in the `master` configuration file:

```
thorium_roots:
  base:
    - /srv/thorium-alt/
```

Like the state system, Thorium requires a `top.sls` file. This is the first of many similarities you'll find between the two subsystems. As with `/srv/salt/top.sls`, you need to specify an environment, a target, and a list of SLS files:

```
base:
  '*':
    - thorium_test
```

To be honest, the environment and target really don't mean much; they are artifacts from the state system, which weren't designed to do anything special inside of Thorium. That said, the target does actually have some useful purposes.

The target here doesn't refer to any minions. Rather, it refers to the master that this top file applies to. For example, if your master's ID is `moe` and you set a target of `curly`, then this top file won't be evaluated for that master.

Sound confusing? In a single-master, non-syndicated environment, it probably is. In such an environment, go ahead and set the target to *. But in an environment in which multiple masters are present, you may wish to divide the workload between them. Take a look at this `top.sls` file:

```
base:
  'monitoring-master':
    - alerts
    - graphs
  'packaging-master':
    - redhat-pkgs
    - debian-pkgs
```

In this multi-master environment, the masters may work in concert to manage jobs among the minions, but one master will also be tasked with looking for monitoring-related events and processing them, while the other will handle packaging-related events.

There is a component of Thorium that we haven't discussed yet called the register. We'll get to it in a moment, but this is a good time to point out that the register is not shared. This means that if you assign two different masters to handle the same events, any actions performed by one master will be invisible to the other. The right hand won't know what the left is doing, as it were.

As you may expect, the list following each target specifies a set of SLS files to be evaluated. But whereas state SLS files are only evaluated when you kick off a state run (`state.highstate`, for instance), Thorium SLS files are evaluated at regular intervals. By default, these intervals are set to every half second. You can change that interval in the `master` configuration file:

```
thorium_interval: 0.5
```

Once you have your `top.sls` file configured, it's time to set up some SLS files.

Writing Thorium SLS files

Let's go ahead and create `/srv/thorium/thorium-test.sls` with the following content in it:

```
shell_test:
  local.cmd:
    - tgt: myminion
    - func: cmd.run
    - arg:
      - echo 'thorium success' > /tmp/thorium.txt
```

I wouldn't restart your master yet if I were you. First, let's talk about what we're looking at here.

This should look very familiar to you, with a few differences. As you would expect, `shell_test` is the ID of this code block; `local.cmd` refers to the module and function that will be used, and everything that follows is arguments to that function.

The local module is a Thorium-specific module. Execution, state, runner, and other modules are not available in Thorium without using a Thorium module that wraps them. The local module is one such wrapper, which provides access to execution modules. As such, `tgt` refers to the target that the module will be executed on, `func` is the module and function that will be executed, and `arg` is a list of ordered arguments. If you like, you may use `kwarg` instead to specify keyword arguments.

Because state modules are accessed via the state execution module, `local.cmd` would also be used to kick those off; `runner.cmd` is also available to issue commands using the runner subsystem.

Now, why did I tell you not to restart your master yet? Because if you did, this SLS file would run every half second, writing out to `/tmp/thorium.txt` over and over again. In order to keep it from running so often, we need to gate it somehow.

Using requisites

Because Thorium uses the state compiler, all state requisites are available, and they all function as you would expect. Let's go ahead and add another code block and alter our first one a little bit:

```
checker:
  check.event:

    - name: salt/thorium/*/test
contains_check
  check.contains:
    - value: trigger

shell_test:
  local.cmd:
    - tgt: myminion
    - func: cmd.run
    - arg:
      - echo 'thorium success' > /tmp/thorium.txt
    - require:
```

```
    - check: contains_check
```

The `check` module has a number of functions that are designed to compare a piece of data against an event and return `True` if the specified conditions are met.

In this case, we're using `check.event`, which looks at a given tag and returns `True` if an event comes in and matches it. The tag that we are looking for is `salt/thorium/*/test`, which is intended to look for `salt/thorium/<minion_id>/test`. This isn't an official event of any sort, just a made-up one for the purposes of this book. The event must also have a variable called `checker` in its payload, with a value of `trigger`.

We have also added a `require` requisite to the `shell_test` code block, which will prevent that block from running unless the right event comes in. Now that we're set up, go ahead and restart the master and a minion called `myminion`, and issue the following command from the minion:

```
# salt-call event.fire_master '{"checker":"trigger"}'
'salt/thorium/myminion/test'
local:
    True
```

You may need to wait a second or two for the event to be processed and the command from `shell_test` to be sent. But then you should be able to see a file called `/tmp/thorium.txt` and read its contents:

```
# cat /tmp/thorium.txt
thorium success
```

This particular SLS, as it is now, mimics the functionality of the reactor system, albeit with a slightly more complex setup. Let's take a moment now to go beyond the reactor.

Using the register

Thorium isn't just another reactor. Even if it were, just running in its own process space makes it more valuable than the old reactor. But the true value of Thorium comes with the register.

The register is Thorium's own in-memory database, which persists across executions. A value that is placed in the register at one point in time is will still be there a half hour later unless the master is restarted.

Is the register really that fragile? At the moment, yes. And as I stated before, it's also not shared between systems. However, it is possible to make a copy of the register on disk by adding the following code block: `myregisterfile`:

```
file.save
```

This will cause the register to be written to a file called `myregisterfile` at the following location:

`/var/cache/salt/master/thorium/saves/myregisterfile`

At the time of writing this, that file will not be reloaded into memory when the master restarts. However, it is expected that persisting the registry to disk and autoloading it on start will be added to Salt very shortly, possibly by the time this book is published.

We're going to go ahead and alter our SLS file. The `shell_test` code block doesn't need to change, but the `checker` code block will. Remove the `name` field and change the function from `check.event` to `check.contains`:

```
checker:
  check.contains:
    - value: trigger
```

We're still looking for a payload with a variable called `checker` and a value called `checker`, but we're going to look at the tag somewhere else:

```
myregister:
  reg.set:
    - add: checker
    - match: salt/thorium/*/test
```

In this code block, `myregister` is the name of the register that you're going to write to. The `reg.set` function will add a variable to that register that contains the specified piece of the payload. In this case, it will grab the variable from the payload called `checker` and add its associated value. However, it will only add this information to the registry if the tag on the event in question matches the `match` specification (`salt/thorium/*/test`).

Go ahead and restart the master, and then fire the same event to the master:

```
# salt-call event.fire_master '{"checker":"trigger"}'
'salt/thorium/myminion/test'
local:
    True
```

If you've added the `file.save` code block from before, we can go ahead and take a look at the register:

```
# cat /var/cache/salt/master/thorium/saves
/myregisterfile
{"myregister": {"val": "set(['trigger'])"}}
```

Looking forward

The Thorium system is pretty new, so it's still filling out. The value of the registry is that data can be aggregated to it and analyzed in real time. Unfortunately, at the time of writing this, the functions to analyze that data do not yet exist.

The Carbon release of Salt is expected to have modules that allow better access to that data and the ability to perform an action based on a series of data that is collected over time. In the meantime, the reactor functionality does already exist (again, in the Carbon release), so we'll bring up a few more examples with it throughout the book.

Using the queue system

The queue system is another component of Salt with the ability to fire events. This can be used by the reactor system. However, before we get ahead of ourselves, let's go through the basics of using the queue system.

Learning how queues work

At its most basic level, the queue is very simple. Items can be added to the queue and then processed at a later time in the order in which they were added. Depending on the queue module being used, items may or may not be required to be unique.

For our examples, we'll use `sqlite`, the default queue module. This module should work in any infrastructure because `sqlite3` is built in Python. It will also automatically generate any database files if they don't already exist. Take note that `sqlite` is one of the queue modules that require items to be unique. If you want to use a different module, just add a backend argument to any of the queue commands. For instance, to explicitly list queues stored in `sqlite`, use the following command:

```
# salt-run queue.list_queues backend=sqlite
```

The queue system is managed by a runner. This means that queue databases will be accessed only by the master. However, as you'll see later on, it can still be used to manage tasks on minions.

Adding to the queue

Before we can do anything with a queue, we need to have some items in it to process. For now, we'll use a queue called `myqueue`. The following command will add a single item to the queue:

```
# salt-run queue.insert myqueue item1
True
```

It is also possible to add multiple items to the queue at a time by passing them as a list. From the command line, we'll do this using a JSON string:

```
# salt-run queue.insert myqueue '["item2", "item3"]'
True
```

Listing queues

As we're using the `sqlite` module, if this queue did not exist before we issued the command, it will be automatically created. The following command will list the queues that are available:

```
# salt-run queue.list_queues
- myqueue
```

Listing items in a queue

Now that we have some items in the queue, let's take a quick look at them. The following command will just list them:

```
# salt-run queue.list_items myqueue
- item1
- item2
- item3
```

To get a count of the number of items in a queue, use the following command:

```
# salt-run queue.list_length myqueue
3
```

Processing queue items

There are two ways to process one or more items in a queue. Simply popping the queue will remove the first item and display it on the command line:

```
# salt-run queue.pop myqueue
- item1
```

Multiple items can also be popped at the same time:

```
# salt-run queue.pop myqueue 2
- item2
- item3
```

This can be useful for programmatic applications that make use of Salt's queue system. However, it doesn't help us in the way of providing system automation. In order to do that, we need to be able to fire events to the reactor system. The following command will pop an item off the queue and fire an event with it:

```
# salt-run queue.process_queue myqueue
None
```

If you are watching the event bus when this command is issued, you will see an event that looks like this:

```
Event fired at Sat Apr 18 22:29:18 2015
*************************
Tag: salt/queue/myqueue/process
Data:
{'_stamp': '2015-04-19T04:29:18.066287',
 'backend': 'sqlite',
 'items': ['item1'],
 'queue': 'myqueue'}
```

As with popping items, you can also process multiple queue items at once, and they will appear within the same event:

```
Event fired at Sat Apr 18 22:30:22 2015
*************************
Tag: salt/queue/myqueue/process
Data:
{'_stamp': '2015-04-19T04:30:22.240045',
 'backend': 'sqlite',
 'items': ['item2', 'item3'],
 'queue': 'myqueue'}
```

Deleting items from a queue

Before we move on, there's one more function available to us-deleting an item from the queue without popping or processing it:

```
# salt-run queue.delete myqueue item1
True
```

It is also possible to delete multiple items at once with the following code:

```
# salt-run queue.delete myqueue '["item2", "item3"]'
True
```

Using queues with the reactor

Queues were originally designed to be used with the reactor system. Minion IDs were added to a queue, and this queue was processed as appropriate. This can be useful in environments with large jobs, which may end up consuming resources on the master.

Spreading out State runs

Let's take a look at a use case. A master that will run on hardware that is not performant enough, for its needs may have difficulty serving large files to all of its minions. Rather than performing a State run on all minions at once, it makes sense to use the queue to spread them out a little.

First, let's get the reactor set up. The queue system will always use the `salt/queue/myqueue/process` tag, so let's go ahead and map this to a reactor SLS file in the master configuration:

```
reactor:
  - salt/queue/myqueue/process:
    - /srv/reactor/salt-queue.sls
```

Now, we need to set up the reactor itself. This will not be a complex reactor; it only needs to issue the `state.highstate` command. Create `/srv/reactor/salt-queue.sls` with the following content:

```
{% if data['queue'] == 'needs_highstate' %}
{% for minion in data['items'] %}
highstate_{{ minion }}:
  cmd.state.highstate:
    - tgt: {{ minion }}
{% endfor %}
```

```
{% endif %}
```

We will use Jinja in this example to filter out queues and only loop through the items that appear in the queue that we want. In this case, the queue that we're looking at is called `needs_highstate`. For each minion ID that is delivered via the event, a reactor called `highstate_<minion_id>` will be created, which issues the `state.highstate` command against that individual minion.

Now that we have our reactor set up, let's go ahead and set up a schedule that only kicks off one State run every 5 minutes. In the master configuration, add the following code:

```
schedule:
  highstate_queue:
    function: queue.process_queue
    minutes: 5
    arg:
      - needs_highstate
```

When you restart the master, this schedule will pop a minion ID off the queue every 5 minutes, starting with the master start time, and perform a State run on it. If there are no minions in the queue, it will wait another 5 minutes and try again.

Dividing tasks among minions

Let's take a look at another use case where a large number of jobs need to be handled by multiple minions. In this example, we have two queues. The first queue contains pieces of data to be posted on a URL as they are received. The second queue contains a list of minions that will perform a job. For the sake of simplicity, we'll assume that the job is able to make use of the data that is posted on the URL without any interaction from us. The example job that will be run only requires that a minion issue the `//usr/local/bin/bigjob` command.

First, we need to populate the `bigjob` queue, which contains data that will be used by the minions:

```
# salt-run queue.insert bigjob '["data1", "data2",
"data3", "data4"]'
```

Then, we will populate a `workers` queue, which contains the names of the minions that are available to perform the big jobs:

```
# salt-run queue.insert workers '["dave", "carl",
"jorge", "stuart"]'
```

As before, the `master` configuration needs to be able to map between the event data and the reactor SLS:

```
reactor:
  - salt/queue/bigjob/process:
    - /srv/reactor/salt-queue.sls
```

For this example, we'll create a new `/srv/reactor/salt-queue.sls` file with the following content:

```
{% if data['queue'] == 'bigjob' %}
{% for job in data['items'] %}
bigdata_{{ job }}:
  runner.http.query:
    - kwarg:
      url: 'http://bigdata.example.com/jobs'
      method: POST
      data:
        job={{ job }}

bigjob_{{ job }}:
  runner.queue.process_queue:
    - arg:
      - workers
{% endfor %}
{% endif %}
{% if data['queue'] == 'workers' %}
{% for minion in data['items'] %}
worker_{{ minion }}:
  cmd.cmd.run:
    - tgt: {{ minion }}
    - arg:
      - '/usr/local/bin/bigjob'
{% endfor %}
{% endif %}
```

There's a lot going on here, so let's jump in. The first thing that we will do is process the `bigjob` queue. Each item in the queue will be POSTed to the `http://bigdata.example.com/jobs` URL. It will also trigger the worker queue to process one item at a time.

The worker queue reactor is simpler: it pops a minion ID off the queue and asks it to execute the `/usr/local/bin/bigjob` command. Again, we'll assume that this command knows how to make use of the data that was posted on the URL.

There are a couple of ways to kick off this workflow. One way is to assume that once a `bigjob` instance is finished, it can kick off an event to the reactor that processes the next item in the `bigjob` queue. Let's go ahead and set up a webhook that accomplishes this. For simplicity, we'll not worry about authentication this time.

First, map a new webhook to a new reactor in the `master` configuration file, as follows:

```
reactor:
  - salt/netapi/hook/bigjob:
    - /srv/reactor/bigjob.sls
```

Then, we will create `/srv/reactor/bigjob.sls` with the following content:

```
process_bigjob:
  runner.queue.process_queue:
    arg:
      - bigjob
```

Now, assuming that the hostname for the master is `salt-master`, we will issue the following cURL command:

```
curl https://salt-master:8080/hook/bigjob -H 'Accept:
application/json' -d '{}'
```

This will kick off the process by processing one queue item. It could also be called by the `/usr/local/bin/bigjob` command after the completion of the job in order to notify the master that it is finished. Of course, the minion should also add its name back to the queue. Let's modify `/srv/reactor/bigjob.sls` so that it can do this as well:

```
process_bigjob:
  runner.queue.process_queue:
    arg:
      - bigjob

add_worker:
  runner.queue.insert:
    arg:
      - workers
      - {{ data['minion_id'] }}
```

We'll also change the cURL command to include the ID of the minion:

```
curl http://salt-master:8080/hook/bigjob -H 'Accept:
application/json' -d minion_id=<this_minion_id>
```

Another option is to use the scheduler to kick off the `bigjob` queue on a regular basis:

```
schedule:
  bigjob_queue:
    function: queue.process_queue
    hours: 1
    arg:
      - bigjob
```

In this case, be sure to remove the `process_bigjob` block from `/srv/reactor/bigjob.sls`, but leave the `add_worker` block.

Summary

The event system in Salt can be extremely powerful when combined with the reactor system. Events can be designed to trigger other events, which can in turn trigger even more events. This moves Salt from the configuration management and automation playing fields to a bigger area, where autonomy rules all.

In the next chapter we will take a look at some of the systems available inside of Salt to provide information both to masters and minions.

6

Taking Advantage of Salt Information Systems

To the newly initiated, one of the stranger aspects of Salt is the absence of a **configuration management database** (**CMDB**). The fact is that Salt was designed to query minions quickly to return the data normally found in a CMDB in real time.

The mechanism used to discover that information was the grains system. However, using the minion itself to manage that information presents some limitations. The pillar system, and later the SDB system, was added to help address these limitations. In this chapter, we'll cover:

- Templating files in `pillar_roots`
- Using the external pillars that ship with Salt
- Understanding SDB, the Simple Database System
- Understanding the differences between pillars and SDB

Understanding pillar_roots

In the early days, pillars didn't exist in Salt. Grains were originally introduced as a mechanism for minions to gather system information. That data was useful to execution modules, and it wasn't long before custom grains were also introduced.

The problem with grains is that they need to be configured directly on minions. While the `grains` execution module does allow easy remote editing of those files, it is often easier and more appropriate to configure data for those minions in a centralized location, such as the master.

As you know, pillars are normally stored in the `/srv/pillar/` directory on the master, in static YAML files. However, those files don't need to be static.

Templating pillar_roots

By `pillar_roots`, we mean the directory that is used as the root directory for pillar files. This setting is configured in the `master` configuration file. By default, it is set to the following:

```
pillar_roots:
  base:
    - /srv/pillar/
    - /srv/spm/pillar/
```

The second entry refers to pillars that are installed by SPM, which was covered in `Chapter 3`, *Managing States*. The first entry is the more traditional storage location for pillar files.

As with other Salt files, pillars are formatted in YAML by default. But as with other Salt files, they are also run through Salt's renderer system, which means that all of the other templating engines are available. Even the `top.sls` file can be templated, so you can do things such as declaring variables in Jinja:

```
{% set tmpvar = 'vim' %}
base:
  '*':
    - base-pkgs
    - {{ tmpvar }}
```

This would be rendered as follows:

```
base:
  '*':
    - base-pkgs
    - vim
```

You could also use the `py` renderer and write your SLS files in pure Python:

```
#!py
def run():
    return {
'base': {
            '*': [
                'base-pkgs',
                'vim',
            ]
```

```
        }
    }
```

This would still render as the follows:

```
base:
  '*':
    - base-pkgs
    - vim
```

Calling out to other modules

The `top.sls` file is still somewhat limited, because it only defines a set of targets and the formulas that are associated with those targets. Other pillar files are more dynamic, as they are rendered specifically for the minion that will be receiving their data. Because the minion ID is known at this point, operations can be performed that are relative to the minion itself.

In particular, three dictionaries are available inside pillars and can be referenced from the renderer system:

- `opts`: A copy of the minion's in-memory configuration
- `grains`: The grains that have been generated for that minion
- `salt`: The execution modules that are available to that minion

If you wanted to access the minion's ID, you would reference it as follows:

```
{{ opts['id'] }}
```

If you wanted to generate a pillar that returned the version of Apache installed on the minion, you would reference this:

```
{{ salt['pkg.version']('apache') }}
```

Keep in mind that while the master does cache a copy of the minion's `opts` and `grains` dictionaries, calling out to an execution module will always generate traffic between the master and the minion. The flow of traffic will be like this:

1. The minion asks the master for pillar data.
2. The master begins rendering the pillar.
3. During the render process, the master makes a callback to the minion to execute a job.

4. The minion executes the job and sends the return data back to the master.
5. The master interpolates that data into the pillar and finishes rendering it.
6. The pillar data is now sent back to the minion.

What seems like an innocuous call to an execution module may actually be very expensive in terms of resources. This is especially true when working with a target that matches hundreds of minions or more. There are times when performing such a call may be the most appropriate option, but you will need to decide that on a case-by-case basis.

Using Salt's external pillars

Pillar files can be very simple and convenient, and having the ability to template data is very powerful, but sometimes going that route is like trying to fit a square peg into a round hole. There are a number of situations where going outside of `pillar_roots` and using an external pillar fits the bill much better.

External pillars are their own type of Salt module, written in Python. You can create your own, but that falls outside the scope of this book. If you would like more information, check out *Extending SaltStack, Packt Publishing*.

Configuring the etcd pillar

Fortunately, a number of valuable external pillar modules already ship with Salt. For instance, a number of users have begun integrating the `etcd` configuration database into their infrastructures. When you use the `etcd` pillar, it might feel as if Salt and `etcd` were designed for each other!

The `etcd` pillar does require that you create a configuration block in your `master` configuration that specifies how to connect to the `etcd` service:

```
my_etcd_config:
  etcd.host: 127.0.0.1
  etcd.port: 4001
```

Once that is configured, you can add a reference to that block to your `ext_pillar` configuration inside the `master` file:

```
ext_pillar:
  - etcd: my_etcd_config
```

When the master is restarted, the contents of the etcd database will be available as pillar items. In this configuration, all minions will have access to the same pillar data. If you would like to store pillar data that is specific to one minion, you will need to set aside a path inside etcd where minion data will be stored. Each minion will then have its own directory named after itself inside that path. The configuration for this model would look more like this:

```
ext_pillar:
  - etcd: my_etcd_config root=/salt/%(minion_id)s
```

Take note of %(minion_id)s, which will be replaced with the minion's ID when that pillar is requested. With that configuration in place, you may add minion-specific data to the etcd database with a command such as this:

```
etcdctl set /salt/myminion/foo bar
```

You could even use multiple etcd servers or at least multiple external pillar definitions for the same server at the same time. Consider the following:

```
etcd_shared:
  etcd.host: 10.1.0.11
  etcd.port: 4001
etcd_private:
  etcd.host: 10.1.0.38
  etcd.port: 4001
ext_pillar:
  - etcd: etcd_shared root=/salt/shared
  - etcd: etcd_private root=/salt/private/%(minion_id)s
```

This configuration makes use of two different etcd servers, each with their own type of data. You could of course set up multiple paths inside the same server and have each pillar definition use a different root:

```
ext_pillar:
  - etcd: etcd_config root=/salt/shared
  - etcd: etcd_config root=/salt/private/%(minion_id)s
```

Using git_pillar

The GitFS external file server has shown to be extremely popular. Somewhat less known is git_pillar, based on the same concepts. Just as gitfs presents a virtual file system that correlates with file_roots, git_pillar presents a virtual file system that corresponds to pillar_roots.

Unlike etcd, this pillar does not require an extra code block to be defined. All that it needs is in the ext_pillar declaration itself. If you were hosting your pillars on GitHub, your configuration might look like this:

```
ext_pillar:
  - git: master https://github.com/myuser/myproject
```

In this example, master refers to the branch of the Git repository to use, and the rest of course is the URL to point to that repository.

The contents of this Git repository must resemble the standard pillar definitions that you would find in pillar_roots. There needs to be a top.sls file and all of the static (or templated) pillar files that it refers to.

If you find the idea of maintaining a single repository just for pillar data to be limiting, don't worry. You can point to a specific directory inside a repository to use as the starting point for the pillar tree. If your repository had a directory called pillar_data/ in it, then your configuration would look like this:

```
ext_pillar:
  - git: master https://github.com/myuser/myproject
    root=pillar_data
```

You can also map your pillars to different Git branches based on the environment that is specified when the pillar data is requested. Your master configuration would look like this:

```
ext_pillar:
  - git: __env__ https://github.com/myuser/myproject
    root=pillar_data
```

And your top.sls file might look like this:

```
{{env}}:
  '*':
    - {{ env }}-pkgs
```

The __env__ and {{ env }} placeholders will be replaced with the specified environment. In this example, I've added a second {{ env }} block to specify a group of packages that belong to that environment. I did this to reinforce that pillar files, even those stored in Git, are processed through the renderer system.

A quick note on {{ env }}: This variable is available in top.sls, but not inside any other pillar SLS files. If you would like to refer to the environment in one of those, use {{ opts['environment'] }}.

I'd like to point out one more thing about `git_pillar` for those of you that are worried about crippling Git servers with excessive pillar calls. This pillar does not connect to the Git server for every single pillar lookup; that would be way too expensive in terms of resources. Instead, it creates a local clone of the remote repository and then queries that. This clone is then periodically updated from that server in order to avoid using resources in a wasteful manner.

Using the mysql pillar

Let's take a look at one final external pillar: `mysql`. This pillar differs from the first two that we looked at in that it allows you to specify an actual query with which to look up data. First, the MySQL server is configured using a `mysql` code block:

```
mysql:
  user: larry
  pass: 123pass
  db: pillar_data
```

Then, an external pillar definition is set up, which contains the query to be run:

```
ext_pillar:
  - mysql:
      query: 'SELECT somefield FROM sometable WHERE
      minion_id LIKE %s'
      depth: 1
```

This query contains a very simple example query, with a depth of 1. The `%s` in the query will be replaced with the minion ID when the query is executed.

The depth refers to how the SQL data is converted to the dictionary that is returned inside the pillar. Depth values start at 1, and the maximum value is based on how many fields are referred to in your query. What this looks like is probably best explained by the documentation in the code:

The depth defines how the dicts are constructed.

Essentially if you query for fields a,b,c,d for each row you'll get:

With depth 1: {a: {"b": b, "c": c, "d": d}}

With depth 2: {a: {b: {"c": c, "d": d}}}

With depth 3: {a: {b: {c: d}}}

Depth greater than 3 wouldn't be different from 3 itself.

Depth of 0 translates to the largest depth needed, so 3 in this case. (max depth == key count − 1)

Then they are merged in a similar way to plain pillar data, in the order returned by the SQL database.

Thus subsequent results overwrite previous ones when they collide.

Okay, so it's still a little rough to understand. What happens with multiple fields is that a dictionary is created that contains the values and, in some cases, the names of the fields. The more fields you specify, the more complex the return result.

My solution to this is to keep my queries simple, with a low `depth` value specified. I tend to like my pillar data to be pretty concise anyway, so this works out well in my implementations.

You may be alarmed by the last line there about collisions being overwritten. This is entirely possible, depending on how loose your query is. If you are concerned about collisions showing up in your pillar data, you can configure it to return those dictionaries in a list format:

```
ext_pillar:
  - mysql:
    query: 'SELECT somefield FROM sometable WHERE
    minion_id LIKE %s'
    depth: 1
    as_list: True
```

This makes it harder to search pillar data without using a loop, but it does get around the collision problem.

Some final thoughts on external pillars

I want to give you some final notes concerning external pillars in general before we move on to the next section.

Using multiple external pillars

You can specify a number of external pillars to be used at a time, by adding new list items to the `ext_pillar` configuration block:

```
ext_pillar:
  - etcd: my_etcd_config root=/salt/%(minion_id)s
  - git: master https://github.com/myuser/myproject
```

There is no imposed limit within Salt itself as to how many of these you use, but depending on your environment and your pillar sources, you may still run into resource issues as you increase the number of configurations that are used. When you specify too many sources, you run the risk of having a lookup from a single minion slowing down the master for all of the other minions. Use as many external pillars as are necessary, but don't go overboard.

Caching pillar data

Some pillar drivers cache data, while others do not. In the case of `git_pillar`, retrieving data from the remote source can be very expensive, so the data is cached locally. But `etcd` tends to be a very light lookup in terms of resources, so its pillar just grabs data from the database in real time. The `mysql` pillar is more resource intensive than the `etcd` pillar, but it still queries in real time. A slow MySQL connection will definitely be problematic, as will overly complex queries.

Understanding SDB

SDB, or Simple Database, was created to serve certain needs that the grains and pillar systems cannot provide. Specifically, grains and pillars are constructs that exist entirely for the benefit of minions, and as such are not available to master-side operations.

This makes SDB more useful for lookups that happen inside the `master` configuration and for Salt Cloud configuration. SDB data is still available via `minion` configurations, and there are both execution and pillar modules for SDB, but in those cases, you may find it more appropriate to store your data inside a pillar.

Before we get into all that, let's talk about the use cases that drove the initial development of SDB.

Securely storing passwords

SDB was originally intended as a mechanism for keeping passwords out of Salt Cloud provider and profile files. As you can imagine, keeping the following code block around in plaintext would constitute security risks:

```
azure-centos72:
  provider: larry-azurearm
  image: OpenLogic|CentOS|7.2|7.2.20160308
  size: Standard_A0
  location: westus
  ssh_username: larry
  ssh_password: 123pass
```

If it were possible to store some of this data in a more secure system, such as with the `keyring` module in PyPi, and then use a simple reference to obtain the data only when necessary, then we could do things such as storing those files in Git without worrying about passwords being stored in the revision history.

I want to make something very clear here. Modules such as `keyring` and `vault` do store data using secure software using trusted encryption-at-rest techniques. But if you can access that data using a module, there is a very good chance somebody else can too. Best practices for properly securing your data will vary between SDB modules, and some offer no encryption at all. Most importantly, if a minion process has access to data, then its master also has access to that same data. Don't assume that data is secure just because it is encrypted!

Staying simple

One point of contention that has presented itself in the past is SDB's insistence on being simple. URIs should be short and easy to use. Complicated URIs make for complicated and often confusing usage. Unfortunately, I cannot promise that every SDB URI that you encounter will be simple. If you use SDB enough, you are bound to eventually run into a driver that makes use of long, complicated configuration and URIs.

That said, the intent is to remain simple. Information on writing SDB modules can be found in *Extending SaltStack, Packt Publishing*, complete with admonitions to keep drivers simple.

Using SDB URIs

SDB is based around a very simple URI format. The scheme of course is `sdb://`, followed by the name of the configuration block being referenced, followed by the key to look up, optionally followed by any options. A sample URI might look like this:

```
sdb://mykeyring/mypassword
```

This particular URI would reference a configuration block inside either the `master`, `minion`, or `cloud` configuration files, which would look like this:

```
mykeyring:
   driver: keyring
   service: system
```

Of course, `mypassword` would refer to a key stored inside the `keyring` system called `mypassword`. We'll get into how that configuration block looks in the next section. For the moment, let's look at how the aforementioned `cloud` configuration would look using SDB URIs to obscure certain data:

```
azure-centos72:
   provider: larry-azurearm
   image: OpenLogic|CentOS|7.2|7.2.20160308
   size: Standard_A0
   location: westus
   ssh_username: sdb://mykeyring/myusername
   ssh_password: sdb://mykeyring/mypassword
```

This file can safely be stored in plaintext or revision control, and even changing the username or password will not affect the file itself.

Configuring SDB

SDB modules all require some sort of configuration block to exist. The name of that block is up to you, but it is best to keep the name short and simple but appropriately descriptive. For instance, when using the `keyring` driver, a name such as `mykeyring` may be all you need. But if you're using SDB with multiple `etcd` databases, then names that describe each one of them (`etcd-private`, `etcd-shared`, and so on) will be easier to make use of.

The first line inside that configuration block is `driver`, which refers to the module that will be used to provide the necessary functionality, for instance, `etcd` or `keyring`.

As far as SDB is concerned, those two lines are the bare minimum required. In fact, the `env` driver will only ever make use of those two lines. For instance, the following configuration is valid:

```
osenv:
    driver: env
```

And the following URI would access data from that environment:

```
sdb://osenv/HOME
```

If you want to try this out yourself, add the aforementioned configuration to your `minion` configuration and run it:

```
# salt-call --local sdb.get sdb://osenv/HOME
local:
    /root
```

Most other drivers require some other sort of configuration. Usually, that configuration will reference a specific point inside that resource where the requested key is to be found. It may even contain connection information. For example, `etcd` supports the same connection information that is used for pillars:

```
myetcd:
    driver: etcd
    etcd.host: 127.0.0.1
    etcd.port: 4001
```

The `keyring` driver specifies which kind of database to perform the lookup in:

```
mykeyring:
    driver: keyring
    service: system
```

Each driver should contain documentation that explains what parameters are required and how to use them.

Performing SDB lookups

SDB URIs are always looked up at runtime, when they are requested. This means a couple of things:

- If you issue a command that performs an SDB lookup and then a separate command that performs the same lookup, you will receive different data if the SDB source was changed between those two commands.
- Configuration files may contain SDB URIs in any place, even above the configuration block that they use to define their source. This is because the URI itself is stored, and it will not be translated to the actual data until requested.

In the case of configuration files, such as `/etc/salt/master` or `/etc/salt/cloud.profiles` (or, say, `/etc/salt/cloud.profiles.d/softlayer.conf`), SDB URIs are entered as is:

```
azure-centos72:
  provider: larry-azurearm
  image: OpenLogic|CentOS|7.2|7.2.20160308
  size: Standard_A0
  location: westus
  ssh_username: sdb://mykeyring/myusername
  ssh_password: sdb://mykeyring/mypassword
```

But if you want to access the data directly, you have some other options.

First of all, if you have direct access to the data source, you can just modify it directly, using whatever command or commands are appropriate to do so. This is in many cases the easiest to manage those data.

However, there are both execution and runner modules that can perform the lookup for you. The usage is the same (outside of `salt` or `salt-call` versus `salt-run`), so we'll use `salt-call` (with the `--local` flag to speed things up) for our examples.

Getting data

We'll start with retrieving data from SDB, which is also the most straightforward. The name of the call is `sdb.get`, followed by the URI to look up:

```
# salt-call --local sdb.get sdb://osenv/HOME
```

This is a good time to point out that when referring to SDB data, the URI is always used, whether getting, setting, or deleting data. It contains all of the data necessary to perform the lookups (or at least the data necessary to access the configuration blocks), and trying to force people to define the location of data in a different way would be contrived and confusing at best.

In the previous example, we are asking SDB to return the HOME environment variable from the minion. If you have the minion running as a special user (such as `salt`) then the environment that has been defined for that process running as that user will be returned. If you're issuing the command using `salt-call`, then you will see variables from your own environment.

Some drivers may support functionality beyond a simple key lookup. Because SDB URIs follow (or should follow) RFC 3986, it is possible for a driver to support URIs that contain data that looks like HTTP GET request data:

```
sdb://mydriver/mytable?username=larry&dept=painters
```

Most drivers do not support this functionality as of this edition of this book, but don't be surprised if drivers like that become more commonplace.

You can look up specifics for RFC 3986 and its predecessor, RFC 2396, on Wikipedia:
`https://en.wikipedia.org/wiki/Uniform_Resource_Identifier`.
While I normally support using underscores in Salt configuration, this is one place not to do it. That's because while compliant URIs may contain dashes, they may not contain underscores. Salt doesn't care (right now, at least), but it is best practice.

Setting data

While every SDB driver must support getting data, not every driver supports setting data. This is in part because in many cases, it is better to manage the data being served through some other tool native to the platform in question.

For those drivers that do support setting data, there is very little difference in the command used:

```
# salt-call --local sdb.set sdb://osenv/EDITOR vim
```

Outside of the function called, the only difference is the presence of a second argument, which contains the information to apply to that key.

The previous example is interesting because it sets an environment variable. However, the scope of that environment is local to the salt worker that performed the command. Once the command is finished, the worker will close up shop and the environment will disappear. Why then would that driver support setting an environment variable?

This is more of a hack, really, but it can be very useful. While execution modules are designed to open a process, execute a command, and then close, not every execution is as shortlived as that. For instance, the `state` execution module can issue a set of commands that are complex and long running.

Calling SDB to set an environment variable at the beginning of a state run (for instance, inside Jinja code) can provide settings which may not otherwise be available in that environment. A number of cloud providers, for instance, provide toolkits that make extensive use of environment variables to authenticate to their services. In this case, it is actually more useful to use SDB to set data (as temporary though it may be) than to retrieve data.

Deleting data

Even more rare than the ability to set data is the ability to delete data. This will vary wildly between drivers, and for some drivers it will never be appropriate for this functionality to exist. Where it does exist, deleting data is as easy as getting it:

```
# salt-call --local sdb.delete sdb://myetcd/mypassword
```

Because there is no data to set, there is only one argument: a pointer to the key to remove. Be wary when using this command: Salt will not ask you whether you're sure you want to delete the data-it will just delete it.

As of Salt version 2016.3, the only driver to support delete is the `etcd` driver. But don't be surprised if other drivers start supporting it soon as well.

Comparing pillars and SDB

It is very important to note that while pillars and SDB do provide much of the same data, there are some differences between them. Understanding these differences will help you decide which is more appropriate for you for each situation you encounter.

Where the data is generated

Pillar data is always generated on the master before being sent to the minion. If that data comes from another source that the master has permission to look at but not the minions, then the minions can still obtain the necessary data from the master without having to have access to that resource themselves.

SDB configuration is obtained using configuration on the system that performs the lookup. If `pillar_opts` is `True` on the master (meaning the minions receive a copy of the master's configuration as its own pillar dictionary), then SDB URIs in the `master` configuration will be translated on the master before being sent to the minion.

However, if it is the `minion` configuration that contains an SDB URI, then the minion will perform the lookup itself. In the case of Salt Cloud, SDB lookups will be performed by Salt Cloud itself before being used to issue cloud commands.

An important example here is the `keyring` driver. The `keyring` driver itself is in fact a wrapper around its own set of drivers that manage secure data. Most of the drivers that it supports are designed for desktop use rather than server use. Data for some of these drivers cannot be accessed without physically typing in a passphrase on the machine running `keyring`, and even then, that data is typically only available inside a specific session.

If a minion has not had this password entered yet, then the master will have no way to obtain data stored inside that database (outside of actually attempting decryption attacks against it). Once the password has been entered, that data is still only available to that user's session.

In the case of secure drivers such as this, SDB can safely access data that is otherwise unavailable via a pillar, because the master has access to that data. That is, however, contingent upon you running the minion in local mode (using `salt-call --local`). As soon as a minion connects to the master, the master can ask it for whatever the minion has access to. If the minion is running in the same session as your `keyring` data, then the master can look it up.

Differences in drivers

While many modules exist in both SDB and pillar form, not all modules do. The previous discussion of the `keyring` driver is one such example. If a particular type of driver does have both SDB and pillar counterparts, they may have been architected differently, as necessity dictates.

Salt Cloud and others

Salt Cloud can be run on either master or minions, but while an execution module does exist for it, its primary purpose is to stand apart from an infrastructure and create, manage, and destroy resources in that infrastructure as required. As such, pillar data will not always be appropriate or available to Salt Cloud.

In the cases of software such as Salt Cloud, runners, or other subsystems that are really designed to be run on the master, pillars will probably not do you a whole lot of good. It is in these cases that SDB can step up to the plate and take over those functionalities.

Summary

There are a number of information systems inside of Salt. Grains are defined on the minions that use them, while pillars are defined on the master. When files inside `pillar_roots` are used, they may take advantage of templates and other modules in the renderer system. External pillars are also available that can give access to dynamic remote sources. Some of those external pillars, such as `git_pillar`, provide a virtual filesystem that behaves like `pillar_roots`, even allowing templating abilities.

SDB can be used to obscure data from configuration files. While it may look secure, there are very few situations in which it can actually be treated as a completely secure storage mechanism. Its power lies in two areas: being able to remove sensitive data from configuration files so that they can be safely stored in plaintext or revision control and being simple to use.

SDB and pillars overlap in some areas of functionality, but not all. With some exception, SDB tends to be more useful for master-side configuration, while pillars are only available to minions.

Next up, we'll take a look at Salt Cloud!

7
Taking Salt Cloud to the Next Level

To many, Salt Cloud has become a crucial part of the stack of Salt tools. Originally designed for little more than creating and "Salting" virtual machines across multiple cloud hosting providers, its functionalities have grown to become much more. In this chapter, we'll discuss the following topics:

- The basics of configuration
- Extending configuration directives
- Using SDB with Salt Cloud
- Building custom deploy scripts
- Working with cloud maps
- Creating reactors to extend Salt Cloud
- Building and using autoscale reactors

Take note that this chapter discusses how to manage compute nodes or instances, which generally refers to virtual machines. However, since some cloud hosting companies also provide cloud resources by creating an entire physical server or bare-metal instance available to the user, we will refer to them all collectively as **compute instances**.

Examining the Salt Cloud configuration

Some of the biggest evidence of how much Salt Cloud has grown resides in its configuration files. Early versions supported several cloud providers, but only one account per provider. It quickly became clear that a number of users did in fact make use of multiple accounts. Let's take a few minutes to look at the basics of how Salt Cloud configuration files work now.

Global configurations

The basis of the Salt Cloud configuration resides in the main configuration file, which is normally found at /etc/salt/cloud. This file used to be very central to the operation of Salt Cloud, but nowadays, there are very few options that can only be used here. We'll cover these later in *Global configurations*; for now, we'll focus on the global aspect of this file.

Salt Cloud has been designed with a top-down configuration mindset. Configurations defined in each type of the configuration file are available in the next configuration set, unless overridden. The order of operation is as follows:

1. /etc/salt/cloud
2. Provider configuration
3. Profile configuration
4. Cloud maps

Some options are relevant to many cloud providers, while others only pertain to one. As the configuration is compiled together to create a new compute instance, a number of options may be made available. These aren't necessary. Don't worry, because any options that are declared as unusable will be ignored.

Let's go through an example. Let's assume that you manage a number of compute instances in Amazon's EC2 cloud and that they span multiple regions. As you'll see in the next section, each region will be configured as a different cloud provider as far as Salt Cloud is concerned. However, you have a number of EC2-specific options that you want to apply to all regions:

```
# cat /etc/salt/cloud
rename_on_destroy: True
delvol_on_destroy: True
```

These two options are specific to EC2. Every region that is set up as a separate provider will inherit these options, saving the user having to specify them multiple times. Simplifying configurations like this will also cut down on errors when broad changes need to be made, because tedious editing of multiple files and configuration blocks will be eliminated.

Provider and profile configuration

Before we go into details on how these two types of configuration work, we should clarify what each one is. You should already be comfortable with these configurations, so we won't go into the details here.

Providers

Provider refers to the compute-cloud hosting company, which should be used to create the new compute instance. A provider configuration block is also used to separate configuration for multiple regions on the same cloud provider. For example, the following configuration blocks refer to the same hosting company, but within two different regions:

```
ec2-east:
  provider: ec2
  id: HJGRYCILJLKJYG
  key: 'kdjgfsgm;woormgl/aserigjksjdhasdfgn'
  keyname: test
  securitygroup: quick-start
  private_key: /root/test.pem
  location: us-east-1
ec2-west:
  provider: ec2
  id: HJGRYCILJLKJYG
  key: 'kdjgfsgm;woormgl/aserigjksjdhasdfgn'
  keyname: test
  securitygroup: quick-start
  private_key: /root/test.pem
  location: us-west-1
```

Take note of the `provider` line in each of these blocks. Inside the provider configuration blocks, this argument refers to the driver that will be used to manage compute instances.

Provider configuration is stored in one of two places. For simpler cloud configuration, it may be most convenient to store it in the `/etc/salt/cloud.providers` file. If you use a number of cloud providers or have a need for smaller configuration files, which are managed by a configuration management suite (such as Salt), it may be better to break them into a number of files in the `/etc/salt/cloud.providers.d/` directory.

 Take note that files inside this directory must have a `.conf` extension in order for Salt Cloud to use them

Profiles

Profile configuration is used to set up configuration blocks. These blocks define a certain type of compute instance. For instance, an infrastructure may have a number of web servers that share identical configuration and a number of database servers that share their own identical configuration, which is likely to be very different from the web servers' configurations.

A profile configuration block is used to divide the separate configurations for each of these types of machines. Take, for example, the following two profiles:

```
azure-centos:
  provider: azure-west
  image: 'OpenLogic-CentOS-65-20150128'
  ssh_username: root
  ssh_password: pass123
  ssh_pubkey: /root/azure.pub
  media_link: 'https://example.blob.core.windows.net/vhds'
  slot: production
  size: Medium
azure-ubuntu:
  provider: azure-west
  image: 'Ubuntu-14_04-LTS-amd64-server-20140724-en-us-30GB'
  ssh_username: larry
  ssh_password: pass123
  ssh_pubkey: /root/azure.pub
  media_link: 'https://example.blob.core.windows.net/vhds'
  slot: production
  size: Medium
  tty: True
  sudo: True
```

These profiles are almost identical; the differences stem from the operating system. Many CentOS images default to using root as the default user, whereas the Ubuntu philosophy prefers to use an unprivileged user as the default. However, since privileged access is required to be able to install Salt, additional options have been added in order for Salt Cloud to be able to issue commands as root, using `sudo`.

 Take note of the `provider` argument in each block. In this case, it refers to the configuration block defined in the `provider` configuration files, as opposed to the name of the driver.

Similar to the provider configuration files, profile configuration may be stored either in the `/etc/salt/cloud.profiles` file or in `.conf` files in the `/etc/salt/cloud.profiles.d/` directory.

Extending configuration blocks

The `provider` and `profile` configuration blocks are unique among Salt configurations, in which they support the `extends` configuration directive. This feature allows you to create a generic `provider` or `profile` configuration block and then use this block as a template for other `provider` or `profile` definitions.

For example, take the following profile:

```
ec2-ubuntu:
  provider: my-ec2
  image: ami-83dee0ea
  size: m3.medium
  ssh_username: ubuntu
  securitygroup: images
  spot_config:
    spot_price: 0.24
```

This profile takes advantage of the **spot instance** feature in Amazon's EC2, which allows you to bid for resources at a potentially lower cost than they would normally be available at. This profile and its spot price may be a good default for most compute instances in your organization, but certain compute instances may need to be a little different.

Let's say you have some web servers that only serve static images, and they don't need to be as large or as expensive as others. You can create a new profile that inherits all the properties from this one and then overwrites arguments as needed:

```
static-image-ec2:
    size: m1.small
    spot_config:
        spot_price: 0.10
    extends: ec2-ubuntu
```

This profile, once compiled by Salt Cloud, will actually create a new profile that looks similar to the following code:

```
static-image-ec2:
    provider: my-ec2
    image: ami-83dee0ea
    size: m1.small
    ssh_username: ubuntu
    securitygroup: images
    spot_config:
        spot_price: 0.10
```

Now is a good time to point out an important restriction with the extends block. There are several configuration items that can be declared as lists. For instance, ssh_username is a common configuration item across multiple providers in the following example:

```
ec2-ubuntu:
    provider: my-ec2
    image: ami-83dee0ea
    size: m3.medium
    ssh_username:
        - ubuntu
        - ec2-user
    securitygroup: images
```

There are two usernames provided. When initially logging in to a compute instance, Salt Cloud will attempt each of these in order until a valid username is found.

If this profile were extended to also include the root user, then the entire `ssh_username` argument would need to be redeclared. This is because list items will be overwritten in their entirety. The following profile would only include the root username in the final configuration:

```
medium-ubuntu:
    ssh_username:
        - root
    extends: ec2-ubuntu
```

This profile would contain all the necessary usernames:

```
medium-ubuntu:
    ssh_username:
        - ubuntu
        - ec2-user
        - root
    extends: ec2-ubuntu
```

This may seem odd because there are list arguments in SLS files appended together, for example, the `require` statement, as shown in the following code:

```
nginx-service:
    service.running:
        - name: nginx
        - require:
            - pkg: nginx-package
            - pkg: mysql-package
```

However, in the case of SLS files, the order is not actually important. So long as all the requirements are met, the state will execute. If the requirements need to be performed in a specific order, then each item will have its own list of requirements declared, which will determine the order.

In the case of lists in Salt Cloud, the order is often very important, whereas in the case of `ssh_username`, each item will be tried in the order in which it is presented. Simply adding lists together will not necessarily result in the order that is actually desired.

Using SDB with Salt Cloud

Salt's simple database system was originally designed with a single idea in mind: to keep passwords out of Salt Cloud configuration files. Of course, they were immediately added to other configuration files as well, but that doesn't diminish their use here.

The classic examples of using SDB to store usernames and passwords still apply, of course:

```
my-provider:
  username: sdb://myetcd/username
  password: sdb://myetcd/password
```

But the new `env` SDB driver will prove valuable to a number of cloud users who make use of environment variables to store their authentication information.

Using SDB with OpenStack

OpenStack users have been making use of environment variables for years to store their personal cloud configuration. It is very common to set up a shell script that exports OpenStack variables to be used with the standard OpenStack commands. One such script might look like this:

```
export OS_USERNAME=larry
export OS_PASSWORD=123pass
export OS_TENANT_NAME=myProject
export OS_AUTH_URL=https://keystone.example.com:5000/v2.0
export OS_REGION_NAME=regionOne
```

In Salt Cloud, these variables would be stored in a provider configuration file, such as `/etc/salt/cloud.providers.d/openstack.conf`:

```
my-openstack-provider:
  driver: nova
  user: larry
  password: 123pass
  tenant: myProject
  identity_url: https://keystone.example.com:5000/v2.0
  compute_region: regionOne
```

Having to maintain two different configuration files can be a pain. What's more, if you're on a system that is shared between multiple users, you don't necessarily want to use a single provider file for all of your users nor do you want to maintain multiple provider files, each with its own private user data, all of which are visible to all users. You could set up the correct user permissions on each provider file, but users still end up relying on admins to manage their configuration.

No-it is much easier in many cases to make use of environment variables instead. Assuming that users already have their environment variables set up (perhaps in their ~/.bash_profile file), you could set up a single, global provider configuration file that looks like this:

```
my-openstack-provider:
  driver: nova
  user: sdb://environ/OS_USERNAME
  password: sdb://environ/OS_PASSWORD
  tenant: sdb://environ/OS_TENANT_NAME
  identity_url: sdb://environ/OS_AUTH_URL
  compute_region: sdb://environ/OS_REGION_NAME
```

In order to make this work, you will also need to enable the env SDB driver in your master, minion, or cloud configuration file:

```
environ:
  driver: env
```

With all of this set up, each user will be able to use their own environment variables with a single global configuration. They could even set up multiple scripts, each with their own set of configuration variables, for different OpenStack installations. Let's say you have two separate shell files, each for a different region of the same provider, called openstack_nyc.sh and openstack_dfw.sh respectively. Each file has the aforementioned OpenStack variables set up in them. You could then set up salt-cloud aliases in your ~/.bash_profile file to run those scripts before issuing a Salt Cloud command:

```
alias salt-cloud-nyc='source ~/openstack_nyc.sh; salt-cloud'
alias salt-cloud-dfw='source ~/openstack_dfw.sh; salt-cloud'
```

Using SDB with AWS/EC2

OpenStack is not the only cloud provider whose users have gotten used to using environment variables for authentication and the like. The AWS command-line tools also make use of these. For instance, you may have the following set in your ~/.bash_profile file:

```
export AWS_ACCESS_KEY_ID=0123456789ABCDEF012345
export AWS_SECRET_ACCESS_KEY=0123456789abcdef0123456789abcdef0123
```

With those variables in place, you can now set up the
`/etc/salt/cloud.providers.d/ec2.conf` file with the following lines in place:

```
id: sdb://environ/AWS_ACCESS_KEY_ID
key: sdb://environ/AWS_SECRET_ACCESS_KEY
```

Don't forget to enable the `env` SDB driver:

```
environ:
  driver: env
```

And now, each AWS user will be able to use their own environment variables with the same global configuration file.

Using SDB with other cloud providers

The aforementioned examples make use of standard environment variables that are used by CLI tools for OpenStack and AWS respectively. I pointed these out because they are two of the most common cloud providers, and each has a user community that is already used to these tools.

Some other providers also have standard environment variables. For instance, the Linode CLI tools make use of `LINODE_API_KEY`, which can be pulled in using the following:

```
my-linode-config:
  apikey: sdb://environ/LINODE_API_KEY
```

Many other cloud providers don't make use of standard environment variables, but that doesn't mean you can't set them up yourself. I would recommend you check the documentation for your cloud provider first in order to see whether such configuration already exists. Then, once you know which environment variables you're going to use, go ahead and set up your cloud provider files and shell scripts that export the appropriate configuration for your users.

Building custom deploy scripts

One of the most critical aspects of Salt Cloud is its ability to not only create compute instances but also deploy Salt (or anything else) once those instances become available. The vast majority of users will use the Salt Bootstrap script to install Salt, but there are times when augmenting or replacing this script with your own files is appropriate.

Understanding the Salt Bootstrap script

The Salt Bootstrap script is the default deployment method to install Salt on non-Windows compute instances with Salt Cloud. By default, it will only install the Salt minion service. It also has the capability to install Salt master and Salt syndic if required.

The Salt Bootstrap script has some special considerations, which dictate the way in which it works. First, it was designed to be run on as many POSIX platforms as possible, including various flavors of both Unix and Linux. In order to accommodate the disparate environments, it was written to be compatible with the **Bourne shell**, also known as sh.

As it's very rare to find a Unix or Linux distribution that does not support the Bourne shell, the Salt Bootstrap script can run pretty much anywhere (except for Windows). It uses this portability to automatically detect the operating system that it's running on so that it can install the necessary dependencies for Salt, followed by Salt itself.

This brings us to another important aspect of Salt Bootstrap. While it will execute on almost any platform, it does need to be written specifically for a platform in order to be able to do its job there. As of Bootstrap version 2015.03.15, the following platforms are supported:

- Amazon Linux 2012.09
- Arch Linux
- CentOS 5/6
- Debian 6.x/7.x (Git installations only)
- Debian 8
- Fedora 17/18
- FreeBSD 9.1/9.2/10
- Gentoo
- Linaro
- Linux Mint 13/14
- OpenSUSE 12.x
- Oracle Linux 5/6
- Red Hat Enterprise 5/6
- Scientific Linux 5/6

- SmartOS
- SUSE Linux Enterprise 11 SP1 – 3
- Ubuntu 10.x/11.x/12.x/13.04/13.10
- Elementary OS 0.2

You've probably noticed the note about Debian Git installations. In its normal mode of operation, Salt Bootstrap will install the latest version of Salt available for that platform using the prebuilt packages that are available in that platform's public repositories. Let's first talk about installing from those.

Installing from prebuilt packages

Most people who use Salt Bootstrap will do so from Salt Cloud, Salty Vagrant, or another similar tool that will automatically place it on the compute node to be deployed and run it for them. However, it is helpful to know how to run Salt Bootstrap manually.

A copy is distributed with Salt so that Salt Cloud can make use of it. If you are running the most recent version of Salt, you probably have the most recent version of Salt Bootstrap as well. If you want to be sure, you can ask Salt Cloud to update it for you with the following code:

```
# salt-cloud --update-bootstrap
```

You can also download the latest stable version manually on the target system. There are a number of different ways to do this from the command line, depending on the downloading tool that your operating system has installed:

```
# curl -L https://bootstrap.saltstack.com -o
bootstrap-salt.sh
# wget -O bootstrap-salt.sh
https://bootstrap.saltstack.com
# python -m urllib "https://bootstrap.saltstack.com"
> bootstrap-salt.sh
# fetch -o bootstrap-salt.sh
https://bootstrap.saltstack.com
```

Once you have it downloaded, you can simply run it with no arguments to install the Salt minion, as shown in the following code:

```
# sh bootstrap-salt.sh
```

If you would like to install Salt master as well, add the -M argument:

```
# sh bootstrap-salt.sh -M
```

To install Salt syndic, add -S:

```
# sh bootstrap-salt.sh -S
```

Also, if you want to install the Salt libraries but not the Salt minion, add the -N argument:

```
# sh bootstrap-salt.sh -N
```

Any of these arguments can be used together as required. When any of the Salt services are installed, they will be started automatically. If you prefer not to start them right away, you can add the -X argument:

```
# sh bootstrap-salt.sh -X
```

This doesn't work everywhere; Debian-based distributions-such as Ubuntu-are designed to start services automatically as part of the package installation process. Salt Bootstrap will warn the user about this. However, efforts have been made to support this argument whenever possible.

Keep in mind that automatically starting a service that has not yet been configured properly can be problematic. By default, the Salt minion will check the DNS for the Salt master at the Salt hostname. It will also poll the minion's own hostname and use that as the minion's ID. If there is no master at the Salt hostname or if a number of minions have the localhost hostname, this will cause problems.

Before you run the Salt Bootstrap script, you can either place configuration files and keys directly where they need to be or put them in a temporary directory and ask the Bootstrap script to put them in place for you:

```
# sh bootstrap-salt.sh -c /tmp/.saltbootstrap/
```

This feature exists so that automated deployment programs, such as Salt Cloud, can spend as few resources as possible getting the files to the target. A simplified version of the commands run by Salt Cloud to create and populate this directory is as follows:

```
(via ssh)# mkdir /tmp/.saltcloud-<randomhash>/
(via ssh)# chmod 700 /tmp/.saltcloud-<randomhash>/
# scp minion target:/tmp/.saltcloud-<randomhash>/
# scp minion.pem target:/tmp/.saltcloud-<randomhash>/
# scp minion.pub target:/tmp/.saltcloud-<randomhash>/
# scp bootstrap-salt.sh target:/tmp/.saltcloud-
<randomhash>/
```

Once the directory has been populated, Salt Cloud will issue the command to run the Bootstrap script. After this has finished, Salt Cloud will clean up the temporary directory on the target and return to the user.

Installing from Git

If you do not wish to use the public repositories for your infrastructure, then you have two options. One is to install from Git. The other is to use a custom deploy script. We'll get to custom scripts in a moment-let's talk about installing from Git first.

To install from Git, you need to pass `git <branch>` to the end of the Salt Bootstrap command:

```
# sh bootstrap-salt.sh git develop
```

By default, this will use SaltStack's own Salt repository on GitHub:

```
https://github.com/saltstack/salt
```

If you want to install Salt from a different Git repository, such as your own fork, you can use the `-g` argument:

```
# sh bootstrap-salt.sh -g https://github.com/myuser
/salt.git git develop
```

Normally, Salt Bootstrap will use a `git://` URL for Salt. If the Git port is blocked, you will need to use the `https://` URL for Git. Instead of manually specifying the `https://` URL, you can use `-G` to use it automatically, as shown in the following code:

```
# sh bootstrap-salt.sh -G git develop
```

If you want to install a version of Salt that is different from the version in your distribution's repositories, using a Git-based installation is often the easiest. SaltStack uses Git tags to keep track of different major versions of Salt. As of January 2014, Salt is versioned with the year and the month, and the tags reflect this. To install the `2016.11` branch of Salt, use this command:

```
# sh bootstrap-salt.sh git 2016.11
```

Looking back at legacy deploy scripts

Before the Salt Bootstrap script, there were a number of different scripts used to deploy Salt. Each operating system had two scripts: one to install from that distribution's own repositories and one to install from Git. Although they have fallen into disuse and are often out of date, they are still included with Salt Cloud.

One of the reasons these scripts still ship is academic: users who are unable to use Salt Bootstrap for some reason can examine the legacy deploy scripts and modify them for their own purposes.

There are also some newer deploy scripts that wrap around the Salt Bootstrap script. These scripts are designed explicitly for user modification: users can add their own commands before or after the Salt Bootstrap script runs. If you have a lot of work that needs to be done by the deploy script before Salt starts up and takes over, then a customized deploy script may be ideal.

Writing your own deploy scripts

In the early days, Salt Cloud was designed to do little more than create a compute instance, install Salt on it, and auto-accept that minion's keys on the master. As the most complex variable here was which operating system was running on the target, this script was specified using the os argument. Before long, it became clear that Salt Cloud needed to support more complexity, so the os argument was changed to script.

Back in those days, custom scripts needed to be added directly to the deploy/ directory of Salt Cloud's source tree. Fortunately, we can now take advantage of a simpler and more predictable directory: /etc/salt/cloud.deploy.d/.

Scripts in this directory may be referred to with or without the .sh extension, which is normally associated with Bourne shell scripts. This doesn't mean that the scripts have to be Bourne scripts, but if no extension is specified and Salt Cloud is unable to find it, then the .sh extension will be added, and Salt Cloud will look again.

The deploy script will generally perform the following tasks:

- Place automatically signed keys on the minion
- Place the minion's configuration file
- Install the Salt minion package for that operating system
- Start the salt-minion service

As with most files in Salt, this file can be templated using Salt's renderer system. By default, the Jinja templating system will be used, but of course, other renderers are also available.

The purpose of using a renderer for this file is to be able to place keys and other files on the minion. Other configuration variables from the provider and profile configuration blocks will also be merged, if specified.

The following is a very basic script to install Salt on an Ubuntu target:

```bash
#!/bin/bash
# Install the minion's keys
mkdir -p /etc/salt/pki/minion
echo '{{ vm['priv_key'] }}' > /etc/salt/pki/minion
/minion.pem
echo '{{ vm['pub_key'] }}' > /etc/salt/pki/minion
/minion.pub
# Write the minion's configuration file
cat > /etc/salt/minion <<EOF
{{minion}}
EOF
# Set up Ubuntu repositories
echo deb http://ppa.launchpad.net/saltstack
/salt/ubuntu `lsb_release -sc` main | tee /etc/apt
/sources.list.d/saltstack.list
wget -q -O- "http://keyserver.ubuntu.com:11371
/pks/lookup?op=get&search=0x4759FA960E27C0A6" |
apt-key add -
apt-get update
# Install Salt
apt-get install -y -o DPkg::Options::=--force-
confold salt-minion
# No need to start services on Ubuntu; it will be
done by apt
```

You can see the template variables for the minion's private and public keys as `{{ vm['priv_key'] }}` and `{{ vm['pub_key'] }}`, respectively. You can also see the minion's configuration file as `{{ minion }}`. Any other work that needs to be performed can be added here as needed.

Of course, the section of this script that sets up the Ubuntu repositories can be a little unwieldy. Also, the Salt Bootstrap script will take care of those for you. Plus, the keys and configuration file will be uploaded manually by Salt Cloud anyway, so unless you have a specific reason to put them here, you can skip those steps and have a greatly simplified file, which is much more multiplatform. The following script is much shorter and makes use of a couple more tricks:

```
#!/bin/sh
wget -O - https://bootstrap.saltstack.com | sudo sh
-s -- "$@"
```

This script makes use of the infamous one-line installer. It's nice because it demonstrates how Salt can be installed with a single command even when extra work needs to be performed, such as setting up repositories. However, it does have issues.

The biggest issue is with the source. You are trusting an arbitrary URL, which you have no control over, to provide a script that will be directly piped to the sh command. This is considered insecure by security professionals and should normally be avoided. However, since Salt Cloud used to only upload a specific set of files, custom scripts that wrapped the Bootstrap script had little other choice. Technically, the following script demonstrates a more secure way to download and use the Salt Bootstrap script:

```
#!/bin/bash
wget -O bootstrap-salt.sh
https://bootstrap.saltstack.com
sudo sh bootstrap-salt.sh "$@"
```

However, since this is run as a script anyway, there is no functional difference. It is much more secure to upload your own copy of the Salt Bootstrap script in addition to the wrapper. In a moment, we'll discuss how to do that. But, first, let's talk about the other trick used here: passing arguments to your script.

Passing arguments to scripts

As you have already seen, the Salt Bootstrap script supports a number of arguments. Also, some of these will be automatically added by Salt Cloud. However, you may wish to specify some arguments directly. This can be especially important for your own custom scripts, which support your own arguments.

Salt Cloud allows script arguments to be passed with the `script_args` argument anywhere in the Salt Cloud configuration files, which are used for the target minion, provider, profile, and so on. The following profile configuration block will not only install Salt as usual, but also attempt to install Apache Libcloud so that the target minion can also be used to run Salt Cloud with a Libcloud-based provider:

```
gogrid-centos:
    provider: my-gogrid
    size: 512MB
    image: CentOS 6.2 (64-bit) w/ None
    script_args: -L
```

We covered a few arguments earlier in this chapter. In addition to those, the following arguments are also available:

- `-v`: This specifies the display script version.
- `-n`: This denotes no colors.
- `-D`: This shows debug output.
- `-k`: This specifies the temporary directory that holds the minion keys that will preseed the master.
- `-s`: This refers to the sleep time used when waiting for daemons to start and restart and when checking for running services. The default is `${__DEFAULT_SLEEP}`.
- `-C`: This only runs the configuration function. This option automatically bypasses any installation.
- `-P`: This allows installations using `pip`. On some distributions, the required Salt packages or their dependencies are not available as a package for that distribution. Using this flag allows the script to use `pip` as a last-resort method.

 This only works for functions that actually implement `pip` installations.

- `-F`: This allows copied files to overwrite existing files (`config`, `init.d`, and so on).
- `-U`: If this is set, the system is fully upgraded prior to bootstrapping Salt.
- `-K`: If this is set, the temporary files are kept in the temporary directories, specified with `-c` and `-k`.

- `-I`: If this is set, insecure connections are allowed when you download files, for example, pass `--no-check-certificate` to `wget` or `--insecure` to `curl`.
- `-A`: This passes the `salt-master` DNS name or IP and will be stored under `${_SALT_ETC_DIR}/minion.d/99-master-address.conf`.
- `-i`: This passes the `salt-minion` ID and will be stored under `${_SALT_ETC_DIR}/minion_id`.
- `-L`: This installs the Apache Libcloud package if possible (required for `salt-cloud`).
- `-p`: This specifies extra packages to install when you install Salt dependencies. You are limited to one package per `-p` flag. You're responsible for providing the proper package name.
- `-H`: This uses the specified HTTP proxy for the installation.
- `-Z`: This enables the external software source for newer ZeroMQ versions (only available for RedHat-based distributions).

Using file maps

In the *Building custom deploy scripts* section, we touched on how to upload your own custom version of the Salt Bootstrap script. You can in fact upload any number of files to a minion before executing the deploy script. However, you may issue only one command, as explained before, with the `script` argument, and any arguments are passed using the `script_args` argument.

Therefore, if you need to upload and execute a number of scripts, you will need to create one master script that executes them for you. This is the script that will be specified with the `script` argument. The other files can be uploaded with a file map.

The `file_map` variable is a dictionary that can be added to any relevant configuration file for the minion. Each key in the dictionary is the name of a local file that is to be uploaded, and the value is the name of the remote path to which it should be uploaded. Consider the following cloud profile:

```
ec2-ubuntu:
    provider: my-ec2
    image: ami-83dee0ea
    size: t2.small
    ssh_username: ubuntu
    securitygroup: default
    script: install.sh
    file_map:
```

```
/srv/salt/scripts/install1.sh: /tmp/install1.sh
/srv/salt/scripts/install2.py: /tmp/install2.py
/srv/salt/scripts/custompkg.deb: /tmp/custom-package.deb
```

This profile will upload a shell script, a Python script, and a package file to the `/tmp/` directory on the minion. It won't necessarily upload them in that order, but that's okay; the `install.sh` script (which will be uploaded from `/etc/salt/cloud.deploy.d/` on the system running Salt Cloud) will execute them in the proper order.

 Take note of the last file in `file_map`. If you specify a different filename on the target system than on the local system, Salt Cloud will rename it for you when it uploads it.

Taking a look at cloud maps

So far, we have only discussed how to work with compute instances on an individual level. However, one of the earliest features of Salt Cloud was the concept of a cloud map file (not to be confused with `file_map`). Cloud maps allow you to specify a group of machines to create all in one shot.

This can be very useful when managing a small infrastructure or small pieces of a large infrastructure. Not only can you declare that certain profiles be used to declare a number of compute instances, but you can also append and override configuration in those profiles.

Let's say that you have an infrastructure that contains database servers, web servers, and load balancers. Each type of server will have its own unique needs, but there will also be multiple instances of each type of server. First, let's define the provider:

```
my-ec2:
  id: FWEHKJ345FSDAFDE34DF
  key: 'fewhgreFRE/FSE+freg3r43FDSDS3334DSFdff4u'
  keyname: mycompany
  private_key: /root/mycompany.pem
  securitygroup: private
  location: us-east-1
  provider: ec2
  rename_on_destroy: True
  delvol_on_destroy: True
  owner: amazon
  minion:
    master: 10.0.0.150
Then, we'll define the profiles as follows:
ec2-load-balancer:
```

```
    provider: my-ec2
    size: t2.micro
    image: ami-83dee0ea
    security_group: public
  ec2-web:
    provider: my-ec2
    size: t2.small
    image: ami-83dee0ea
    security_group: public
  ec2-database:
    provider: my-ec2
    size: m3.xlarge
    image: ami-83dee0ea
```

To finish, we'll define a map that makes use of each of these profiles, as shown in the following code:

```
ec2-database:
  db001:
    grains:
      role: database
ec2-load-balancer:
  lb001:
    grains:
      role: load-balancer
      note: primary load-balancer
  lb002:
    grains:
      role: load-balancer
      note: secondary load-balancer
{% set webservers = ('web001', 'web002', 'web003') %}
{% for server in webservers %}
ec2-web:
  {{ server }}:
    grains:
      role: web
{% endfor %}
```

Three different techniques have been used in this map to define server names. However, only one database server has been defined: db001. It also has a custom grain set, which declares its role to be database. However, two load balancers, called lb001 and lb002, have been defined. They both have their role grains set to load-balancer, but they also have a unique value for their note grains.

The last profile, `ec2-web`, defines three different web servers, but it does so using Jinja templating. As with other files, cloud map files use Salt's renderer system, making templating easy. In this map, there's nothing special about each of the web servers; they will be identical. So, we just declared a tuple in Jinja with their names and then looped through each of them to create the final map file, which will look like the following code:

```
ec2-database:
  db001:
    grains:
      role: database
ec2-load-balancer:
  lb001:
    grains:
      role: load-balancer
      note: primary load-balancer
  lb002:
    grains:
      role: load-balancer
      note: secondary load-balancer
ec2-web:
  web001:
    grains:
      role: web

  web002:
    grains:
      role: web

  web003:
    grains:
      role: web
```

In order to run this map, we will use the `-m` or `--map` command-line argument:

```
salt-cloud -m /etc/salt/cloud.maps.d/mymap.map
```

By default, Salt Cloud will create these machines serially. In order to create them in parallel, we will add `-P` or `--parallel`:

```
salt-cloud -P -m /etc/salt/cloud.maps.d/mymap.map
```

You may have noticed the `cloud.maps.d/` directory. This is a directory suggested by SaltStack, which matches the naming scheme for other Salt Cloud directories. However, it is not required, and in fact, Salt Cloud will not even look in this directory unless it is pointed directly to it. If you do not specify an absolute path to a map file, Salt Cloud will look in the current working directory.

Using reactors with Salt Cloud

Salt Cloud is powerful on its own, but it can be made even more powerful by tying it in Salt's own event bus. Let's go ahead and set up a workflow to kick off whenever a new server is spun up using Salt Cloud. The steps that we need to perform, in order, are as follows:

1. Request a new cloud server.
2. Upon its creation, kick off a test suite to validate the servers.
3. If the tests fail, fire an alert and stop.
4. If they succeed, add the server to the load balancer.

We won't create a full test suite here as that is well beyond the scope of this book. However, because we can make use of Jinja templates, we will go ahead and perform some configuration for the load balancer.

Setting up the event tags

We're going to use a combination of both standard cloud tags and our own custom tags in our example. Go ahead and edit the `master` configuration file, and add a `reactor` section:

```
reactor:
  # Look for new web servers
  - 'salt/cloud/web-*/created':
    # Start the test suite
    - '/srv/reactor/web-tests.sls'
  # Look for failures
  - 'qa/live-tests/web-*/fail':
    # Fire an alert
    - '/srv/reactor/web-test-fail.sls'
  # Look for success
  - 'qa/live-tests/web-*/success':
    # Add server to load balancer
    - '/srv/reactor/web-haproxy-add.sls'
```

In this example, all our web servers start with `web-`. Undoubtedly, you'll want to run different tests against different types of servers, but this will get us through our example.

Now, we need to set up a reactor to kick off our test suite. This example assumes that there is a custom module called `mytestsuite` that has a series of functions, including one called `web`, for testing servers. We'll use a minion called `testmanager` that has been set aside just for this purpose. Create this file as `/srv/reactor/web-tests.sls`:

```
test-new-web-server:
  cmd.mytestsuite.web:
    - tgt: testmanager
    - kwarg:
        minion_id: {{ data['name'] }}
```

We'll also need to set up an alert that can notify us when a new server does not pass the test suite. This reactor will make use of another minion, called `monitoring`, which has been configured to fire alerts using PagerDuty. Save this file as `/srv/reactor/web-test-fail.sls`:

```
new-web-failure:
  cmd.pagerduty.create_event:
    - tgt: monitoring
    - kwarg:
        description: "Test fail: {{ data['name'] }}"
        details: "A new cloud instance on {{
        data['provider'] }} called {{ data['name'] }} has
        failed the web test suite"
        service_key: 0123456789abcdef0123456789abcdef
        profile: my-pagerduty-account
```

We're assuming that this `mytestsuite.web` function will fire an event that looks like `qa/live-tests/web-*/fail` when a server fails the test suite. We're also assuming that that function will fire an event that looks like `qa/live-tests/web-*/success` when a server passes the test suite. The reactor for this will be a little more complex, because we need to do some specific things in sequence:

1. Notify the load balancer about the new server.
2. Rewrite the load balancer configuration file.
3. Restart the load balancer.

We'll make use of grains to manage the list of active servers because there is already an execution module to manage grains. We'll use a state to handle the configuration file and load balancer because that can be included later in a highstate run.

We'll set up a file at `/srv/reactor/web-haproxy-add.sls`, which adds the grain and then kicks off a state run:

```
add-grain:
  cmd.grains.append:
    - tgt: 'haproxy-*'
    - kwarg:
      key: webservers
      val:
        minion: {{ data['name'] }}
        hostname: {{ data['hostname'] }}

run-state:
  cmd.state.sls:
    - tgt: 'haproxy-*'
    - arg:
      - haproxy
```

This file assumes that two pieces of data were sent in the event from the test suite: the ID of the minion (as `name`) and the hostname or IP address (as `hostname`).

Then, we'll set up `/srv/salt/haproxy.sls`, to be stored on any minion whose ID starts with `haproxy-`:

```
/etc/haproxy/haproxy.conf:
  file.managed:
    - source: salt://haproxy/haproxy.conf
    - template: jinja
    - mode: 644
    - user: root
    - group: root
haproxy:
  service.running:
    - enable: True
    - reload: True
    - require:
      - file: /etc/haproxy/haproxy.conf
```

Finally, we'll set up a template to be used to generate the `haproxy.conf` configuration file. This will be stored at `/srv/salt/haproxy/haproxy.conf`. To avoid confusion, I'll only show the part of the configuration file here that we're actually interested in:

```
listen http-webservices 0.0.0.0:80
  acl servers_down nbsrv(servers) lt 1
  monitor-uri /haproxy?monitor
  monitor fail if servers_down
{%- for minion in grains['webservers'] %}
  # Configuration for {{ minion['minion'] }}
  server {{ minion['hostname'] }}:80 {{ minion['hostname'] }}:80 maxconn 25
check inter 5s rise 3 fall 2
{%- endfor %}
```

With everything in place, we can now create new servers using the `salt-cloud` command, which kicks off this whole process:

```
# salt-cloud -p webserver web-093
```

If everything goes well, then each server whose name starts with `haproxy-` will end up having the following appear in its `/etc/haproxy/haproxy.conf` file:

```
listen http-webservices 0.0.0.0:80
  acl servers_down nbsrv(servers) lt 1
  monitor-uri /haproxy?monitor
  monitor fail if servers_down
  # Configuration for web-093
  server 10.0.0.93:80 10.0.0.93:80 maxconn 25 check inter 5s rise 3 fall 2
```

Working with autoscale reactors

Some cloud providers are able to actively send updates to automated systems, such as Salt, which Salt Cloud can act on, but even if they don't, Salt Cloud is able to poll cloud providers for the information it needs and use that information when the cloud provider automatically scales your infrastructure for you.

Cloud cache

There are in fact two caches kept by Salt Cloud, but one is more of an index than anything. Both are kept in the `cloud/` directory inside Salt's own `cache` directory. The normal location for the cloud cache is `/var/cache/salt/cloud/`.

If you've used Salt Cloud to create a compute instance, then there will be a file in this directory called `index.p`. This file, which is in the `msgpack` format, contains a list of all the compute instances that have been created by Salt Cloud (minus any that have been subsequently destroyed by Salt Cloud). There is no configuration variable to turn this on or off; it will be generated automatically.

If you were to open this file with `msgpack`, you would find the list of compute instances with a very small amount of information about them, as shown in the following code:

```
{
    "testinstance01": {
        "driver": "ec2",
        "id": "testinstance01",
        "profile": "centos65",
        "provider": "my-ec2"
    }
}
```

This information can be used by various components, such as the `cloud` roster, for Salt SSH to quickly determine which provider a compute instance belongs to and which profile was used to create it.

However, it is possible to extend the `cloud` cache to include more information. Be warned that this may slow Salt Cloud execution for some providers, but you may find it worth the extra time. To turn on the full cloud cache, set the following value in the main cloud configuration file:

```
update_cachedir: True
```

With this option turned on, Salt Cloud will make an entry in this directory for every single compute instance that is queried when either a `--full-query` operation is performed against a cloud provider or when a `show_instance` action is performed against a single compute instance.

Once the cache is updated, a new set of directories will show up under
`/var/cache/salt/cloud/`. First, there will be a directory called `active/`. In this
directory, there will be another directory for each driver (`ec2`, `linode`, `softlayer`, and so
on) that has been queried. In each of these directories, there will be another directory for
each user-defined provider-configuration block (`my-ec2-config`, `my-linode-config`,
`my-softlayer-config`, and so on). In each of these directories, there will be a `msgpack`
file with a `.p` extension for each node that has been queried for that provider. Such a
directory structure will look like the following code:

```
/var/cache/salt/cloud/
├── active
│   ├── ec2
│   │   └── my-ec2
│   │           ├── autoscalemaster.p
│   │           └── basepi-master.p
│   ├── linode
│   │   └── my-linode
│   │           └── techhat-master.p
│   └── softlayer
│           └── my-softlayer
│                   ├── cro-master.p
│                   └── rallytime-master.p
└── index.p
```

The content of each file is the output that will be shown for that compute instance in either a
`--full-query` or `show_instance` action. For example, take a look at the following code:

```
{
  "amiLaunchIndex": "0",
  "architecture": "x86_64",
  ...SNIP...
  "tagSet": {
    "item": {
      "key": "Name",
      "value": "techhat-master"
    }
  },
  "virtualizationType": "paravirtual"
}
```

The contents of these files become especially useful when Salt Cloud is instructed to fire
events when something changes. In order to do this, set the following value in the main
cloud configuration file:

```
diff_cache_events: True
```

When this is turned on, Salt Cloud will fire events when `--full-query` is executed. If a compute instance is found that was not previously in the cache, an event tagged `salt/cloud/<vm_name>/cache_node_new` will be fired. If a compute instance that previously existed in the cache is no longer there, then an event tagged `salt/cloud/<vm_name>/cache_node_missing` will be fired. Also, if a piece of information about a compute instance has changed (such as its running status), then an event tagged `salt/cloud/<vm_name>/cache_node_diff` will be fired.

Using cloud cache events

These cloud cache events can be used in conjunction with autoscaling systems. Many cloud providers offer their own autoscaling solutions but do not actively issue notifications to users when compute instances are created or destroyed. A small handful of cloud providers do, which can speed things up dramatically.

If you are working with one of the many cloud providers that do not actively send notifications, do not despair; Salt Cloud can still help. If set on a schedule, it will poll the cloud provider for you on a regular basis, firing events when it finds any changes.

Setting up a schedule

To use Salt's own scheduler on the master, add the following code to your master configuration file:

```
schedule:
  cloud_query:
    function: cloud.full_query
    minutes: 10
```

When this master configuration is applied, Salt Cloud will perform a full query for you every 10 minutes, updating the cache.

It is recommended to keep the time value conservative: bear in mind that each time this is run, it will query the cloud provider directly. If you are using a cloud provider that meters API calls and you query them too often, you risk getting blocked on a number of queries.

It may also be useful to set aside a dedicated minion to perform cloud queries. A number of infrastructure managers have decided to go this route to keep the load off the master. If you feel this is the right move for you, go ahead and install the necessary Salt Cloud configuration files on your chosen minion, and set the `schedule` option in the minion configuration file, which is exactly the same as on the master:

```
schedule:
  cloud_query:
    function: cloud.full_query
    minutes: 10
```

You don't even have to install the Salt Cloud package on the minion that will be performing the work. This is because Salt Cloud itself is built in to the core Salt libraries; the Salt Cloud package provides little more than the `salt-cloud` command. However, since there is a cloud execution module (which mirrors the cloud runner module on the master), you don't actually need the `salt-cloud` command to exist in order to use Salt Cloud. However, you will still need any dependencies (Libcloud, Azure, and so on) that are required for your cloud provider of choice.

Of course, if your infrastructure uses the cron system instead of Salt's built-in scheduler, you can still kick off events. However, you will need the `salt-cloud` command. Go ahead and set the following record in your crontab:

```
*/10 * * * * /usr/bin/salt-cloud --full-query
```

This will also issue a `--full-query` operation every 10 minutes, which is based on clock time rather than the time that the `salt-master` or the `salt-minion` services started up.

Catching cloud cache events

Once you have events set up to fire when the cloud cache changes, you can set up a reactor to respond to them. However, before we get into the details of how to set up the reactor, let's talk about the workflow that is going on here.

When Salt Cloud is asked to create a compute instance using either a `--profile` or `--map` argument, it will perform the following:

- Request that the cloud provider create a compute instance
- Wait for an IP address to become available for that compute instance
- Wait for SSH/SMB to become available at that IP address

- Upload files to that IP address
- Execute the deploy script or the Windows installer
- Clean up temporary files
- Return to the user

Some cloud providers do more than this, but every cloud provider performs at least these steps.

When Salt Cloud detects that a new minion has appeared, we know that the first of these steps (request a compute instance) has already been performed. We don't necessarily know that any other steps were performed, but that's okay; each step naturally leads to the next. All we need to do is tell Salt Cloud to skip Step 1 and start with Step 2, using the ID of the compute instance that we provide it.

 Keep in mind that not every cloud provider currently supports skipping the first step. As of Salt version 2015.5, the EC2 driver and all OpenStack-based drivers support it.

When Salt Cloud finds a new compute instance, it will fire an event using the `show_instance` function that contains all the information that will be shown for that node:

```
Tag: salt/cloud/mynewinstance/cache_node_new
Data:
{'_stamp': '2015-05-03T18:34:40.267845',
 'event': 'new node found',
 'new_data': {'amiLaunchIndex': '0',
              'architecture': 'x86_64',
              'id': 'i-deadcafe',
              'instanceId': 'i-deadcafe',
...SNIP...
              'tagSet': {'item': {'key': 'Name', 'value':
'mynewinstance'}},
              'virtualizationType': 'paravirtual'}}
```

The most important piece of information here is the `id` field. We'll assume that the ID of the compute instance is also the name that you'll want to refer to the minion with (which is probably true for a compute instance that was created by an autoscaler). For simplicity, we'll also assume that you're only working with one provider.

First, let's go ahead and create a map for the reactor in the master configuration file:

```
reactor:
  - salt/cloud/*/cache_node_new:
    - /srv/reactor/new_compute_instance.sls
```

Then, we'll set up a simple Jinja-based reactor to kick off a Salt Cloud process, as follows:

```
cat /srv/reactor/new_compute_instance.sls
new_compute_instance:
  runner.cloud.create:
    instances: {{ data['new_data']['id'] }}
    instance_id: {{ data['new_data']['id'] }}
    provider: my-ec2
```

Profile configuration is not necessary here because the compute instance has already been created. However, provider configuration does need to be specified so that Salt Cloud knows how to access the compute instance and its metadata.

However, this information is not necessary when Salt Cloud detects that a compute instance has disappeared. Salt Cloud doesn't need to do anything by itself, including destroying the node, because it's already been destroyed. However, the old public key for that minion should still be cleaned up on the master. Let's add one more reactor. The event that will be generated looks like the following code:

```
Tag: salt/cloud/mymissinginstance/cache_node_missing
Data:
{'_stamp': '2015-05-03T18:57:03.931963',
 'event': 'cached node missing from provider',
 'missing node': 'mymissinginstance'}
```

First, let's map it out in the master configuration:

```
reactor:
  - salt/cloud/*/cache_node_missing:
    - /srv/reactor/missing_compute_instance.sls
```

Then, we'll set up a reactor that cleans up the key from the master using the `wheel` subsystem:

```
cat /srv/reactor/missing_compute_instance.sls
missing_compute_instance:
  wheel.key.delete:
    - match: {{ data['missing_node'] }}
```

Now, when Salt Cloud detects that a node is missing, its key will be cleaned up right away.

Summary

Salt Cloud can be a very powerful tool in the hands of an experienced user. It has moved from its humble beginnings as a simple tool for creating virtual machines to a crucial component of many production infrastructures with complex provisioning needs.

The Salt Cloud configuration can be simple, but it also has the flexibility to be very complex if required. The Salt Bootstrap script is also very powerful but not a one-size-fits-all solution. Fortunately, we can replace it when another solution is better for our needs.

Cloud maps are also very useful for managing infrastructures and they bring with them the power of Salt's renderer system. The reactor system can be used to manage tasks such as starting test suites and updating configuration. Also, when third-party systems manage clouds for you, it is still possible to bring Salt Cloud into the game using autoscale reactors.

In the next chapter, we'll take a look at how Salt works with REST interfaces, both as a client and as a server.

8
Using Salt with REST

We've discussed using Salt not only to manage an infrastructure from within, but also to grow the infrastructure with Salt Cloud. But what happens when you need to manage your infrastructure from the outside? Or if you want your infrastructure to take advantage of external systems? In this chapter, we'll explore how Salt makes use of REST interfaces, both as a client and as a server. We'll be covering the following topics:

- Taking advantage of Salt's HTTP library
- Setting up the Salt API
- Communicating as a client or a server
- Parsing data
- Reacting with Thorium

Looking at Salt's HTTP library

An increasing number of subsystems inside Salt are designed to make use of external APIs. At the moment, most of these are drivers for Salt Cloud, and most use either the Apache project's Libcloud library or the SDK maintained by the cloud provider.

Things have been changing in recent releases, though. Salt now has a library designed to make a generic, Salty HTTP client available to modules and for direct use by users. This library is already being used by some compute cloud providers as well as other services that provide a REST interface to their users.

Why a Salt-specific library?

Why go to all this trouble instead of just using an SDK? The biggest reason is portability. Take for example PagerDuty, which is a powerful service that manages incident alerting. The original Salt module used a community driver for PagerDuty. At the time, this driver didn't do much, but it did allow Salt to create alerts, which was all that was needed.

However, in practical use, it was realized that if a minion wanted to create an alert in PagerDuty, it needed that community package installed. This would mean having one more package to maintain on each minion across the infrastructure, and with a cluster filled with thousands of nodes, that was just unreasonable.

So Salt said farewell to the community driver, and an entirely new set of Salt modules was written from scratch using PagerDuty's REST API directly. Now any server that has Salt installed automatically has access to create alerts in PagerDuty.

This explains why so many modules in Salt skip the SDK and use REST APIs directly. But why provide a library when so many other fine libraries exist and do a nice job of providing access to HTTP?

The first reason is that while these libraries are easy to use when it comes to connecting to Salt, they aren't really designed to take advantage of the Salt toolset. Salt provides templating, an event bus, reactors, and a number of other subsystems that are very powerful. The Salt HTTP library ties these components together in a manner consistent with Salt's own mannerisms.

But which library to use? There are a number of excellent HTTP libraries available, each with its own pros and cons. The `requests` library is easily the most popular, and even upstream Python documentation recommends it over its own built-in `urllib` and `urllib2` libraries. But due to packaging issues, requests cannot be made a hard dependency for Salt.

However, Salt does have a hard dependency on the `tornado` web library for internal use with the event bus. And while Tornado is primarily designed to be used as a web server, it also has its own HTTP client built in.

The Salt HTTP library allows any of these three libraries to be used: `tornado` (the default), `requests`, and `urllib2`. In order to set a system-wide default, set the backend argument in either the master or the minion configuration, as appropriate:

```
backend: tornado
backend: requests
backend: urllib2
```

You can also declare, per execution, which backend to use, but let's not get too far ahead of ourselves. First, let's go over the basics of how to use the client.

Using the http.query function

The Salt HTTP client is widely available throughout Salt. Using it as a runner on the master is identical to using it as an execution module on a minion, apart from the obvious differences between how those two types of modules operate:

```
# salt myminion http.query https://www.google.com/
# salt-run http.query https://www.google.com/
```

We'll use the runner for the rest of the examples in this section, but all the arguments are identical in usage between the two.

By default, these functions will not return anything. If return data is expected, then you need to tell the function what kind to return. The following will return a dictionary containing the HTTP status code and headers and the content of the result body:

```
# salt-run http.query https://www.google.com/ text=True status=True
headers=True
headers:
    ----------
    Accept-Ranges:
        none
    Alternate-Protocol:
        443:quic,p=1
    Cache-Control:
        private, max-age=0
    Connection:
        close
    Content-Type:
        text/html; charset=ISO-8859-1
    Date:
        Mon, 04 May 2015 08:24:59 GMT
    Expires:
        -1
    Server:
        gws
    Vary:
        Accept-Encoding
status:
    200
text:
    <!doctype html>...SNIP...
```

For simplicity, our examples from here on won't include these arguments unless they are explicitly needed for the example in question.

A cookie jar is also available if necessary. To turn it on, set `cookies` to `True`:

```
# salt-run http.query https://www.google.com/
cookies=True
```

By default, this cookie jar will be stored as `cookies.txt` in the Salt `cache` directory. This will normally be `/var/cache/salt/cookies.txt`. It will also be saved in the (**LWP (lib-www-perl)**) format by default since it is a text-based file. To change the location of the cookie jar and set it to use (old-style) Mozilla cookies instead, use the `cookie_jar` and `cookie_format` arguments:

GET versus POST

By default, requests made with `http.query` will use the `GET` method. The `GET` arguments can either be added to the URL manually or passed as `params` values. The following two arguments are functionally identical:

```
# salt-run http.query http://mydomain.com/?user=larry
# salt-run http.query http://mydomain.com/
params='{"user": "larry"}'
```

However, it is possible to use any other valid HTTP method. `POST` is the most common argument to be used after `GET`, but these techniques are also valid with `PUT`, `PATCH`, and so on:

```
# salt-run http.query http://mydomain.com/ POST
data='{}'
```

If the `POST` data to be sent is stored inside a file, then that file may be specified instead:

```
# salt-run http.query http://mydomain.com/ POST
data_file=/tmp/post.txt
```

This is where the Salt HTTP client starts to differ from other clients: if a POST data file is used, then it may be templated using any of the renderer engines.

For instance, a number of older web APIs are based on XML. Unlike JSON, which can be easily generated without specialized tools, XML often requires templates to be used, with data merged in. The Salt HTTP client makes quick work of this. Consider the following template:

```
<?xml version="1.0" encoding="utf-8"?>
<soap:Envelope xmlns:soap="http://schemas.xmlsoap.org/soap/envelope/"
xmlns:xsi="http://www.w3.org/2001/XMLSchema-instance"
xmlns:xsd="http://www.w3.org/2001/XMLSchema"
xmlns:xmime="http://www.w3.org/2005/05/xmlmime"
xmlns:ns="http://schemas.hp.com/SM/7"
xmlns:cmn="http://schemas.hp.com/SM/7/Common">
  <soap:Body>
    <ns:DeleteHostRequest>
      <ns:model>
        <ns:keys>
          <ns:VMName type="">{{ minion_id }}</ns:VMName>
        </ns:keys>
        <ns:instance/>
      </ns:model>
    </ns:DeleteHostRequest>
  </soap:Body>
</soap:Envelope>
```

It looks daunting, doesn't it? This is actually a very small request compared to a number of XML queries, and the only piece of information that needs to be changed is the VMName value, which has been templatized in Jinja as minion_id. To issue a request using this file to insert a minion_id of web099, use this:

```
# salt-run http.query http://mydomain.com/ POST
data_file=/srv/xml/delete.xml data_render=True
template_dict='{"minion_id": "web099"}
```

The two important arguments here are data_render, which must be set to True in order to use the renderer, and template_dict, which contains the variables to be merged into the template. The default renderer is Jinja, but you can change it by specifying a data_renderer argument as well.

POST data is not the only data that can make use of Salt's renderer system. Header data may be represented as a dictionary, a properly formatted list, or a file that can be rendered if necessary. To send a header dictionary, use header_dict:

```
# salt-run http.query http://example.com/
header_dict='{"Content-Type": "application/json"}'
```

To send a list of headers (making sure that they are already properly formatted), use `header_list`:

```
# salt-run http.query http://example.com/
header_list='["Content-Type: application/json"]'
```

To use a file containing all the headers (again, properly formatted), use `header_file`:

```
# cat /srv/headers/headers.txt
Content-Type: application/json
# salt-run http.query http://example.com/
header_file=/srv/headers/headers.txt
```

If the `header_file` is templated, set `header_render` to `True`, and pass the values using the `template_dict` argument as before:

```
# cat /srv/headers/headers.txt
Content-Type: {{ content_type }}
# salt-run http.query http://example.com/
header_file=/srv/headers/headers.txt
header_render=True template_dict='{"content_type":
"application/json"}'
```

As with the `POST` data templates, if you want to use a different renderer for the headers, set it with `header_renderer`.

Decoding return data

Another important aspect of the Salt HTTP client is the ability to automatically decode data that is received. If `decode` is set to `True`, Salt will try to autodetect whether the return data is XML or JSON, unless `decode_type` is explicitly set to either `xml` or `json`:

```
# salt-run http.query https://api.github.com/
decode=True decode_type=json
dict:
    ----------
    authorizations_url:
        https://api.github.com/authorizations
    code_search_url:
        https://api.github.com/search/code?q={query}
{&page,per_page,sort,order}
    current_user_authorizations_html_url:
        https://github.com/settings/connections
/applications{/client_id}
    current_user_repositories_url:
        https://api.github.com
```

```
    /user/repos{?type,page,per_page,sort}
    current_user_url:
        https://api.github.com/user
    emails_url:
        https://api.github.com/user/emails
    emojis_url:
        https://api.github.com/emojis
...SNIP...
```

 Note that when `decode` is set to `True`, the data will be returned in the `dict` field rather than the `text` field that is used when `text` is `True`.

You should also note that while JSON is perfectly suited to being decoded as a dictionary, XML is very poorly suited to being translated like that. Salt will do its best, but any XML attributes won't be decoded. If you are working with XML that does not decode properly this way, it is best to set decode to `False` and use a more XML-specific program to translate it (or use straight Python).

Now that you've seen the basics of the Salt HTTP client and some of the more advanced features that are specific to Salt, let's take a look at how we can use that functionality with our state files.

Using the http.query state

The `http.query` state differs slightly from most other states in that it serves not to actually make changes on the minion running the state but to provide assistance to the operations of a state run. Webhooks can be called to do things such as reporting on failures or providing status updates.

Take, for example, the following SLS:

```
code_tree:
  file.recurse:
    - name: /srv/web/code
    - source: salt://code/
    - onfail_in:
      - http: alert_admins

alert_admins:
  http.query:
    - name: http://alerts.example.com/?type=code_deploy_fail
```

This SLS will attempt to recursively copy a directory to a minion. In the event of a failure, it will call a URL that reports to an alerting service if a failure has occurred.

Of course, multiple calls to `http.query` can be made within a single SLS file. We can trigger a separate webhook for each of the states if we want:

```
code_tree:
  file.recurse:
    - name: /srv/web/code
    - source: salt://code/
    - onfail_in:
      - http: alert_admins_code

alert_admins_code:
  http.query:
    - name: http://alerts.example.com/?type=code_deploy_fail

web_service:
  service.running:
    - name: nginx
    - require:
      - file: code_tree
    - onfail_in:
      - http: alert_admins_web

alert_admins_web:
  http.query:
    - name: http://alerts.example.com/?type=web_restart_fail
```

Alternatively, we can just provide status via a webhook as each state is called:

```
code_tree:
  file.recurse:
    - name: /srv/web/code
    - source: salt://code/

alert_admins_code:
  http.query:
    - name: http://alerts.example.com/?type=code_deploy_finished
    - require:
      - file: code_tree

web_service:
  service.running:
    - name: nginx
    - require:
      - file: code_tree
```

```
alert_admins_web:
  http.query
    - name: http://alerts.example.com/?type=web_restart_finished
    - require:
      - service: web_service
```

This may have started to look like a lot of work-why doesn't Salt just have something built in that can send updates as each state is completed?

Using http.query with reactors

You may recall using `http.query` in Chapter 5, *Managing Tasks Asynchronously*, in conjunction with reactors. Each time a state is completed, an event is fired to the master containing the result data for that event. This has an advantage over using the `http.query` state, in that the return data from the state will also be available.

Go ahead and fire up the event listener on the master (as described in Chapter 5, *Managing Tasks Asynchronously*), and try out this set of commands:

```
# salt myminion state.single file.touch /root/somedir
local:
----------
          ID: /root/somedir
    Function: file.touch
      Result: True
     Comment: Created empty file /root/somedir
     Started: 02:55:59.237320
    Duration: 0.881 ms
     Changes:
              ----------
              new:
                  /root/somedir
Summary
------------
Succeeded: 1 (changed=1)
Failed:    0
------------
Total states run:     1
# salt myminion state.single file.directory /root/somedir
local:
----------
          ID: /root/somedir
    Function: file.directory
      Result: False
     Comment: Specified location /root/somedir exists and is a file
     Started: 02:56:09.708133
```

```
          Duration: 0.787 ms
           Changes:
Summary
------------
Succeeded: 0
Failed:    1
------------
Total states run:     1
# salt myminion state.single file.absent /root/somedir
local:
----------
               ID: /root/somedir
         Function: file.absent
           Result: True
          Comment: Removed file /root/somedir
          Started: 02:56:47.408437
          Duration: 0.837 ms
           Changes:
                   ----------
                   removed:
                       /root/somedir
Summary
------------
Succeeded: 1 (changed=1)
Failed:    0
------------
Total states run:     1
# salt myminion state.single file.directory /root/somedir
local:
----------
               ID: /root/somedir
         Function: file.directory
           Result: True
          Comment: Directory /root/somedir updated
          Started: 02:56:59.564577
          Duration: 22.386 ms
           Changes:
                   ----------
                   /root/somedir:
                       New Dir
Summary
------------
Succeeded: 1 (changed=1)
Failed:    0
------------
Total states run:     1
```

Because one of the states intentionally had an error, you will see three successes overall and one failure. In the event listener, you will see messages that look like the following:

```
Event fired at Sun May 10 02:55:59 2015
*************************
Tag: salt/job/20150510025559240942/ret/myminion
Data:
{'_stamp': '2015-05-10T08:55:59.241475',
 'arg': ['file.touch', '/root/somedir'],
 'cmd': '_return',
 'fun': 'state.single',
 'fun_args': ['file.touch', '/root/somedir'],
 'id': 'myminion',
 'jid': '20150510025559240942',
 'out': 'highstate',
 'retcode': 0,
 'return': {'file_|-/root/somedir_|-/root/somedir_|-touch':
                    {'__run_num__': 0,
                     'changes': {'new': '/root/somedir'},
                     'comment': 'Created empty file /root/somedir',
                     'duration': 0.881,
                     'name': '/root/somedir',
                     'result': True,
                     'start_time': '02:55:59.237320'}},
 'tgt': 'myminion',
 'tgt_type': 'glob'}
Event fired at Sun May 10 02:56:09 2015
*************************
Tag: salt/job/20150510025609711804/ret/myminion
Data:
{'_stamp': '2015-05-10T08:56:09.712309',
 'arg': ['file.directory', '/root/somedir'],
 'cmd': '_return',
 'fun': 'state.single',
 'fun_args': ['file.directory', '/root/somedir'],
 'id': 'myminion',
 'jid': '20150510025609711804',
 'out': 'highstate',
 'retcode': 2,
 'return': {'file_|-/root/somedir_|-/root/somedir_|-directory':
                    {'__run_num__': 0,
                     'changes': {},
                     'comment': 'Specified location /root/somedir exists and
is a file',
                     'duration': 0.787,
                     'name': '/root/somedir',
                     'result': False,
                     'start_time': '02:56:09.708133'}},
```

```
 'tgt': 'myminion',
 'tgt_type': 'glob'}
Event fired at Sun May 10 02:56:47 2015
*************************
Tag: salt/job/20150510025647412099/ret/myminion
Data:
{'_stamp': '2015-05-10T08:56:47.429361',
 'arg': ['file.absent', '/root/somedir'],
 'cmd': '_return',
 'fun': 'state.single',
 'fun_args': ['file.absent', '/root/somedir'],
 'id': 'myminion',
 'jid': '20150510025647412099',
 'out': 'highstate',
 'retcode': 0,
 'return': {'file_|-/root/somedir_|-/root/somedir_|-absent':
                     {'__run_num__': 0,
                      'changes': {'removed': '/root/somedir'},
                      'comment': 'Removed file /root/somedir',
                      'duration': 0.837,
                      'name': '/root/somedir',
                      'result': True,
                      'start_time': '02:56:47.408437'}},
 'tgt': 'myminion',
 'tgt_type': 'glob'}
Event fired at Sun May 10 02:56:59 2015
*************************
Tag: salt/job/20150510025659589886/ret/myminion
Data:
{'_stamp': '2015-05-10T08:56:59.590486',
 'arg': ['file.directory', '/root/somedir'],
 'cmd': '_return',
 'fun': 'state.single',
 'fun_args': ['file.directory', '/root/somedir'],
 'id': 'myminion',
 'jid': '20150510025659589886',
 'out': 'highstate',
 'retcode': 0,
 'return': {'file_|-/root/somedir_|-/root/somedir_|-directory':
                     {'__run_num__': 0,
                      'changes': {'/root/somedir': 'New Dir'},
                      'comment': 'Directory /root/somedir updated',
                      'duration': 22.386,
                      'name': '/root/somedir',
                      'result': True,
                      'start_time': '02:56:59.564577'}},
 'tgt': 'myminion',
 'tgt_type': 'glob'}
```

You can see the kinds of information we get along the event bus and we can make use of in our reactors. Let's go ahead and set up something that will fire a webhook every time any state is run. Because we're specifically interested in the return data, let's start by mapping that out in the master configuration file. Go ahead; edit the master configuration and add the following mapping:

```
reactor:
  - 'salt/job/*/ret/*'
    - /srv/reactor/state_notify.sls
```

This will catch any job (the first *) coming from any minion (the second *). Now, let's set up the reactor itself:

```
# cat /srv/reactor/state_notify.sls
#!jinja|json
{% if data['fun'].startswith('state.') %}
{"react_to_state":
  {"runner.http.query":
    [
      {
        "url": "http://alerts.example.com/",
        "method": "POST",
        "data": "{{ data }}"
      }
    ]
  }
}
{% endif %}
```

We have to be very careful here, since this reactor is going to analyze any job return data that appears on the bus. This would be especially critical if we were calling out to an execution module, which itself would create another return event. So, we start off by making sure we only process the events whose function starts with state (that is, `state.highstate`, `state.top`, `state.sls`, and so on).

With that out of the way, this reactor is actually very simple: call the `http.query` runner with the URL `http://alerts.example.com/`, a `POST` method, and the contents of the return data as the `POST` data.

Notice how we used JSON instead of YAML here. That's because the return data may contain characters that wouldn't translate properly in YAML. JSON is a more exacting serialization method and much less likely to cause syntactical errors.

But let's say that we're only interested in raising an alert when we get an error. Let's add another condition to our reactor SLS:

```
# cat /srv/reactor/state_notify.sls
#!jinja|json
{% if data['fun'].startswith('state.') %}
{% set return_key = data['return'].keys()[0] %}
{% set result = data['return'][return_key]['result'] %}
{% if result == False %}
{"react_to_state":
  {"runner.http.query":
    [
      {
        "url": "http://alerts.example.com/isfalse",
        "method": "POST",
        "data": "{{ data }}"
      }
    ]
  }
}
{% endif %}
{% endif %}
```

We've left in the check to make sure that we're looking at a state, because we don't want anything else happening if it's not. Beyond that, we've actually done a couple of things here. First, we had to find out what the return value of the state was. You may recall that the return dictionary has a single key in it, which looks kind of like this:

```
file_|-/root/somedir_|-/root/somedir_|-directory
```

That's going to be pretty much impossible to autodetect, and in our case, it doesn't matter anyway. But Jinja still does need to know what that key is so that it can access the result inside the return dictionary. So, we pull it out first and assign it to return_key. Then, we use that to access the rest of the dictionary.

Once we know what the result is, we just do a check on its truth value. Python coders take note: Jinja requires that our check, even for a boolean, use == instead of is.

Understanding the Salt API

We've spent some time looking at how to send requests, but many users would argue that receiving requests is just as important, if not more so. Let's take a moment to understand the Salt API.

What is the Salt API?

Very simply, the Salt API is a REST interface wrapped around Salt. But that doesn't tell you the whole story. The `salt` command is really just a command-line interface for Salt. In fact, each of the other Salt commands (`salt-call`, `salt-cloud`, and so on) is really just a way to access various parts of Salt from the command line.

The Salt API provides a way to access Salt from a different interface: HTTP (or HTTPS, preferably). Because web protocols are so ubiquitous, the Salt API allows software, written in any language that has the capability of interacting with web servers, to take advantage of it.

Setting up the Salt API

So far, this book has assumed that you have a copy of Salt installed, with both a master and a minion service running. But we're going to take a moment to talk about setting up the Salt API, since it's somewhat less intuitive than the rest of Salt.

Being a REST interface, the Salt API acts as a web server over and above Salt. But it doesn't actually provide the server interface itself. It uses other web frameworks to provide those services and then acts as more of a middleman between them and Salt. The modules that are supported for this are:

- CherryPy
- Tornado
- WSGI

These modules are set up in the master configuration file. Each has its own set of configuration parameters and possible dependencies. Let's take a look at each one.

CherryPy

CherryPy is a minimalist web framework that is designed to be very Pythonic. Because it is based around creating web code in the same way that other Python code is created, it is said to result in code that is much smaller and more quickly developed. It has a mature codebase and a number of notable users. It has also been the de facto module of the Salt API for some time.

This module does require that the **CherryPy** package (usually called `python-cherrypy`) be installed.

The basic setup for CherryPy doesn't involve much configuration. At a minimum, you should have the following:

```
rest_cherrypy:
  port: 8080
  ssl_crt: /etc/pki/tls/certs/localhost.crt
  ssl_key: /etc/pki/tls/certs/localhost.key
```

We'll discuss creating certificates in a moment, but first let's talk about configuration in general. There are a number of configuration parameters available for this module, but we'll focus on the more common ones here:

- `port`: This is required. It's the port for the Salt API to listen on.
- `host`: Normally, the Salt API listens on all available interfaces (`0.0.0.0`). If you are in an an environment where you need to provide services only to one interface, then provide the IP address (that is, `10.0.0.1`) here.
- `ssl_crt`: This is the path to your SSL certificate. We'll cover this in a moment.
- `ssl_key`: This is the path to the private key for the SSL certificate. Again, we'll cover this in a moment.
- `debug`: If you are setting up the Salt API for the first time, setting this to `True` can be very helpful. But once you are up and running, make sure to remove this option or explicitly set it to `False`.
- `disable_ssl`: It is highly recommended that the default value of `False` be used here. Even when just getting started, self-signed certificates are better than setting this to `True`. Why? Because *nothing is as permanent as temporary*, and at least self-signed certificates will remind you each time that you need to get a real set of certificates in place. Don't be complacent for the sake of learning.

- `root_prefix`: Normally, the Salt API will serve from the root path of the server (that is, `https://saltapi.example.com/`), but if you have several applications that you're serving from the same host or you just want to be more specific, you can change this. The default is `/`, but you could set it to `/exampleapi` in order to serve REST services from `https://saltapi.example.com/exampleapi`, for example.
- `webhook_url`: If you are using webhooks, they need their own entry point. By default, this is set to `/hook`, which in our example would serve from `https://saltapi.example.com/hook`.
- `webhook_disable_auth`: Normally, the Salt API requires authentication, but this is quite commonly not possible with third-party applications that need to call it over a webhook. This allows webhooks to not require authentication. We'll go more in depth on this in a moment.

Tornado

Tornado is a somewhat newer framework that was written by Facebook. It is also newer than Salt but is quickly becoming the web framework of choice inside Salt itself. In fact, it is used so much inside Salt that it is now considered a hard dependency for Salt and will be available on all newer installations.

Tornado doesn't have as many configuration options inside the Salt API as CherryPy. The ones that are supported (as defined in the *CherryPy* section) are:

- `port`
- `ssl_crt`
- `ssl_key`
- `debug`
- `disable_ssl`

While the Tornado module doesn't support nearly as much functionality as the CherryPy module just yet, keep an eye on it; it may become the new de facto Salt API module.

WSGI

WSGI, or **Web Server Gateway Interface**, is a Python standard, defined in PEP 333. Direct support for it ships with Python itself, so no external dependencies are required, but this module is also pretty basic. The only configuration option to worry about here is `port`.

However, this module is useful in that it allows the Salt API to be run under any WSGI-compliant web server, such as Apache with `mod_wsgi` or Nginx with FastCGI. Because this module does not provide any sort of SSL-based security, it is recommended that one of these options be used, with those third-party web servers being properly configured with the appropriate SSL settings.

Creating SSL certificates

It is highly advisable to use an SSL certificate for the Salt API even if you currently only plan to use it on a local, secured network. You should probably also purchase a certificate that is signed by a **certificate authority** (**CA**). When you get to this point, the CA will provide instructions on how to create one using their system. However, for now, we can get by with a self-signed certificate.

There are a number of guides online for creating self-signed certificates, but finding one that is easy to understand is somewhat more difficult. The following steps will generate both an SSL certificate and the key to use it on a Linux system:

First, we'll need to generate the key. Don't worry about the password-just enter one for now, take note of it, and we'll strip it out in a moment.

```
# openssl genrsa -des3 -out server.key 2048
Generating RSA private key, 2048 bit long modulus
...............+++++
.................................................+++++
e is 65537 (0x10001)
Enter pass phrase for server.key:
Verifying - Enter pass phrase for server.key:
```

Once you have the key, you need to use it to generate a certificate signing request, or CSR. You will be asked a number of questions about you that are important if you want a certificate signed by a CA. On your internal network, it's somewhat less important.

```
# openssl req -new -key server.key -out server.csr
Enter pass phrase for server.key:
You are about to be asked to enter information that will be incorporated
into your certificate request.
What you are about to enter is what is called a Distinguished Name or a DN.
There are quite a few fields but you can leave some blank
For some fields there will be a default value,
If you enter '.', the field will be left blank.
-----
Country Name (2 letter code) [AU]:US
State or Province Name (full name) [Some-State]:Utah
```

```
Locality Name (eg, city) []:Salt Lake City
Organization Name (eg, company) [Internet Widgits Pty Ltd]:My Company, LLC
Organizational Unit Name (eg, section) []:
Common Name (e.g. server FQDN or YOUR name) []:
Email Address []:me@example.com
Please enter the following 'extra' attributes
to be sent with your certificate request
A challenge password []:
An optional company name []:
```

At this point, we can go ahead and strip the password from the key.

```
# cp server.key server.key.org# openssl rsa -in server.key.org -out
server.key
Enter pass phrase for server.key.org:
writing RSA fkey
```

Finally, we'll create a self-signed certificate.

```
# openssl x509 -req -days 365 -in server.csr -signkey server.key -out
server.crt
Signature ok
subject=/C=US/ST=Utah/L=Salt Lake City/O=My Company,
LLC/emailAddress=me@example.com
Getting Private key
```

At this point, you will have four files:

- server.crt
- server.csr
- server.key
- server.key.org

Copy server.crt to the path specified for ssl_crt and server.key to the path specified for ssl_key.

Configuring authentication

Normally when using Salt, the salt command is accessed from the command line as the root user, an unprivileged user with sudo access, or as the user that is running the salt-master daemon. However, it can be configured to allow other user accounts to be used instead, from other authentication platforms.

Because the Salt API is not available from the command line (outside command-line clients such as `wget` and `curl`), it requires external authentication (often referred to as `eauth`) to be configured. This is done in the same way as with the other areas of Salt that support `eauth`.

The external authentication module

The external authentication module is one of the pluggable areas of Salt that does not currently have many modules and is not likely to in the near future. Why is that so? That is because so many of the authentication schemes that could be used here are already supported by**PAM**, Linux's **Pluggable Authentication Module** .

For instance, even though LDAP is supported, many administrators find it easier to just use PAM bindings, since the users they want to authenticate are already available through PAM's LDAP bindings.

External authentication is set up inside the master configuration file with a block called `external_auth`. The module that is used is then declared, followed by users to be provided by that module and their permissions. Here's an example:

```
external_auth:
  pam:
    larry:
      - .*
      - '@runner'
      - '@wheel'
    darrel:
      - test.*
      - '@runner'
      - '@wheel'
    darryl:
      - test.*
      - network.*
      - '@runner'
      - '@wheel'
```

The `larry` user has three permissions defined here:

- `.*`: These are the execution modules that the user has access to. Note that this is a regular expression.
- `@runner`: These are the runner modules that the user has access to (in this case, all runner modules).

- @wheel: These are the wheel modules that the user has access to (in this case, all wheel modules).

The darrel and darryl users have slightly more restricted access: both have access to any of the functions inside the test module, and darryl also has access to any of the functions inside the network module.

Taking your first steps with the Salt API

Once you have the proper settings in the master configuration file, you can start up the Salt API. For now, go ahead and set debug to True, and start up the service in the foreground:

```
# salt-api
[11/May/2015:00:55:22] ENGINE Listening for SIGHUP.
[11/May/2015:00:55:22] ENGINE Listening for SIGTERM.
[11/May/2015:00:55:22] ENGINE Listening for SIGUSR1.
[11/May/2015:00:55:22] ENGINE Bus STARTING
[11/May/2015:00:55:22] ENGINE Started monitor thread
'_TimeoutMonitor'.
[11/May/2015:00:55:22] ENGINE Started monitor thread
'Autoreloader'.
[11/May/2015:00:55:23] ENGINE Serving on
http://0.0.0.0:8080
[11/May/2015:00:55:23] ENGINE Bus STARTED
```

As you issue commands to the Salt API, you will see information about them printed to this console. Because the Salt API requires extra headers and often POST data, we'll use curl for our examples.

Before we do anything else, we need to obtain a token to issue commands. We will need to submit the proper credentials to get this token but, once we have it, we can use it to confirm our authentication with each request. To get a token, type the following:

```
# curl -ski https://localhost:8080/login \
      -H 'Accept: application/json' \
      -d username='larry' \
      -d password='123pass' \
      -d eauth='pam'
```

The -s in this command will tell the Salt API to be silent (it shouldn't show any superfluous messages). The -i will tell it to show the headers that were returned from the server. We'll use -s in the rest of our examples, but we'll leave out -i.

The -H option allows us to send a specific header to the remote server. The Salt API requires that the application/json header be sent; we are interested in receiving responses back in the JSON format.

The -d options are used to send POST data to the server-in this case, in a set of key-value pairs. The eauth parameter explicitly specifies which eauth module to use to authenticate this user. The username and password, of course, refer to the credentials that will be used with that module.

This command will return something that looks like the following (the return data is formatted here for clarity):

```
HTTP/1.1 200 OK
Content-Length: 196
Access-Control-Expose-Headers: GET, POST
Vary: Accept-Encoding
Server: CherryPy/3.6.0
Allow: GET, HEAD, POST
Access-Control-Allow-Credentials: true
Date: Mon, 11 May 2015 07:12:13 GMT
Access-Control-Allow-Origin: *
X-Auth-Token: 0bbb7e20dfb6093528636202e706ebc4d4c8493c
Content-Type: application/json
Set-Cookie: session_id=0bbb7e20dfb6093528636202e706ebc4d4c8493c;
expires=Mon, 11 May 2015 17:12:13 GMT; Path=/

{"return": [{
        "perms": [".*", "@runner", "@wheel"],
        "start": 1431328333.460601,
        "token": "0bbb7e20dfb6093528636202e706ebc4d4c8493c",
        "expire": 1431371533.460602,
        "user": "larry",
        "eauth": "pam"}]}
```

In the return body, you'll see a token-in this case, 0bbb7e20dfb6093528636202e706ebc4d4c8493c. You'll need to pass this exact token in each of your subsequent requests but, since it's pretty long, we'll just use <token> to represent it in our examples.

Once we have our token, we add it to subsequent requests to the server using the X-Auth-Token header. For example, to perform a simple test.ping operation against a minion, we will issue the following command:

```
# curl -sk https://localhost:8080/minions -H 'Accept: application/json' -H
'X-Auth-Token: <token>' -d client='local' -d tgt='*' -d fun='test.ping'
{
    "_links": {"jobs": [{"href": "/jobs
/20150511024432503750"}]},
    "return": [{
        "jid": "20150511024432503750",
        "minions": ["myminion"]}]}
```

> Note that this command was issued against the /minions URL. This is used for executing a number of commands-for example, against an execution module-over the Salt API.

There are also some extra arguments in the command that we need to look at before we get to the return data. The first is client='local', which tells the Salt API to use an execution module. The others may look more familiar. The tgt argument sets the target-in this case, all minions. The fun argument sets the function that will be run-test.ping in this case.

As with other components of Salt, we can also specify tgt_type to change the target type from glob to something else and we can add arg and kwarg as needed in order to pass arguments and keyword arguments to Salt.

There are two pieces of return data in the response body. First, we see _links, which contains a reference path that we'll use in a moment. But we also have a return dictionary that contains a job ID (jid) and a list of the minions affected by this command.

What we did not get was an actual response from the minions in this command. Remember that Salt is asynchronous by nature and, while it makes sense for the salt command to wait a few seconds for the response by default, it doesn't make sense to force web clients to wait the same amount of time.

In order to retrieve the response data, we'll need to issue another command that includes the job ID. This command will be performed using a GET method, so be sure there are no -d options in your command:

```
# curl -sk https://localhost:8080/jobs/20150511024432503750 -H 'Accept:
application/json' -H 'X-Auth-Token: <token>'
{
    "info": [{
        "Function": "test.ping",
        "jid": "20150511024432503750",
        "Target": "*",
        "Target-type": "glob",
        "User": "larry",
        "StartTime": "2015, May 11 02:44:32.503750",
        "Arguments": [],
        "Minions": ["myminion"],
        "Result": {"myminion":
            {"return": true}}}],
    "return": [{
        "myminion": true}]}
```

This is more like what we expect to see! You can see a breakdown of all the options used, the success of the command on each minion, and the return data from the command on each minion.

 Note: The /jobs path in the URL requires a job ID to be passed after it.

Just to make this a little easier to read, let's go ahead and tell the Salt API to return the data in YAML format. Note how we change the Accept header to application/x-yaml:

```
# curl -s localhost:8080/jobs/20150511024432503750 -H 'Accept:
application/x-yaml' -H 'X-Auth-Token: <token>'
info:
- Arguments: []
  Function: test.ping
  Minions:
  - myminion
  Result:
    myminion:
      return: true
  StartTime: 2015, May 11 02:44:32.503750
  Target: '*'
  Target-type: glob
  User: larry
```

```
    jid: '20150511024432503750'
return:
- myminion: true
```

Issuing one-off commands

So far, we've only issued commands using a token. We can in fact issue one-off commands that authenticate on every single call. This is not the normal operation of the Salt API, but it can be helpful in troubleshooting issues with custom modules. It may also be helpful for working with webhooks, which we will cover in a moment.

In order to issue a one-off command, we will use the /run path in our URL instead of the /minions path. The rest of the command contains arguments that you're already familiar with:

```
# curl -sk http://localhost:8080/run -H 'Accept: application/json' -d
username='larry' -d password='123pass' -d eauth='pam' -d client='local' -d
tgt='*' -d fun='test.ping'
{"return": [{"myminion": true}]}
```

Working with webhooks

As mentioned previously, it is possible to use webhooks with the Salt API. Webhooks are designed to be commands that can be issued over HTTP/HTTPS in a single call-no getting tokens first. This can be problematic from a number of standpoints.

The first roadblock involves services that make use of tokens or any other authentication scheme that requires multiple web requests to be made to a server. Since webhooks need to be able to work in a single shot, using a Salt API token is out of the question.

As you have seen, the Salt API does allow commands to be issued in a single call as long as all the credentials are passed along. This is okay if the service making the call allows you to define things such as custom headers and POST data. In some situations, this is acceptable, but some services do not provide that capability.

That leaves us with unauthenticated web requests. This is also doable inside the Salt API, but the user will have to provide their own authentication mechanism. We'll see how to do that in a moment.

First, let's go ahead and configure the Salt master to accept webhooks in the first place. This functionality will require the CherryPy module, so make sure you're set up with that. It will also require a `webhook_url` value, as specified in the *CherryPy* section. And, for our purposes, we'll go ahead and set `webhook_disable_auth` to `True`:

```
rest_cherrypy:
  port: 8080
  ssl_crt: /etc/pki/tls/certs/localhost.crt
  ssl_key: /etc/pki/tls/certs/localhost.key
  webhook_url: /hook
  webhook_disable_auth: True
```

This means that all webhook URLs will have a path of `/hook`, for example, `https://saltapi.example.com/hook`. We have also disabled authentication for webhooks, because our examples will not need authentication. If you are working with a service that does support passing custom headers and `POST` data, go ahead and leave it out, or explicitly set it to `False`.

You will not need to restart `salt-api` explicitly; it will do so on its own when it detects changes in its configuration.

Go ahead and fire up the event listener. We'll issue a request to the webhook URL using `curl`:

```
# curl -sk http://localhost:8080/hook -H 'Accept: application/json' -d
foo=bar
In the event listener, we'll see the following message:
Event fired at Mon May 11 09:09:09 2015
*************************
Tag: salt/netapi/hook
Data:
{'_stamp': '2015-05-11T15:09:09.719958',
 'body': '',
 'headers': {'Accept': 'application/json',
             'Content-Length': '7',
             'Content-Type': 'application/x-www-form-
             urlencoded',
             'Host': 'localhost:8080',
             'Remote-Addr': '127.0.0.1',
             'User-Agent': 'curl/7.42.0'},
 'post': {'foo': 'bar'}}
```

There are two items of interest here. First of all, the event was tagged as `salt/netapi/hook`. All events fired from the Salt API will start with `salt/netapi/` and then contain the path that was used in the web request, including `webhook_url`.

The other item is the `POST` data, which was translated inside Salt to a dictionary. In this case, the dictionary is very short: there is a key of `foo` with a value of `bar`.

Reacting with Thorium

Let's go ahead and take a look at a Thorium example using the popular website Slack (`https://slack.com/`). Slack provides a communication medium in the form of a chatroom for members of a team or a company.

While Slack is obviously useful for chatting with team members, some teams also use it to receive messages from external sources. For instance, you may have GitHub set up to post messages to Slack when new code is committed, or you may have Twitter set up to post new messages from specific users.

For now, let's focus on what to do when Slack receives new messages. You can configure Slack to post outgoing webhooks, which we can then look at with Thorium.

 Information about outgoing webhooks in Slack can be found at `https://api.slack.com/outgoing-webhooks`.

For our example we'll assume that we have a user named `codebot`, who will post a message that says `new_commit` when it picks up new code. We will add messages from `codebot` to the Thorium register as they come in, and then we will examine them for the `new_commit` string. If the string is found, then we'll kick off a request to a Jenkins server (using their own web API) to run a build.

The URL that we'll use for our Salt API server will be this:

```
https://salt.example.com/hook/slack/commit
```

This means that when new messages come in, they will have the following tag:

```
salt/netapi/hook/slack/commit
```

Slack has two fields that we'll want to look for: user_name and text. However, we'll go ahead and store the user_id and the timestamp values in the register too-create /srv/thorium/slack.sls with the following content:

```
slack:
  reg.list:
    - add:
        - user_name
        - user_id
        - text
        - timestamp
    - match: salt/netapi/hook/slack/commit
    - stamp: True
  file:
    - save

user_name:
  check.contains:
    - value: codebot

text:
  check.contains:
    - value: new_commit

start_build:
  runner.cmd:
    - func: http.query
    - kwarg:
      url: http://jenkins.example.com/job/<job_name>/build
      token: 0123456789abcdef
    - require:
      - check: user_name
      - check: text
```

You can see the slack code block, which adds incoming data to the register. We also have a code block for user_name, which checks to see whether it contains codebot, and one for text, which looks for new_commit. The file.save part of the slack code block will let us keep an eye on things while we're working. This will generate a file here:

```
/var/cache/salt/master/thorium/saves/slack
```

Those blocks will always run. However, the start_build code block will only run if both the user_name and the body code blocks find what they're looking for. If codebot posts a message that doesn't contain new_commit, it will be ignored.

When `start_build` does run, it will kick off the `http.query` runner to start a new build job on the Jenkins server. We can test this manually by faking a message from Slack. Use `curl` to issue the following command:

```
# curl http://localhost:8080/hook/slack/commit \-d user_name=codebot -d
text=new_commit \
    -d user_id=U12345 -d timestamp=1355517523
```

If you check the contents of the save file, you should find something that looks like this:

```
{"slack": {"val": [{"user_name": "codebot", "text": "new_commit",
"user_id": "U12345", "timestamp": "1355517523", "time":
"2016-08-17T05:13:26.267182"}]}}
```

If you check your Jenkins server, you should find that a new build process has started.

Security considerations

Anyone who can access the Salt API port on your Salt master will be able to send messages. There are a couple of simple means of authenticating requests, neither of which are very secure, but they are important to take a look at.

First, you can authenticate by URL. If a user knows the correct URL to use, they can send requests. This type of security is known as **security through obscurity**: it only remains secure as long as an easily obtainable piece of information is obscured.

You can also authenticate based on the address of the remote machine that made the request. This is known as **host-based security**. Unfortunately, since known proofs of concept exist to spoof both hostnames and IP addresses, this method is also not terribly secure.

That leaves us with using the `POST` data to send secure data. If we're using HTTPS, then this data will be encrypted already, which mitigates **man-in-the-middle** attacks. In such an attack, a user watching the communication between two parties is able to obtain enough information to imitate one or both of the parties.

If you are able to pass custom `POST` data, this may be enough; just set some secret data inside the `POST`, and watch for it on the Salt master.

Let's go ahead and set up a reactor that handles this use case. First, we'll configure reactor mapping in the master configuration:

```
reactor:
  - salt/netapi/hook/sample/url
    - /srv/reactor/webhook_simple_post.sls
```

Then, after restarting the master, we'll set up the reactor SLS itself:

```
# cat /srv/reactor/webhook_simple_post.sls
{% if data['post']['foo'] == 'bar' %}
simple_post_auth:
  cmd.file.touch:
    - tgt: myminion
    - arg:
      - /tmp/simple_post_auth.txt
{% else %}
simple_post_auth_failed:
  cmd.file.touch:
    - tgt: myminion
    - arg:
      - /tmp/simple_post_auth_failed.txt
{% endif %}
```

This time, we've not only triggered a file to be touched if the authentication succeeded, but also a different file if authentication failed. Go ahead and try it out:

```
# curl -s localhost:8080/hook/sample/url -H 'Accept: application/json' -d
foo=bar# salt myminion cmd.run 'ls -l /tmp/simple_post_auth*'
myminion:
    -rw-r--r-- 1 root root 0 May 11 10:43 /tmp/simple_post_auth.txt
# curl -s localhost:8080/hook/sample/url -H 'Accept: application/json' -d
foo=baz
# salt myminion cmd.run 'ls -l /tmp/simple_post_auth*'
myminion:
    -rw-r--r-- 1 root root 0 May 11 10:43 /tmp/simple_post_auth.txt
    -rw-r--r-- 1 root root 0 May 11 10:44 /tmp/simple_post_auth_failed.txt
```

More complex authentication

It may be that you're working with something more complex than simply passing through POST arguments. In this case, you'll probably need something more powerful than Jinja mixed with YAML. There are three Python renderers that ship with Salt and, as long as it doesn't take very long, writing a reactor using one of them may be appropriate for your needs.

Because the focus of this book is Salt and not Python, we won't go into a lot of detail here. But I'll include a Python version of the aforementioned reactor to get the Python users among you started:

```py
#!py
def run():
if data.get('post', {}).get('foo', '') == 'bar':
    return {'simple_post_auth': {
        'cmd.file.touch': [
            {'tgt': 'myminion'},
            { 'arg': ['/tmp/simple_post_auth.txt'] }
        ]
    }
else:
    return {'simple_post_auth_failed': {
        'cmd.file.touch': [
            {'tgt': 'myminion'},
            { 'arg': ['/tmp/simple_post_auth_failed.txt'] }
        ]
    }
```

Summary

Salt provides some very powerful capabilities for interacting with the REST interfaces, both as a client and as a server. When combined with the reactor system, especially, these capabilities change the scope of autonomous operations from being local to the internal infrastructure to being usable with the vast majority of third-party services available today.

Now that we've spent some time looking at some of the more traditional aspects of Salt, it's time to get really serious. The next chapter will focus on Salt's new transmission protocol, Reliable Asynchronous Event Transport, and Salt's pure TCP transport mechanism.

9
Understanding the RAET and TCP Transports

You may have heard of SaltStack's **Reliable Asynchronous Event Transport** (**RAET**) protocol. However, there's a very good chance you haven't heard much about it. To the average user, RAET may not seem like much. Salt commands haven't changed, output from the commands hasn't changed, and you certainly don't need to update your SLS files. In fact, if you've enabled RAET but haven't changed your workflow, you probably haven't noticed much of anything, which is by design. So what's the big deal? In fact, RAET introduces some interesting concepts that are new to the configuration-management game.

We will also take a look at the TCP transport that now ships with Salt. ZeroMQ already uses TCP, but this transport uses the protocol directly. Its introduction also came with the addition of a package to Salt called Tornado, which is an asynchronous programming library.

In this chapter, we'll cover the following topics:

- RAET versus ZeroMQ
- Understanding flow-based programming
- Using estates, roads, and lanes
- Understanding asynchronous programming
- Using the TCP transport

Comparing RAET and ZeroMQ

To understand Salt, it really does help if we understand what ZeroMQ is and why Salt was originally based on it. Having a solid foundation of knowledge when it comes to ZeroMQ will also help in getting a handle on RAET. It will also help if we understand HTTP and why Salt doesn't make use of it.

It's important to understand that when ZeroMQ came out, there was nothing like it. There are alternatives now, such as `nanomsg`, but ZeroMQ was the first, and it came on the scene just in time for Salt.

Many of the design principles behind Salt are inspired by previously existing projects, some of which were in use by Salt's creator at the time of its conception. However, it was not simply a copy of a bunch of other projects hacked together. If existing projects did what Salt was designed to do, then Salt would not have been created. The corollary here is that a number of design principles were used because what was out there wasn't cutting it.

Starting with HTTP

A very common technology in distributed management systems is HTTP, which makes sense from a number of points of view. It's ubiquitous and easy to understand and use. However, its functionality is somewhat limited: you request and are served a document. Doing so was originally a static process. Features were quickly added to support dynamic content, but the basic premise still stands.

Security was an afterthought with HTTP and, in the beginning, competing standards existed to supply it. In the end, HTTPS won out, but the numerous iterations of SSL, followed by TLS, that have presented themselves only highlight a number of limitations with the protocol. However, we will focus on HTTP and HTTPS together as a single concept.

A configuration-management system based on HTTP necessarily requires a web server to be in the mix. Maintaining a web server for clients opens up innumerable potential security risks and introduces a lot of overhead, so having clients connect to a single server instead makes a whole lot more sense.

This means that the web server must be able to handle a lot of load. Also, the more clients that connect to it, the more concurrent connections it must handle. For instance, **Puppet** is barely usable when configured to use **WEBrick** because WEBrick wasn't designed to handle much traffic. Switching to Mongrel or Apache significantly improves the performance of Puppet.

However, no matter how performant a web server is, it is still limited to pull-based connections. It is not possible to have the server initiate a connection to the client with only a web server. This is why web-based configuration-management systems are frequently set to check with their master on a regular basis, such as every 30 minutes.

SSH – the old favorite

Possibly the world's most common means of managing a Unix or Linux server is SSH. This is because Telnet was the king for several decades, whereas SSH is a secure tunneling mechanism. Its default application is Telnet. For a very long time, SSH-based management was an entirely manual process. However, as popular as it was, it was only natural that it would eventually acquire automation tools.

The earliest of these tools was a simple, shell-based loop to perform one-off commands. Other tools that could perform SSH-based tasks in parallel or maintain multiple concurrent SSH windows were introduced and gained popularity. Soon, entire frameworks were built around SSH-based management.

However, there are architectural similarities between HTTP and SSH that demonstrate several limitations of an SSH-based management system. Like HTTP, a server can accept multiple simultaneous connections. However, a client can only connect to one server at once. In order to connect to multiple machines in parallel, multiple clients must also be started at once, and the number of parallel clients is limited by the resources on the client machine.

Also, like HTTP, an SSH connection requires a server to exist on the other end. However, it is extremely uncommon for machines that need to be configured to call home to a central server over SSH. Instead, each machine that is to be configured over SSH will generally be running an SSH server itself. This carries exactly the same risks as running an HTTP server on each client, and the risk is more if the SSH user has root access to the machine. This will probably be the case if the goal of the SSH connection is to configure the machine.

Using ZeroMQ

ZeroMQ was never designed for configuration management. It was designed as a faster, simpler replacement for the (**AMQP**Advanced Message Queuing Protocol (AMQP), which its author had also designed. However, message queues work well with large-scale environments and tend to be very performant.

Message queues are different from HTTP and SSH because rather than a single client initiating a single connection to a single server, multiple clients can subscribe to one or more servers (message queues) and watch for messages that apply to them. The connection is very lightweight. As it is persistent, the overhead of successive client/server handshakes is eliminated.

Let's look at some analogies that demonstrate the architectural differences between HTTP, SSH, and ZeroMQ. A team of workers is headed by a manager, who will assign tasks to workers on a regular basis.

With an HTTP-based architecture, each worker will call the manager on the phone on a regular basis to check for new tasks. If the manager is already busy talking to other workers when another worker calls in, then the other worker must continue to try calling until the manager's phone is no longer busy.

With an SSH-based architecture, the manager will call each worker when they have a task to assign. When there are few tasks to be performed, this will result in less work for everybody involved. It also allows the manager to initiate tasks as soon as they are received rather than waiting for the intended recipient to check in.

In a ZeroMQ-based architecture, each worker will watch a TV channel that broadcasts the tasks as they become available. When a worker sees a task that applies to them, they perform it and then call the manager with the results. Any TV executive can tell you that broadcasting messages in this manner is a far more scalable way to reach an intended audience, especially when the potential audience is quite large.

Salt actually makes use of two message queues. **Port 4505** is the port that workers subscribe to (or the channel that they watch) in order to receive messages from their manager. **Port 4506** is a second queue that the manager watches to receive the result data back.

ZeroMQ and security

ZeroMQ did not originally implement any kind of security. This is because it was meant to be run inside environments that were already secure on their own. Without the encryption overhead, ZeroMQ was able to achieve significant performance.

However, Salt was not designed to be only run inside secure networks. It was designed to run on networks where not every user was necessarily trusted. Because of this, it was crucial that Salt messages be encrypted. Even today, it is not possible for Salt to communicate on a nonencrypted channel.

However, as ZeroMQ did not have security built in at that time, a secure layer was built on top of it, that is, inside Salt. This layer was based on the SSH standard, which is widely trusted worldwide. SaltStack has never used its own encryption libraries; it has always made use of other known, vetted libraries, such as **PyCrypto**. Although there have been a couple of hiccups in the past with applying these libraries, Salt's encryption layer is now regularly audited by third-party corporations that have a vested interest in it running securely.

The need for RAET

Salt is now used in a number of extremely large clusters. It is not uncommon for groups of 15,000 servers or more to be running on a single Salt master. As the scale of these infrastructures increased, it became evident that a transport was needed that was designed specifically for the needs of a tool such as Salt.

One the other hand, a ZeroMQ bus is similar to having all the workers watch a single TV channel; RAET is more like having each worker watching their own, dedicated TV channel that nobody else can watch.

ZeroMQ, similar to most popular Internet protocols (including HTTP and SSH), is based on TCP, which is known for its reliability. RAET is based on UDP, which is known for its unreliability. While TCP is commonly encrypted, UDP is nearly impossible to encrypt. So why use it?

The biggest advantage that UDP has is speed. As it doesn't bother with things such as handshakes and always makes sure that network packets reach their destination, the ones that do make it tend to be very fast.

RAET itself provides the missing components, such as handshakes and reliability. Also, rather than using the classic encryption libraries that HTTPS and SSH have traditionally been based on, RAET uses a type of **elliptic curve-based cryptography** (**ECC**) called **Curve25519**. This algorithm is considered by many to be the most secure today and is now the default encryption method for OpenSSH. RAET doesn't manage the encryption either; it lets a library called `libsodium` (no relation to SaltStack) handle all the work.

The architecture of RAET is far less known than its older siblings-HTTP, SSH, and ZeroMQ-but before we get into that, let's cover some of the concepts that RAET is based on.

Flow-based programming

We've talked about just a few of the differences between RAET and ZeroMQ. However, to really understand the benefits of RAET and how it affects you, it really helps to get at least a basic handle on **flow-based programming (FBP)**, which RAET is designed on.

The pieces of the puzzle

All this may sound a little intimidating, but don't worry. We'll break it into smaller components first and then look at how these pieces fit together. FBP is based on three concepts:

- Black boxes
- Shared storage
- Concurrent scheduling

These three types of components fit together to form a framework that can manage tasks very quickly and efficiently. Let's take a look at them individually.

Black boxes

The first puzzle piece is the black box. More accurately, black boxes really are the puzzle pieces themselves: they are organized by the scheduler and connected with shared storage.

Most simply, a black box is one thing that does another thing. That's not very specific, so let's go into more detail.

A black box is a simple construct that performs an action. This action can be as complex as necessary, but it's often better to keep it simple. There should be a simple interface to start using the black box and a simple interface to obtain the result of its work.

An everyday example of a black box is a toaster. It has a simple interface, in which slices of bread are inserted into slots, a timer is set to control how dark the toast is, and a lever is pressed to warm up the heating coils; this begins the toasting process. Once the process is complete, the timer runs out, the toast is ejected, and the heating coils are cooled.

The cook who uses this black box may also employ other black boxes to complete a larger task. To prepare breakfast, one may employ the toaster black box and a blender black box as well to create a smoothie, or a frying pan black box, which in turn makes use of a stove black box. This requires more frequent input from the user.

Shared storage

Shared storage is something that just about every professional programmer and systems administrator has dealt with in their career: a database. As the name implies, all the black boxes have access to it in some way.

Going back to our breakfast example, we may refer to the refrigerator as our shared storage. It stores juice, fruits, eggs, butter, and, with some users, even the bread used to make the toast.

We may even employ a slightly more complex shared-storage solution by adding pantry storage. You can even refer to it as archival storage, in which the user processes jams, jellies, fruits, pickles, and so on in a boiling-water canner and then stores them until they are needed. When they are retrieved from the archive, they are moved to the refrigerator, where they are accessed more frequently.

Concurrent scheduling

It's nice to have shared storage to keep our food and black boxes to cook our food, but these items are useless without something or someone to combine their functionalities. The food cannot be cooked until it is moved from storage to black box, and doing so in the right way at the right time is critical to the success of our breakfast. Simply putting an egg in a frying-pan black box without properly opening it will not result in an edible product; putting the egg in the toaster black box is likely to cause a fire.

In order to tie these elements together, we need a scheduler. The scheduler will determine when each process needs to happen and which black boxes get which pieces of data.

In our breakfast example, the cook is the scheduler. The cook will remove the bread from the pantry or refrigerator, unpack it from its bag, move it to the toaster, and start the timer. The cook will also take the eggs out of the refrigerator, unpack them by cracking them open in the frying pan, and occasionally provide input to properly cook them.

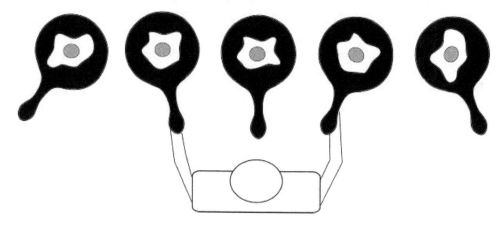

The cook, as the scheduler, will also decide when it is best to start each action. A well-tuned scheduler (or a seasoned cook) will be able to use historical data to help make these decisions.

Both the eggs and the toast highlight a couple of important aspects of the kinds of processing data centers regularly deal with. There are tools to help with the processing of the eggs, but it is still largely a manual process. However, once the data (bread) and parameters (the darkness setting) are given to the toaster, the process of toasting the bread happens without any further user input.

We've talked about scheduling, but what is concurrency? It's actually best to explain both parallel processing and concurrent processing because understanding one will help us understand the other. It's also important to understand both because they are so easy to confuse, as the terms are often used interchangeably.

When two or more processes happen literally at the same time, they happen in parallel. For instance, when two slices of bread are inserted into the toaster at the same time, they will be toasted in parallel.

Concurrency looks as if two or more processes are happening at the same time, but in fact, each step of each process will be performed individually and sequentially. As computers are so fast and the work is hidden from the user, concurrent processing often looks like parallel processing.

Let's go back to our kitchen example: our cook is making breakfast for his whole family. He owns a large toaster and is able to process a dozen slices of bread at once. He also owns a griddle and is able to cook several eggs at once. He also owns a cutting board and knife, and he plans to add fresh fruits to the breakfast.

The cook starts by turning on the griddle. While it is warming up, he puts bread in the toaster and turns it on. Then, he pulls a melon out and sets it on the cutting board. He goes to the griddle and cracks a few eggs in it. Then, he goes back to the cutting board and slices some of the melon. He goes back to the griddle and flips the eggs. Then he finishes cutting the melon.

The toast pops up just as he finishes cutting the melon. The eggs are just about finished as well. He grabs some plates, puts toast on each, uses the spatula to distribute the eggs between them, and finishes up by distributing the slices of melon between them.

The breakfast in this example has in fact been prepared both in parallel and concurrently. The cook concurrently switched between processing the eggs and processing the melon. He also had the toast processing in parallel by another process.

Driving with RAET

We've talked about the concepts behind RAET, but now it's time to get down to business. Let's go ahead and enable it; we can then get started.

Configuring RAET

Setting up Salt to use RAET is actually not a big deal. In the master and the minion configuration files, set `transport` to `raet`:

```
transport: raet
```

As of version 2016.3, this is still set to `zeromq` by default, but this may change in future releases.

There are some other changes that come with RAET. As RAET uses a different encryption scheme, it also has its own set of keys. The master used to store its minions' public keys in the following directories (inside `/etc/salt/pki/master/`):

- `minions_pre/`: This specifies the minions that have identified themselves to the master but whom the master has not yet accepted
- `minions/`: This denotes the minions that have been identified to and accepted by the master
- `minions_rejected/`: This specifies the minions that have identified themselves to the master but with whom the master has explicitly disallowed communication

Instead, RAET uses the following names for these directories respectively:

- `pending/`
- `accepted/`
- `rejected`

As ZeroMQ-based Salt uses RSA encryption, its keys look like this:

```
-----BEGIN PUBLIC KEY-----
MIICIjANBgkqhkiG9w0BAQEFAAOCAg8AMIICCgKCAgEAxL69cuR0Z2lbrAeAq9Ry
pJeBP6lAHL6nUD71cVTxI0OOJC6t2Yb6jzFngvVoPXpCImdBbRFBp6KBG69nmbKu
WXbaeymoDobb5DpYSjGDForfEDvH/f03dj3ovXvf+CEJfir2r/f+IoYeEIdLOVsW
3KmpaHGie9cElitmd6df+gAapG4qdqZ2xzrM1VTaxvP0idmGOtiYOxZx9hj3Xf7J
yE3Xk65CJv5a/xbB+O9or6aEtbLC5tHZ9I7aLaCZ+dO0kDop4HBFjP1ZFe4gJG6d
L25PFOWPLqMmOyeBmCiC+yWIs3Fw9Eu1zH8GhCMonorA1Ih8sr6MmxS9rxmrQ/uA
+HJIaBAvmfjG2CuggkdbAjev2vPDkTgYvqwdeICM3RANH6SV8YdqXtf6lpsAFT/K
LhufO3/bI9s8DfFY7L+9+jf60cGDxkFQKvD0NU+88lscUSPxXDMv0sgy05U1BcyW
cPJy4x9RLwNC1C9EBKPtzvB/fD2carfKm3RDscsqP62V4P1jBfXDE2Jjzd2dC228
gdVTFjhD/c8oDisLrzHzsbd5k1Py8TFEuMlo6y0nDgTxQzCAz9HbpNVlcZOrrvzo
uZncih0nUXiV01rtU29qOUPpz/JhVFz4vYMbxJNsZeb3hwjDGo63WpsGqPKQdJ+t
U/jMDIJXt8mk5dywtho9RLcCAwEAAQ==
-----END PUBLIC KEY-----
```

As RAET-based Salt uses **Curve25519**, its keys look like this:

```
verify@616bb1c637cbbd186932ab2d5f8ea6e3d1f380ea07c1ffd8bc407799894b755fpub@
fb577ea5be149005450ee6a3f4d18698365bdf674f6779151cb3dea032cce972minion_idmy
minion
```

However, beyond these differences, using Salt with RAET is not different, from a user perspective, from using it with ZeroMQ.

> While the RAET libraries ship with Salt, the dependencies needed to run it may not, depending on your distribution. For instance, in Arch Linux, there are two different Salt packages:
> ```
> salt-zmq
> salt-raet
> ```
> Each pulls its own set of dependencies. As they both provide many of the same files, they cannot both be installed at once.

Once the master and minion(s) have been properly configured, Salt should function as normal. Go ahead and try out a couple of commands:

```
# salt myminion test.ping
myminion:
    True
# salt myminion status.loadavg
myminion:
    ----------
    1-min:
        0.27
    15-min:
        0.73
    5-min:
        0.61
# salt myminion status.diskusage /dev/sdc1
myminion:
    ----------
    /dev/sdc1:
        ----------
        available:
            8247476224
        total:
            8247476224
```

The RAET architecture

RAET has a slightly different internal architecture from what most people are used to. On the surface, RAET is just a peer-to-peer connection. Salt uses it in a client/server model but, outside Salt, it can be used for any machine to talk to any other machine. However, before we talk about how machines address each other, we should get some terminology out of the way.

The basics

Hosts on the RAET bus are called estates. Each estate has one or more yards. Estates are connected to each other via roads or lanes. Lanes are used to connect estates on the same physical machine, whereas roads are used to connect estates on separate physical machines.

On Unix and Linux, lanes are actually an abstraction of **Unix domain sockets** (**UXD**), whereas on Windows, lanes are an abstraction of mail slots. Also, on all platforms, roads are an abstraction of a UDP Internet connection:

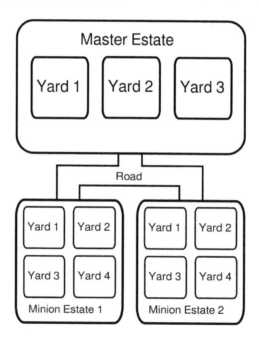

When one machine needs to send a message to another machine, it needs to package this message and address it to the recipient. The address needs to contain the name of the estate and the yard within that estate that needs to receive the message.

A yard is like a process inside the host (but not an actual, full-fledged Unix or Windows process). A host can have multiple yards, each of which is uniquely addressable. This introduces an important change internal to Salt.

Traditionally, Salt commands have been treated as one-off actions. When a command is sent to a minion, a process will be fired off to execute it. Even if this process were to stay open indefinitely, there would be no way to guarantee that any subsequent command will be able to make use of this same process. However, since a process in RAET must be addressed specifically (as a yard), applications can make continued use of them:

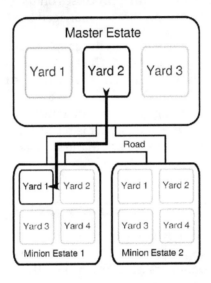

The RAET scheduler

Like ZeroMQ, RAET is based on the concept of queues, which it calls **stacks**. However, the stacks in RAET work a bit differently from what one may expect.

When the master issues a command to a minion in RAET, no work actually happens right away; the command is placed in the appropriate stack to wait for processing purposes. RAET's concurrent scheduler will loop through each stack and, as it finds tasks to be completed, it will process them as appropriate. This gives RAET stacks the property of being nonblocking. When multiple tasks come in, they are immediately sent to the appropriate stack and then processed concurrently by the scheduler.

Estates and yards

We've already mentioned that hosts are referred to as estates. Let's take a closer look at the relationships that are going on inside an estate.

An estate contains yards. While estates are connected to each other via roads, yards are connected to each other via lanes.

We could say that each yard is a process, but that's a little misleading because individual yards do not correlate directly to individual processes on the OS level. Rather than being parallel processes, yards are concurrent threads managed by the estate.

Think back to our breakfast scenario earlier in the chapter. Our cook is a scheduler: he manages all of the tasks that need to be done. The appliances that he is cooking with correlate directly to yards. He flips an egg in one yard, moves to another yard, and flips another egg. Then, he moves to the next yard and cuts a slice of melon. You may also recall that our refrigerator is a shared-storage mechanism, which each of the yards has access to and can make use of. Eggs are a type of data that is retrieved from the shared storage, processed, and, if there are leftovers, sent back to the storage device.

Looking at asynchronous programming

Considering that *asynchronous* is in RAET's name itself, it should come as no surprise that RAET is a type of asynchronous protocol. TCP is not an asynchronous protocol by nature, but it can be used for asynchronous tasks. UDP isn't exactly asynchronous either; it uses more of a "fire and forget" methodology.

So what is asynchronous programming? First of all, let's examine what synchronous programming is. Classical programming is synchronous by its very nature. A program issues a command and then waits for it to complete before issuing the next command.

In terms of more complex software, a program will start with a series of commands, which will usually end up calling subroutines or functions, which themselves may call more subroutines and functions. Each time a piece of code calls another piece of code, it must wait until that code completes before moving onto its next step.

This kind of code is limited by **blocking**. This means that if you have a number of functions that need to run, each one is blocked by the one before it. If a queue of tasks starts to build up, then each will be blocked by the one before it. And if one of those tasks takes a long time, it will negatively impact the queue.

You've probably seen this effect in real life. When going to the grocery store, the bank, or the concert hall, there is often a queue of people ahead of you. Grocery stores solve this by having another cashier open up another register. Banks have tellers open new windows. And concerts...well, nobody's perfect, I suppose.

Opening up new registers and teller windows is a type of parallel processing. The results may look asynchronous, but it's a different solution. In fact, asynchronous programming can be used in conjunction with parallel processing.

Now, before we go any further, I want to clarify something. It may start to look as if concurrent and asynchronous processing are the same, but they are not. Remember our cook earlier in the chapter? Let's go ahead and expand our analogy further.

Cooks in a restaurant

Our example of concurrency involved a cook that was concurrently processing multiple tasks. If there were two cooks, both handling the same tasks in the same way, they would be concurrently processing their tasks in parallel. But there is an essential component that is missing from this equation: how do the cooks know what to cook and when to cook it in the first place?

Let's introduce a new actor: the waiter or waitress, whom we'll conveniently refer to as the server. The server processes requests from guests and delivers them to the kitchen. In our example, they'll attach the order to an order wheel. This is a device used by many restaurants as a means of managing orders coming in. The cooks will routinely check the order wheel for new orders and process them as new ones come in.

Once a cook receives an order, they will prepare it as requested and then place the order under a heat lamp for the server to pick up. The server will then deliver the order to the customer.

The order wheel is a type of queuing system. The algorithm in this example is a first-come-first-serve model: the task will be processed by the first cook who accepts it. If the server directly asked the cooks to prepare the order, then the queuing system is removed from the equation.

In either version of this example, the server (who may or may not be assisted by the queue) represents the asynchronous aspect of a program. One scheduler (in this case, the server) requests a task to be performed by a separate entity (the cooks) and then does other things while waiting for the task to complete. Once the task is completed, the cooks notify the server by placing the completed dish under the heat lamp.

Examining the TCP transport

The previous example illustrates how a complex set of processes can make use of a number of different concepts at once. If you consider that each cook must follow a set of tasks (a recipe) in the correct order in order to produce a dish, our example makes use of asynchronous, parallel, concurrent, and synchronous task management, combined with queue-based task distribution, all flowing together harmoniously.

The TCP transport makes use of most of these concepts, though the concurrent nature of RAET has been replaced with an asynchronous model.

The TCP transport makes use of a Python library called **Tornado**, which is an asynchronous networking library. With the introduction of the TCP transport, the ZeroMQ transport was also retrofitted to be managed by the Tornado library. To sum up, this means that while SSH is synchronous and RAET is concurrent, ZeroMQ and TCP are both asynchronous. However, while the ZeroMQ transport uses ZeroMQ to handle queuing and communication, the TCP transport handles those things by itself.

Under the hood, Tornado provides the TCP transport with a type of function called a coroutine. A collection of coroutines is defined to accept a certain type of data and return an object (called a *future*), which can be used to check on that coroutine's status. Coroutines have the ability to call other coroutines ad nauseam to ensure that all of their tasks can be accomplished without blocking any of the other tasks.

These coroutines are all managed with an *event loop*. Coroutines may *run forever*, meaning they continue waiting for tasks until halted by some outside force, or they may *run until complete*, meaning they will stop as soon as their task is complete. Both types of coroutines are used throughout the TCP transport and inside Salt itself. The event loop manages the coroutines themselves.

Using the TCP transport

Unlike RAET, which uses a different type of keys, the TCP transport uses the same keys as the ZeroMQ transport. This means that you can switch from ZeroMQ to TCP and back as you wish, bearing in mind that the master and minions must also be restarted to pick up the change.

Both master and minion use the same setting to switch to the TCP transport:

```
transport: tcp
```

However, as of the Carbon release of Salt, minions may instead be configured to use a setting of `detect`:

```
transport: detect
```

When a minion is configured this way, it will check with the master while starting up to see which transport it is configured to use. It will first check to see whether the master is configured to use `zeromq`. If it can't connect that way, then it will attempt to connect using `tcp`. If that also fails, then the minion will behave as if the master is unavailable.

Whether you expect to use `tcp` in the future or stick with `zeromq`, I recommend you give the `detect` option a trial run and keep it in place if you feel comfortable with it.

Summary

RAET is a very powerful protocol that extends the functionality of Salt in unexpected ways. We discussed other options for communication management used in other frameworks. We also looked at why they aren't used in Salt.

Next, we'll discuss some of the many techniques that are built in to Salt to handle large-scale infrastructures and a few techniques that can be added to the mix.

10
Strategies for Scaling

Up until now, we've generally covered topics that are relevant to any size of infrastructure, big or small. But when an infrastructure starts getting really big, there is an entire class of strategies that must be considered in order to handle the load. In this chapter, we'll cover the following topics:

- Building a hierarchy with `syndics`
- Using multiple masters
- Testing load with `minionswarm.py`
- Using external filesystems
- Managing the master using the wheel system
- Using reactors and Thorium to manage the master

All about syndication

In order to understand what syndication is all about in Salt, let's step back a few years to when an infrastructure's size did not often go beyond a few dozen nodes. Server management software didn't really need to handle a lot of connections, and often didn't.

Different folks, different strokes

Puppet was one of the earlier configuration-management platforms that really started addressing scale. Since Puppet uses an HTTP-based methodology, early documentation discussed the pros and cons and the various configurations of different web servers.

As we discussed in the previous chapter, Salt doesn't use HTTP and so needs to employ different strategies to address scale. On its own, some users report using Salt to manage over 10,000 machines. However, not everybody has the kind of beefy hardware that those users have available for their masters.

The syndic system was designed for infrastructures where the master was not expected to be powerful enough to handle the load from all the minions that it needed to communicate with. Rather than using a classic architecture, where one master communicates directly with all its minions, the syndic system allows a master to communicate directly with one or more other masters in addition to its own minions. Each master in the hierarchy may also communicate directly with one or more other masters in addition to its own minions. There is no imposed limit to the depth of such a hierarchy.

While this concept was designed to mitigate the load on the master, it is now much more commonly used as an organizational technique. For instance, an organization may maintain data centers in Houston, New York, London, Dubai, Singapore, Tokyo, and Sydney. Each data center may have a single master, which in turn is connected to another centralized master.

When dealing with Salt traffic over the Internet, security is going to be a concern. Limiting minions to only communicate with a master in their own data center will also simplify firewall configuration, as the centralized master will only need to worry about accepting connections from a small set of IP addresses. Additionally, administrators can perform tasks in each data center by connecting to a single master only.

No need for micromanaging

Each master in a syndicated Salt infrastructure knows only about the minions and masters that directly report to it. Say we have master A, which has a group of minions, plus two syndics called master B and master C. Master A is able to issue commands that are propagated down the line to the minions belonging to master B and master C, but it doesn't need to store copies of the public keys for those minions or even know that they exist.

This is because the syndic system provides little more than a pass-through connection. Commands that are published on master A's bus will be sent to master B and master C, each of which will republish those commands to their own buses. As return data is received by master B and master C, it will be consolidated and aggregated back up to master A.

This also means that minions that request other resources from their master, such as files or pillar data, will only be able to receive that data from the master that they report directly to. A syndic will not be able obtain data from its own master to be served to a minion that reports to it. Fortunately, this is not a problem if all that data is provided by an external filesystem or an external pillar, as discussed later in this chapter in *Incorporating external data sources*.

Configuring syndication

Each master in the infrastructure must, of course, be running the `salt-master` daemon. Masters that report to an upper-level master must also be running the `salt-syndic` daemon (which may need to be installed separately, depending on your operating system).

Each syndic must also be configured to know which master they report to. In the master configuration on the syndic, the host or IP address of the master is configured as a `syndic_master`:

```
syndic_master: 10.0.0.10
```

If necessary, you can also change the `syndic_master_port`, which defaults to the value of the `master_port` option (`4506`):

```
syndic_master_port: 4506
```

The master that presides over the syndic will treat it like any other minion, meaning it will need to accept that syndic's public key, which will show up as a minion key. However, it will also need to know that it will be controlling syndics. To know that it will be sending orders to other syndics (who are masters themselves), the `order_masters` option needs to be `True` in the configuration of the master at the upper level:

```
order_masters: True
```

High availability with multiple masters

The traditional Salt setup only involves a single master with multiple minions. This is fine for a number of smaller shops, and even some of the bigger ones, but definitely not for everybody. High availability has become increasingly crucial in the modern infrastructure, and Salt is a part of that.

Built-in high-availability configuration

Salt does have some built-in configuration to handle multiple masters, but it's smaller and simpler than what one might expect. Interestingly, the actual Salt configuration is all on the minion; the masters don't have any configuration inside Salt itself. We'll talk about that in a moment.

First, let's talk about minion configuration. Normally, minions have a single master defined in their configuration file:

```
master: 10.0.0.10
```

However, a list of masters may be defined instead:

```
master:
  - 10.0.0.10
  - 10.0.0.11
```

There is no limit imposed to how many masters may be declared for a single minion. However, once the list of masters has changed, the minion must be restarted in order to pick up the new configuration.

The masters themselves do not need to be aware of other masters in the infrastructure. However, all masters should be identical in every way possible. They must all share the same public/private key pair and should have a synchronized copy of the minions' public keys. Any other files in the `/etc/salt/` or `/srv/` directories must also be identical.

The process of synchronizing files among the masters is not currently supported by Salt; it is up to the administrators to define and implement their own workflow to accomplish that. However, most of the work can be accomplished using other subsystems of Salt, as we'll discuss in a moment.

Old-school high availability

Before Salt got the ability to set multiple masters inside a single minion, it was still possible to create a multi-master setup; it just required a little work outside Salt.

When a minion is pointed to a master, the address used may be either an IP address (that is, `10.0.0.10`) or a DNS-resolvable hostname address (that is, `saltmaster` or `saltmaster.example.com`). Techniques to map either type of address to multiple servers have been around for years, and some even for decades.

The round-robin DNS

DNS may be the oldest method for mapping a single address to multiple machines. It inherently supports several IP addresses to be assigned to one name. When a client makes a request to a DNS server for an IP address matching the specified hostname, the DNS server serves a list of IP addresses to the client. The client can choose which IP address to use, often the first one. When another client makes the same request, the same list is served, but in a different order.

By cycling through a pool of configured addresses, load is effectively spread out across each server. This technique is known as **round-robin DNS** and is often referred to as a *poor man's load balancer*. It's nowhere near perfect, but it usually does a decent job.

Despite the diminutive nickname, round robin DNS does have its place. More advanced configurations are still employed by a number of gigantic infrastructures, which still make use of this style of DNS, combined with more intelligent software that can analyze current traffic information and patterns before deciding which IP address is best to give to a client.

IP-based load balancing

One of the original design goals of Salt was for minions to not have to rely on DNS in order to reach their master. This is because as crucial as DNS is to the modern Internet, it still has a number of shortcomings, which are inherent to its necessarily hierarchical nature. Because DNS is based on a series of lookups, which may require constant synchronization between several DNS servers just to resolve one address, there are a lot of gears that may break while a minion attempts to maintain contact with its master.

Fortunately, DNS is not the only way to map a single address to multiple hosts. A number of open source and commercial load balancers exist that can map one or more public IP addresses to one or more private IP addresses. Depending on the solution used, the intelligence used may be as simple as a round-robin style or as advanced as actually monitoring the load and delivering traffic accordingly.

This is a good time to point out that when we talk about a *public* IP address, we're not necessarily talking about an Internet-facing IP address. What we're talking about is an IP address that is visible to the clients that need to use it. It could be that Master 1 has an address of 10.0.0.11 and Master 2 has an address of 10.0.0.12 and that they share the *public* address of 10.0.0.10 through the load balancer.

Synchronizing files

Whether you configure minions to point to multiple masters or use a shared address solution, or some combination of them, there is still the matter of keeping files in sync among the masters themselves.

Before we talk about how to keep the files synchronized, let's talk about which files need to be kept in sync, why, and which of those we actually need to worry about.

Base configuration files

Inside the `/etc/salt/` directory, there is a base set of files that are necessary for Salt to even run in the first place, and they form the bulk of the files that we'll need to worry about.

- `/etc/salt/master`
- `/etc/salt/master.d/*.conf`

The `master` file, plus any files with a `.conf` extension in the `master.d/` directory, comprises the master configuration. None of these files technically need to exist; if they are absent, then the default master configuration will be used. However, things such as external pillars, caches, and filesystems are not configured by default. Because those things are important to a high-availability setup, it's best to keep this managed.

Fortunately, once these files are dialed in, it's rarely necessary to change them. However you manage these files, you are unlikely to need anything more than a manual process unless you are managing them via some other external process that requires regular, automatic changes to be made.

- `/etc/salt/pki/`

This is where the keys are stored, both for the master and for the minions. It is very crucial to keep this directory synchronized among the masters so that when a key is accepted or, even more importantly, removed from one master, the others know about it as quickly as possible.

- `/etc/salt/cloud`
- `/etc/salt/cloud.profiles`
- `/etc/salt/cloud.profiles.d/`
- `/etc/salt/cloud.providers`
- `/etc/salt/cloud.providers.d/`
- `/etc/salt/cloud.maps.d/`

- `/etc/salt/cloud.deploy.d/`

All these files and directories belong to Salt Cloud, and their necessity and management varies with the needs of the organization. Because Salt Cloud is designed to auto-accept keys on the master, many organizations choose to use Salt Cloud only on the master. However, it is possible to issue commands to Salt Cloud from a minion, and a growing number of users have decided to go that route and handle key management outside Salt Cloud.

If you are not using Salt Cloud at all on a master, then these files can obviously be ignored. If you are using it on a master, keeping these files synchronized is far less crucial. They will only be utilized when issuing Salt Cloud commands, and unless Salt Cloud is being called from an autonomous process such as the reactor, these files can be manually synchronized as needed.

- `/var/cache/salt/`

This directory is used by a number of different processes inside Salt, including the master, minion, Salt Cloud, and others. Salt Cloud uses this directory primarily for increasing performance. However, if `diff_cache_events` is set to `True` in `/etc/salt/cloud` and reactors that make use of those events are configured, then keeping `/var/cache/salt/cloud/` synchronized is as important as keeping `/etc/salt/pki/` synchronized.

The files in `/var/cache/salt/master/` are important for those who make use of Salt's various job-lookup capabilities. If you are using multiple masters, then these capabilities are not only used, but crucial. Fortunately, the job cache can be offloaded onto another server or service, which can be shared by multiple masters. We'll cover the external job cache later on in this chapter, in the *Incorporating external data sources* section.

- `/srv/salt/`
- `/srv/pillar/`
- `/srv/reactor/`

How much you use these directories, if at all, depends entirely on your use cases. However, if you use them, then keeping them synchronized among the masters is pretty important.

The good news is that `/srv/salt/` can be provided in its entirety by one of Salt's external filesystem drivers, and `/srv/pillar/` can be provided entirely by one of Salt's external pillar drivers. Both are covered in the next section.

The bad news is that /srv/reactor/ does not have a specific Salt driver to handle it. However, using this location for reactors is also not required; it was a naming convention that was recommended because it made sense. These files could just as easily be stored in, say, /srv/salt/reactor/ if desired, as long as they aren't referenced by any files used by the state system.

- /var/run/salt/

The files in this directory are specific to an individual host and should not be synchronized.

Synchronizing the nonexternal files

As we saw, there are some files that can be managed externally, and we'll cover those in a moment. For now, let's look at the ones that need to be managed outside Salt.

It's probably fair to say that the majority of infrastructures have a minion set up on the master. If this is the case, then any file in the /etc/salt/ directory (outside of /etc/salt/pki/) may be managed by a Salt state, which means that any of these files can be stored using one of Salt's external filesystem drivers. If your infrastructure meets this model, then this will greatly simplify the storage and management of those files.

If this model doesn't work for you, then you'll need to look at one of the options that will be necessary for /etc/salt/pki/ to handle the rest of the files in the /etc/salt/ directory.

The simplest option, in terms of configuration, may be to mount /etc/salt/ (or just /etc/salt/pki/) using an external filesystem outside Salt, such as NFS or SMB. However, because this strategy will be subject to network conditions, you may find yourself in a situation wherein the stability of Salt degrades or disappears because of a network user or process that is misbehaving.

Even though it may be more complex to set up, it's far better to maintain local copies of the files in these directories and set up a process, be it manual or automatic, to maintain consistency among all masters.

Using rsync

A periodic `rsync` command among the masters will accomplish much of what is needed. Setting this up on a regular cron will eventually make the data among the masters consistent, which in many cases is *good enough*. The following cron line will synchronize files from one master to another every 5 minutes:

```
*/5 * * * * rsync -avz /etc/salt/pki/* othermaster:/etc/salt/pki/
```

Setting up lines similar to this on each master is one step towards eventual consistency. However, `rsync` can be an expensive process to be running on a regular basis, especially with a large set of files. Worse, mismatches between masters can cause keys to show up in multiple directories, putting a minion in a state where it is both *accepted* and *unaccepted*. Fortunately, Salt does give us the ability to be more intelligent with the files that we copy between the masters.

Using the event reactor

It is best to only perform work when it needs to be performed, and ideally, that work is performed as soon as possible. Because key management triggers events, we can use the event listener to let us know when keys have changed so that we can propagate those changes as quickly as possible.

If you were to fire up the event listener and accept and delete the keys for a minion, you would see events that look like this:

```
Event fired at Thu Jun  4 17:34:18 2015
*************************
Tag: salt/key
Data:
{'_stamp': '2015-06-04T23:34:18.583865',
 'act': 'accept',
 'id': 'testminion',
 'result': True}
Event fired at Thu Jun  4 17:35:50 2015
*************************
Tag: salt/key
Data:
{'_stamp': '2015-06-04T23:35:50.853794',
 'act': 'delete',
 'id': 'testminion',
 'result': True}
```

Chances are that these are the only two events you'll be dealing with for key management (unless you have an active policy of rejecting keys, which would result in an act of rejection), so we can go ahead and start building reactors based on them.

First, we'll map the tag to a reactor file inside of /etc/salt/master:

```
reactor:
  - salt/key
    - /srv/reactor/saltkey.sls
```

Then, we'll create /srv/reactor/saltkey.sls with the following content:

```
{% set minion = data['id'] %}
{% set pkidir = '/etc/salt/pki/master' %}
{% if data['act'] == 'accept' %}
copy_accepted_key:
  cmd.cmd.run:
    - tgt: master1
    - name: scp {{pkidir}}/minions/{{minion}} master2:{{pkidir}}/minions/

remove_unaccepted_key:
  cmd.file.remove:
    - tgt: master2
    - name: {{pkidir}}/minions_pre/{{minion}}
{% elif data['act'] == 'delete' %}
{% for keydir in ('minions', 'minions_pre', 'minions_rejected') %}
delete_{{keydir}}_key:
  cmd.file.remove:
    - tgt: master2
    - name: {{pkidir}}/{{keydir}}/{{minion}}
{% endfor %}
{% endif %}
```

Again, we're letting Jinja do a lot of work for us. Let's take a look at what's happening in the preceding code.

First, we define the ID of the minion. We get that from the id field inside the data value provided by the event. We could skip this line and just refer to data['id'] throughout the file, but this is a little more readable and gives us more flexibility if we decide to change the behavior of that variable later. We've done the same thing with the PKI directory by defining it as pkidir.

Then we check to see whether we're dealing with a key that has been accepted or deleted. If it is accepted, we have two tasks to perform: copy the key to the minions/ directory on the target master and then make sure it is no longer in the minions_pre/ directory.

It's temping to issue a `salt-key` command here, but don't do it! First off, the minion in question may not have attempted to contact the other masters yet, and therefore, there won't be a key to accept in the first place. But more importantly, since every master should be configured with this reactor, using the `salt-key` command on all the other masters would trigger an infinite loop, which would be crippling for all the masters, and possibly even the network.

If the key is not being accepted but being deleted, then we just need to make sure that it is absent from all the other masters. There are three directories that it needs to be absent from, so we use a loop to go through each of them. Order is important here: we want to make sure that the minion to be deleted is unable to receive tasks before removing it from the other two directories.

Incorporating external data sources

We've taken care of Salt keys, but we have some other directories that we need to distribute among the masters. Let's start with a component that is used every time you issue a command from the master to one or more minions: the job cache.

The external job cache

Before we dive into this component, let's review the master job cache:

1. When a command is issued, a job ID (JID) is created on the master.
2. Information about that job is stored in the job cache, such as what the command and its arguments are and which minions will be affected.
3. The job data is posted to the message queue, where the affected minions pick it up and perform the requested work.
4. When each minion finishes the task, it sends the return data back to the master, where it is also stored in the job cache.
5. If the `salt` command is still running, it will pick up the job data and display it to the user.

In this workflow, the minion will always return data to the master, whether or not the `salt` command is there to receive it. The master will always cache it so that it can be looked up later.

Using returners on the minions

If we introduce a returner to the equation, then the minions will send the return data to an external data source in addition to sending it to the master. In this case, since the minion is connecting to the data source, the minion will need to be configured with the connection options for that data source. For instance, to use `redis`, one might add the following to the minion configuration:

```
redis.db: saltdb
redis.host: saltdb.example.com
redis.port: 6379
```

Then, to use that returner, specify it when issuing your `salt` command:

```
# salt '*' disk.usage --return redis
```

Any returner that ships with Salt can be used in this manner. All that will be sent to the external database will be the return data for the job. This is useful for monitoring-style tasks, where a minion is constantly being asked for information about system vitals, such as disk or memory usage. Using an external database to store that information allows later analysis of it by another piece of software.

The master can be configured to ask its minions to always return data to an external data store. However, this introduces a couple of changes to the equation. When a default returner is configured, all the job data will be sent to it, not just the return data. Not every returner is set up to do this. As of version 2015.5, the returners that can do this are:

- couchbase
- couchdb
- etcd
- influxdb
- memcache
- mongo
- mysql
- odbc
- pgjsonb (Postgres, with the jsonb data type)
- postgres
- redis
- sqlite3

You may have noticed that only a handful of the many returners that ship with Salt are suitable for use in the external job cache. That's because several returners are designed to be used with systems that are write-only as far as Salt is concerned. When job data is sent to the returner for the Slack service, for instance, it will be posted to a chatroom, which cannot be queried later by Salt. When job data is sent to the returner for the Nagios package, it will be used exclusively for monitoring and alerting purposes.

In order to send job data to an external data source by default, the ext_job_cache setting must be set in the master configuration file. This will just be set to the same name as would normally be passed in using the --return flag:

```
ext_job_cache: redis
```

When this is set, minions will be directed to send the data to the external data source every time. With the master also configured with the same returner credentials as the minions, the jobs runner will also access the external data store to pick up its data about jobs.

Many administrators may feel squeamish about storing database credentials inside the minion configuration files, where anyone with access to the minion can view them, and rightfully so. Returners such redis and etcd can be even more problematic, as they require no credentials and therefore allow unfettered access to everybody.

With some of these returners, it is possible to mitigate some of these concerns. Many of the databases available have the ability to restrict access to reads or overwrite data inside a database, based on the credentials used to access it. However, there is another way out.

Using the master job cache

Starting with version 2014.7, Salt has the ability for the master to store the job return data in the external data store instead of asking the minions to do it. Administrators who are concerned about storing database credentials on minions can set their minds at rest in knowing that only the master has the credentials.

In order to do this, set the master_job_cache option in the master configuration file to the same returner that would be used with ext_job_cache on the minions:

```
master_job_cache: redis
```

Keep in mind that, by default, minions still have access to the master configuration data inside a pillar called master. In order to keep this information from the minions, the `pillar_opts` option can be turned off in the master configuration file:

```
pillar_opts: False
```

 Keep in mind that the default for this option has changed. Previous to version 2015.5.0, it was `True`. As of 2015.5.0, the default is now `False`.

When these options are configured across all masters, the contents of the `/var/cache/salt/` directory that are important to synchronicity will be immediately (not just eventually) available to all masters.

External filesystems

The next set of files and directories that need to be made available to all masters are those found in the `/srv/salt/` directory. As it turns out, the option that many administrators consider to be the best even with a single master is also the option that makes it possible to share this directory structure with all other masters as well.

GitFS

The first component to offer the option of storing files outside the master's local filesystem was the `gitfs` driver. This option was so immediately popular that the entire filesystem model of Salt was refactored in order to allow other drivers to be added as well.

GitFS was a godsend, because so many organizations anyway prefer keeping all their code in a software versioning system such as Git, and having Salt access repositories directly cuts out a lot of work.

As time has passed, a number of features have been added to this driver. So, let's get through the basics first and then cover the bonus features.

External filesystems are set up in the master configuration file, using the `fileserver_backend` option. By default, this option is set to `roots`, which is the driver that manages files on the master's local filesystem:

```
fileserver_backend:
  - roots
```

To switch over from local storage to Git-based storage, change the `roots` line to `gitfs`:

```
fileserver_backend:
  - git
```

Before we get into the rest of the configuration for `gitfs`, this is a good time to point out that multiple fileserver backends can be specified, in the order in which they are to be searched:

```
fileserver_backend:
  - git
  - roots
```

When a file is requested, Salt will search through each external fileserver, in the order in which they are specified, until the requested file is found.

Once the fileserver backend is configured, Salt needs to know where to find the Git repositories:

```
gitfs_remotes:
  - git://github.com/mycompany/salt.git
```

This is the most simple configuration, which will set the root of the Git repository to act as if it were `/srv/salt/` on the local filesystem.

The `git://` URL is not the only protocol that is supported by GitFS. You can also use remotes with `https://`, `file://`, or `ssh://` URL schemes.

As with `fileserver_backend`, multiple Git remotes can be specified, and when a file is requested, Salt will search through each repository in the order in which it is declared.

Starting with version 2014.7, a number of options have been added that allow individual configurations to be specified per Git repository. The following options are available:

- `base`
- `root`
- `mountpoint`
- `user`
- `password`
- `insecure_auth`
- `pubkey`
- `privkey`
- `passphrase`

A number of different backend drivers are available to power GitFS. The base, root, and `mountpoint` options are available across all drivers. But all the other options are only available using the `pygit2` driver. To make sure that you are using the `pygit2` driver, specify it as the `gitfs_provider`:

```
gitfs_provider: pygit2
```

The purpose of some of these options may not be immediately obvious, so let's go through them and see how they are used.

base

As you know from configuring Salt states, the default environment in Salt is called `base`. Other environments such as `dev`, `qa`, and `prod` are normally configured in the `top.sls` file. With GitFS, these environments are configured via tags or branches instead. Files that are in the `prod` branch will be served to servers in the `prod` environment, and so on.

Rather than forcing users to create a branch or tag called `base` to serve files, the `base` option can be used to specify a different branch. For instance, if you needed to use files inside the `trunk` branch inside your base environment, your configuration might look like the following:

```
gitfs_remotes:
  - git://git.example.com/myproject.git:
    - base: trunk
```

Note that if the base is not specified, the default will be the master branch on the repository, whether or not it exists.

root

Normally when Salt serves files from Git, the `root` of the repository behaves as if it were `/srv/salt/`. This may be impractical, depending on the organization of the repository in question. If the directory tree in your repository is set up in a way that, say, the `code/salt/states/` directory needs to be treated as if it were `/srv/salt/`, you can redirect the `root` to point to that directory:

```
gitfs_remotes:
  - git://git.example.com/myproject.git
    - root: code/salt/states
```

mountpoint

Sometimes, you need the opposite of what the root option provides. Perhaps you want the root of your repository to show up deeper inside the directory tree inside Salt. Using a mount point will append a virtual path to the beginning of the repository root. For instance, say your repository has a file called `https.conf` in its `root` directory, and you need it to be served as if it were located at `/srv/salt/apache/files/httpd.conf`. Your configuration would look something like the following:

```
gitfs_remotes:
  - git://git.example.com/myproject.git:
    - mountpoint: salt://apache/files
```

user and password

When working with Git repositories using the `https://` URL scheme, a username and password may be required. These are passed using the `user` and `password` options:

```
gitfs_remotes:
  - https://git.example.com/myproject.git:
    - user: larry
    - password: 123pass
```

insecure_auth

By default, Salt will refuse to authenticate against repositories using the `http://` URL scheme. In order to force Salt to authenticate using this insecure transfer method, set `insecure_auth` to `True`:

```
gitfs_remotes:
  - http://git.example.com/myproject.git:
    - user: larry
    - password: 123pass
    - insecure_auth: True
```

pubkey, privkey, and passphrase

Normally, Git repositories that use SSH are configured using the `git://` URL scheme. However, Git can be configured to allow access using an SSH-like syntax. The following two declarations are functionally identical:

```
https://git@git.example.com/user/myproject.git
git@example.com:user/myproject.git
```

Using Git over SSH will require authentication, and key-based security is the way to go. The `pubkey` and `privkey` options are used to specify the locations of the public and private key files, respectively.

```
gitfs_remotes:
  - git://git.example.com/myproject.git:
    - pubkey: /root/.ssh/myproject_rsa.pub
    - privkey: /root/.ssh/myproject_rsa
```

If the private key is protected by a passphrase, it may be specified using the `passphrase` option:

```
gitfs_remotes:
  - git://git.example.com/myproject.git:
    - pubkey: /root/.ssh/myproject_rsa.pub
    - privkey: /root/.ssh/myproject_rsa
    - passphrase: 123pass
```

Any of these options may also be specified globally by prepending them with `gitfs_`. When doing this, the options will be applied to all GitFS remotes, but they can be overridden individually, as seen in the preceding code. For example, to use `trunk` as the global branch for the base environment while overriding it and using `develop` on the last remote, your configuration might look like the following:

```
gitfs_base: trunk
gitfs_remotes:
  - git://git.example.com/myproject.git
  - git://git.example.com/yourproject.git
  - git://git.example.com/ourproject.git:
    - base: develop
```

Other source-control backends

By far, the most popular fileserver backend is GitFS, and so the maximum time and most features have been spent on that filesystem. However, it is certainly not the only player in the game. Both **Subversion** (**SVN**) and **Mercurial** (**HG**) are available using the `svnfs` and `hgfs` drivers, respectively. Both have many of the options that are available with GitFS, but there are some differences.

SVNFS

In order to use SVNFS, there must be a fileserver backend of `svn` configured:

```
fileserver_backend:
  - svn
```

A URL to the remote SVN repository or repositories must also be configured:

```
svnfs_remotes:
  - svn://svn.example.com/myproject
```

The following options may also be added to any of the `svnfs_remotes`:

- root
- mountpoint
- trunk
- branches
- tags

As with GitFS, these options may be used globally across all SVN repositories by prepending them with `svnfs_`.

root and mountpoint

The `root` and `mountpoint` options behave as with GitFS, but the other three options do need some explanation.

trunk

SVN is based on `trunk`, each of which is made from other branches. This option specifies where a `trunk` is located, relative to the SVN remote URL in question. The default is `trunk`:

```
svnfs_trunk: trunk
```

branches

Also, relative to the SVN remote URL is the location of the branches inside the repository. The default is `branches`:

```
svnfs_branches: branches
```

tags

Once again, SVN tags are also relative to the SVN remote URL. As you might expect, the default is `tags`:

```
svnfs_tags: tags
```

As with GitFS, environments are mapped to `tags` and `branches`. However, with a repository that contains a large number of either of these, limiting the tags and branches that are made available to Salt may increase performance.

This can be accomplished using the `svnfs_env_whitelist` or the `svnfs_env_blacklist` options. They both function as one might expect: items that are not specified in the whitelist are not made available, and items that are specified in the blacklist are not made available.

Items in either of these lists may be specified as either an entire name or a pattern specified as either a glob or a regular expression:

```
svnfs_env_whitelist:
  - oldproject
  - accounting.*
  - 'sales19\d+'
```

These two options may also be used together. When doing so, the whitelist will be evaluated first, and then items that match the blacklist will be removed.

HGFS

Of course, we would be remiss if we skipped over using Mercurial as a fileserver backend. In order to use this driver, set `hg` in the `fileserver_backend`:

```
fileserver_backend:
  -hg
```

Then, set up Mercurial repositories using the `hgfs_remotes` option:

```
hgfs_remotes:
- https://larry@hg.example.com/larry/myproject
```

As with SVNFS, the following options are available globally:

- `hgfs_root`
- `hgfs_base`
- `hgfs_mountpoint`
- `hgfs_env_whitelist`
- `hgfs_env_blacklist`

Once any of these global options are declared, `root`, `base` and, `mountpoint` may be overridden on a per-repo basis:

One more global option is also available, which is specific to HGFS: `hgfs_branch_method`. This specifies whether `branch` or `bookmarks`, or both, will be used in conjunction with tags to provide Salt environments. The available settings for this are:

- branches
- bookmarks
- mixed

S3FS

Version control systems are not the only external filesystem drivers that ship with Salt. After GitFS was introduced, it did not take long for the **S3FS** driver to be committed. This driver has proven to be extremely popular with the customers of Amazon Web Services.

Before we get into the configuration of this driver, take note: it does not provide version control. When working with text-based files, I'm going to put my foot down and recommend that they all be checked into some sort of a revision control system. In any production environment, this provides far more advantages than just using the master's local filesystem.

However, binary files are impractical to be stored in version control. They make repositories bulky and slow and cannot be properly managed as text files can. This is where using a driver such as S3FS can really be useful.

In order to use this driver, add `s3fs` to the list of fileserver backends:

```
fileserver_backend:
  - s3fs
```

Credentials to connect to S3 must also be provided. Once you have received them from Amazon, add them to the master configuration file as `s3.keyid` and `s3.key`:

```
s3.keyid: 0123456789ABCDEF0123
s3.key: abcdefghijklmnop/0123456789qrstuvwxyz
```

There are two ways to set up your S3 buckets to serve files: one environment per bucket or multiple environments per bucket.

One environment per bucket

The most straightforward way to configure S3FS, and the one that requires the least amount of thought before the bucket is created in the first place, is to treat each bucket as its own separate environment. With this model, each environment, and the bucket (or buckets) that belongs to it, are specified with the `s3.buckets` option:

```
s3.buckets:
  base:
    - code
    - design
  prod:
    - prod_code
    - prod_design
```

Multiple environments per bucket

It may make more sense to keep all your environments together in a single bucket or in a group of buckets that are combined together. This requires that the buckets be set up beforehand to include directories named after the environments. First, list the bucket or buckets in the `s3.buckets` list:

```
s3.buckets:
  - code
  - design
```

Then, create the buckets (in this case, one called `code` and one called `design`). Inside each bucket, create one directory per environment (in our case, `base` and `prod`). Then, files are placed inside those directories, as usual.

Were you to abstract your directory tree out into an `s3://` URL scheme, our example would have a file structure that looked like this:

```
s3://code/base/<files>
s3://code/prod/<files>
s3://design/base/<files>
s3://design/prod/<files>
```

AzureFS

Not to be outdone by Amazon, Azure also has a cloud storage solution available, which can be used as an external filesystem with Salt.

In order to use AzureFS, add `azurefs` to the list of fileserver backends:

```
fileserver_backend:
  - azurefs
```

However, this driver is a little different because of the difference between Azure storage and S3. First of all, Azure uses storage containers, not buckets; so we'll refer to them as containers from here on (not to be confused with container systems such as Docker and CoreOS RKT). Secondly, AzureFS is configured only to allow one environment per container.

Azure configures access to each container using the name of the `storage_account` that the container lives in and a `storage_key` that authenticates access to that container.

```
azurefs_envs:
  base:
    storage_account: development
    storage_key: 0123456789abcdefABCDEF==
```

External pillars

The last component that can be moved into an external service is the pillar system. Let's go over the basic configuration first. To use an external pillar driver, add it to the `ext_pillar` list inside the master configuration:

```
ext_pillar:
  - cmd_json: /usr/bin/mypillar
```

There are two components to every pillar declaration: the name of the module (in this case, cmd_json) and any arguments that are to be passed to that driver (in this case, the /usr/bin/mypillar command, which is expected to return pillar data in JSON format).

There are quite a number of external pillar modules available-too many to go through. So, we'll pick out a few key pillars that are likely to be of use in your organization.

 The full list of pillars that are available can be found online at http://docs.saltstack.com/en/latest/ref/pillar/all/index.html.

cmd_yaml/cmd_json

The cmd_yaml and cmd_json aren't pillars that are likely to be useful in scaling out to multiple masters, but they do effectively demonstrate how the pillar system works.

The argument for both of these modules is a command that returns a dictionary of data in either the YAML or the JSON format, respectively. If this command includes a %s in it, it will be replaced with the name of the minion that is requesting the pillar data.

For instance, the following code will return data that would be provided to all of the minions:

```
cmd_json: cat /srv/pillar/common.json
```

This code will search for pillar data that is specific to the requester:

```
cmd_json: cat /srv/pillar/minions/%s.json
```

These modules are good for getting a feel of how the external pillar system works. However, to start scaling out, it's time to look at more advanced external pillars.

git

It should not be surprising that one of the most popular external pillars makes use of Git repositories. However, the configuration of this module is a little different from the GitFS configuration.

There are two arguments that are required: the branch inside the repository that is to be used and the URL to the repository. Here's an example:

```
ext_pillar:
  - git: master git://git.example.com/myproject.git
```

Like GitFS, an alternate `root` may also be specified:

```
ext_pillar:
  - git: master git://git.example.com/myproject.git root=code
```

In this case, `code` refers to a directory inside the Git repository called `code`.

If you want to specify that the `branch` be mapped to a different environment name, you can specify both the branch and the environment together, separated by a colon:

```
ext_pillar:
  - git: master:base git://git.example.com/myproject.git
```

There are a couple of different ways to expose the branches as their own environment. If the special __env__ branch is specified, then each branch will automatically be mapped to a corresponding environment of the same name:

```
ext_pillar:
  - git: __env__ git://git.example.com/myproject.git
```

If you don't want to expose all the branches in the repository as their own environments, it's better to define them all individually, adding a `branch` value to the environment mappings as appropriate:

```
ext_pillar:
  - git: master:base git://git.example.com/myproject.git
  - git: dev git://git.example.com/myproject.git
  - git: prod git://git.example.com/myproject.git
```

redis

The `redis` module is a natural fit for pillar data, because it stores data in the same kind of key/value pairs used for pillar data.

If you are already using `redis` for your external job cache, you can reuse the connection settings inside the master configuration:

```
redis.db: 0
redis.host: 10.0.0.5
redis.port: 6379
```

Then, configure how the data will be pulled out of `redis`. Data can be stored in `redis` as either a JSON object or as a string, hash, or list.

If the data is stored as JSON, then the external pillar declaration will be as follows:

```
ext_pillar:
  - redis: {function: key_json}
```

 Take note that unlike other examples in this book, this one is printed exactly as it should appear in your configuration, character for character.

With this type of data, the key of the JSON object is the name of the minion that has requested the pillar data. If no such object exists in the database, an empty dictionary will be returned.

If the data is stored as a string, hash, or list, then the external pillar declaration will be as follows:

```
ext_pillar:
  redis: {function: key_value}
```

Again, this is the exact configuration that is to be used. And again, the key that is used to access the data must match the name of the minion that has requested it.

mysql

The `mysql` module may not seem as natural as `redis`, since SQL isn't normally thought of as having key/value pairs. But, in fact, nothing could be further from the truth. SQL is all about key/value pairs; it just happens to refer to the keys as fields, and it organizes the data as rows.

To use this module, connection details must be set up inside the master configuration:

```
mysql:
  user: salt
  pass: 123pass
  db: saltdb
```

Then, configure the `mysql` pillar with a query that can be used to collect the data from the database:

```
ext_pillar:
  - mysql:
    fromdb:
      query: 'SELECT role FROM minions WHERE id LIKE %s'
```

Using the master API

The master API has a somewhat confusing name for users that are used to traditional Unix terminology. Because the master is what steers a Salt infrastructure, the API that is used to configure it is called the wheel system. To put it clearly, Salt's wheel system bears no relation or resemblance to the wheel group found in many Unix and Linux distributions.

Like most of Salt, the wheel system is pluggable. However, while a few modules do exist, most of them will never be used by most end users. For our purposes, we'll focus on the ones that are used.

The Salt keys

The part of the wheel system that is most commonly seen by administrators is key management. When keys are accepted, rejected, or deleted, that action is usually performed by the wheel system. The `key` module doesn't actually do much: it creates keys when necessary, moves them between directories as requested, and fires events along the event bus when doing so.

Configuration

The `config` module is used to manage the master configuration files. Again, it does very little: it can write one or more values to the master configuration file, and it can return the contents of that file. Be warned: when this module is used to modify the master configuration, any comments that exist in that file will be stripped. If you take comfort in the presence of friendly comments to help you out, this module is best avoided.

One important note about this module: while it manages configuration files, it does not manage the internal master configuration. Once changes have been made, the master must still be restarted in order to apply those changes.

The file and pillar roots

The `file_roots` and `pillar_roots` modules behave in largely the same way, the only functional difference being the directory they operate on. Each supports searching for files, listing environments, and reading and writing the contents of a file. As the name implies, they are designed to be used with local files, not external filesystems or external pillars.

Using the wheel reactor

So, what good are these modules? Again, the vast majority of commands will use the `key` module, though the small set of use cases surrounding the other modules may meet your needs.

While accepting keys on the master will require some logic that is specific to your needs, in order to securely accept keys only from minions that are considered trustworthy, deleting keys from the master is reasonably safe, at least from a security point of view. While accepting the wrong key may allow rogue minions into your infrastructure, deleting the wrong key never will.

A process that is able to detect that a minion's key should be deleted can be set up to fire an event that triggers that key's deletion. For now, we'll assume that the process in question is able to issue a standard Salt command. For instance, a minion that has been tasked with keeping watch may issue the following command:

```
salt-call event.fire_master '{"id": "myminion"}'
custom/key/myminion/delete
```

On the master, the tag is mapped to a `reactor` file:

```
reactor:
- custom/key/*/delete
- /srv/reactor/deletekey.sls
```

Inside the `/srv/reactor/deletekey.sls` file, the wheel system is called to delete the key for the minion in question:

```
delete_minion_key:
  wheel.key.delete:
    - match: data['id']
```

Using wheel with Thorium

Let's go ahead and take a look at what this reactor would look like using the Thorium system. Instead of using the `reactor` section in the master configuration file, let's set up our Thorium engine:

```
engines:
  - thorium: {}
```

Then go ahead and create `/srv/thorium/deletekey.sls`:

```
delete_key_tag:
  check.event:
    - name: custom/key/*/delete
delete_key:
  wheel.cmd:
    - fun: key.delete
    - match: {{ __reg__['data']['name'] }}
    - require:
      - check: delete_key_tag
```

Lastly, we map our code in Thorium's `top.sls` file:

```
base:
  '*':
    - delete_key
```

Testing the load in the infrastructure

Now that we've talked about the various ways to scale out your infrastructure, you will probably find it useful to know how to throw tests at your infrastructure to test its ability to handle the load that will be thrown at it.

Using the minionswarm.py script

The `minionswarm.py` script was originally used to test the performance of execution modules as they were written. But while it is still used for that today, it can also be used to test the performance of a state tree against a large number of minions.

 The `minionswarm.py` script does not ship inside any of the Salt packages, but it can be downloaded from the `tests/` directory in Salt's GitHub repository at `https://github.com/saltstack/salt`.

The `minionswarm.py` script is designed to create a user-defined number of minions, which can then accept commands from the master. Keep in mind that this script will only run on a single host, so it won't help much in testing syndic architecture. However, it will effectively test how well your external filesystems and pillars are able to interact with each other.

To use the script, copy it into a directory and start it up with Python:

```
# python minionswarm.py
```

By default, this will create five minion processes. Once they are spun up, standard Salt commands can be issued against those minions. If you want to spin up a master as well to talk to those minions, you can do so by specifying the –M option:

```
# python minionswarm.py –M
```

The first thing you will probably want to do is create more minions to test with. The –m option will set the number of minions that will be created.

```
# python minionswam.py –m 500
```

 Be careful here! Each minion that is created will leave its own footprint in memory, and each footprint will be the size of a regular minion process. Specifying too many minions may overload an underpowered system.

Swarm internals

Obviously, the swarm of minions that is created cannot be considered viable for production use; it is for testing purposes only. This should be kept in mind should you decide to take a look at the various files that are created during this process.

In the `/tmp/` directory, a directory whose name starts with `mswarm-root` will be created. This directory will contain a `pki/` directory with entries for each minion. And if you look at the keys for each minion, you will notice that they are all identical!

If the need presents itself, it is possible to replace keys for individual minions so long as you make sure to keep them in sync with the temporary keys stored by the master. But the point of the minion swarm is not to test keys or security-it's to test load!

So, go ahead and fire up a few test commands to get a feel of how load testing works with the minion swarm:

```
# salt '*' test.ping
# salt '*' network.interfaces
# salt '*' disk.usage
```

Then, try testing out a state run, preferably in test mode:

```
# salt '*' state.highstate test=True
```

If you decide to do a state run without enabling the test mode, it will be best to do so on an otherwise blank machine that can safely be trashed if the state run gets out of control. Don't feel bad if you end up having to wipe it and start over several times; if you're storing all your data in an external filesystem or an external pillar (both of which are read-only), you won't have to do much work to get things rolling again.

Summary

In this chapter, we covered the hierarchical and failover configurations of Salt, using syndication and multiple masters. We also talked about load testing and offloading resources from the master to other servers. We even talked about managing the master using the wheel system.

There are plenty of ways to help your Salt infrastructure scale to meet the demands of thousands of servers. But once they're up-and-running, how do you keep an eye on them? Next up, we'll discuss how we can use Salt to help monitor our systems.

11
Monitoring with Salt

Many users are unaware that Salt wasn't originally intended to be used as a configuration management system. One of its first uses was to collect and store information on system vitals, such as memory, CPU, and disk usage. It can still be used this way today, and in fact, it has quite a bit more functionality now, which can be useful in monitoring. In this chapter, we'll discuss the following topics:

- Using returners to establish a historical baseline
- Using monitoring states
- Incorporating beacons into your workflow
- Setting up alerts
- Using Thorium in your monitoring systems

Monitoring basics

There are a number of different monitoring systems available today, some of which have modules inside Salt to support them. However, different systems provide different types of monitoring.

Establishing a baseline

Take, for example, the classic `sysstat` monitoring package in Linux. By default, it collects data on various system vitals every 10 minutes. Over a period of time, analysis of this data will paint a picture of what the system looks like under normal load. Spikes or dips are likely to occur from time to time, which may or may not be normal.

For instance, after monitoring a web server for a few weeks, it may become evident that load average gradually increases throughout the morning and in the afternoon before spiking for a few hours in the evening and dropping off before midnight. Depending on the type of website, weekends may experience more traffic than weekdays. This will manifest itself in tools, such as `sysstat`. This is how the output from `sysstat` looks:

```
# sar
Linux 4.0.5-1-ARCH (dufresne) 06/13/2015 _x86_64_(4 CPU)
02:09:11 PM       LINUX RESTART(4 CPU)
02:10:22 PM     CPU     %user     %nice   %system   %iowait    %steal
%idle
02:20:12 PM     all      3.37      6.56      1.88      4.44      0.00
83.75
02:30:12 PM     all      2.68      5.88      1.51      1.50      0.00
88.43
Average:        all      3.02      6.22      1.69      2.96      0.00
86.11
```

This information will form a standard baseline. Also, when unexpected abnormalities occur that differ from the baseline, it may be a cause for concern. This is where alerting comes in, which we'll cover in the *Setting up alerts* section later in the chapter.

As wonderful a tool `sysstat` is, it doesn't tell the whole story. It reports on a predefined set of system information, such as load average and IO wait times. It does not report on which processes are running or how many users are logged in to the system.

Reading the system vitals in Salt

Most of the earliest modules inside Salt were designed to collect information about various aspects of the system and return them to the user in a format that has been parsed and formatted for ease of usability. Much of what is normally associated with system vitals is inside the status module, but there are others as well. Let's take a look at a few of them.

status.loadavg

The `status.loadavg` module returns load average, using the same information present in the popular `top` program that ships with most Unix and Linux distributions. Establishing a baseline will help you know what specific servers normally look like. In general, so long as the number reported in the 1-minute average is less than the total number of processors in the system, the system is considered to be idle:

```
# salt myminion status.loadavg
```

```
myminion:
    ----------
    1-min:
        0.23
    15-min:
        0.52
    5-min:
        0.42
```

status.cpustats

Much of the information that is stored by sysstat will be contained inside the return of the status.cpustats function, although it may look a little different. Most Linux monitoring systems, including Salt, collect information from virtual files in the /proc/ directory. In this case, the information presented is from the /proc/stat file. The output is likely to be pretty long, but a shortened version would look like the following code:

```
# salt myminion status.cpustats
myminion:
    ----------
    btime:
        1434226009
    cpu:
        ----------
        idle:
            868157
        iowait:
            35603
        irq:
            0
        nice:
            57994
        softirq:
            42
        steal:
            0
        system:
            16190
        user:
            28560
    cpu0:
        7575
    cpu1:
        6872
    cpu2:
        8043
```

```
    cpu3:
        6069
    ctxt:
        9069187
```

status.meminfo

Information on memory usage is vital. Most operating systems have various strategies to cope with running low on memory, but it is far better to not run out in the first place. The `status.meminfo` function will provide information about memory usage and try to be helpful by also presenting the unit that the information is being presented in. A shortened version looks similar to the following code:

```
# salt myminion status.meminfo
myminion:
    ----------
    Active:
        ----------
        unit:
            kB
        value:
            3837372
    Active(anon):
        ----------
        unit:
            kB
        value:
            3549304
    Active(file):
        ----------
        unit:
            kB
        value:
            288068
    AnonHugePages:
        ----------
        unit:
            kB
        value:
            1257472
    AnonPages:
        ----------
        unit:
            kB
        value:
            3547932
```

status.vmstats

Just as status.meminfo reports on physical memory, status.vmstats reports on virtual memory. This is one of the strategies that operating systems use to cope with running out of physical memory. In Linux, this information is pulled from /proc/vmstat. This is how a shortened version of the output looks:

```
# salt myminion status.vmstats
myminion:
    ----------
    nr_active_anon:
        854510
    nr_active_file:
        72671
    nr_alloc_batch:
        4165
    nr_anon_pages:
        854154
    nr_anon_transparent_hugepages:
        641
    nr_bounce:
        0
    nr_dirtied:
        206578
    nr_dirty:
        633
    nr_dirty_background_threshold:
        295696
    nr_dirty_threshold:
        591393
```

disk.usage and status.diskusage

Disk usage is just as critical as memory usage, and in some situations, even more so. There are two different functions inside Salt to display this information. Each behaves differently based on where they obtain their information from. In Linux, the disk.usage function obtains its information from the du command, whereas the status.diskusage function uses information from the /proc/mounts file. The command for disk usage is as follows:

```
# salt myminion disk.usage
myminion:
    ----------
    /:
        ----------
        1K-blocks:
```

```
            414569456
        available:
            270870348
        capacity:
            32%
        filesystem:
            /dev/sda4
        used:
            122633484
# salt myminion status.diskusage
myminion:
    ----------
    /:
        ----------
        available:
            277371793408
        total:
            424519122944
```

status.w

The strangely-named `status.w` function should actually look familiar to old-school Linux or Unix users. This calls out to the `w` command, which reports who is logged in to the system and what they are doing. The command for `status.w` is as follows:

```
# salt myminion status.w
myminion:
    |_
        ----------
        idle:
            7:16m
        jcpu:
            25:24
        login:
            07:56
        pcpu:
            0.00s
        tty:
            tty1
        user:
            larry
        what:
            xinit /home/larry/.xinitrc -- /etc/X11/xinit/xserverrc :0 vt1 -
auth /tmp/serverauth.t5P7FTvG7q
```

status.all_status and status.custom

If you've been following along on your own computer and testing out these commands, you've probably noticed that some of these functions return a lot of data. If you want a firehose of data, try out the `status.all_status` function, which returns everything from the following functions:

- `status.cpuinfo`
- `status.cpustats`
- `status.diskstats`
- `status.diskusage`
- `status.loadavg`
- `status.meminfo`
- `status.netdev`
- `status.netstats`
- `status.uptime`
- `status.vmstats`
- `status.w`

This kind of report is useful because it returns a lot of information in only a single call. However, chances are that it returns far more information than you actually want or need.

The `status.custom` function is designed to cull out the information that isn't necessary. It returns only what is actually needed. By default, it returns nothing; you will need to specify the functions and fields from these functions that you want to run in the minion configuration.

To configure a function, add a line to the minion configuration, containing the name of the function and a list of the fields that you want returned from that function. The format is as follows:

```
status.<function>.custom:
  - <item1>
  - <item1>
  - <etc>
```

Consider the following configuration:

```
status.cpustats.custom:
  - 'cpu'
  - 'processes'
status.loadavg.custom:
- '1-min'
```

This will return a custom output that looks like the following code:

```
# salt myminion status.custom
myminion:
    ----------
    1-min:
        0.27
    cpu:
        ----------
        idle:
            1929298
        iowait:
            46791
        irq:
            0
        nice:
            129568
        softirq:
            61
        steal:
            0
        system:
            34416
        user:
            57184
    processes:
        3737
```

Monitoring with returners

As we discussed in the previous chapter, returners have the ability to store the job return data from minions in an external data store. This is ideal for monitoring situations because the external data store can be used to establish a baseline.

One of the best ways to set up Salt so that it starts to collect data is to use the minion's scheduler. For our example, we'll assume that you're using the `mysql` returner. Go ahead and add the following code to your minion configuration:

```
schedule:
  loadavg_monitoring:
    function: status.loadavg
    minutes: 10
    returner: mysql
  diskusage_monitoring:
    function: status.diskusage
    minutes: 10
    returner: mysql
```

Note that both of these have the returner set to `mysql`. If you are scheduling a lot of tasks that use the same returner, you may just want to add a `schedule_returner` line instead:

```
schedule_returner: mysql
schedule:
  loadavg_monitoring:
    function: status.loadavg
    minutes: 10
  diskusage_monitoring:
    function: status.diskusage
    minutes: 10
```

These configurations will set the minion to run two monitoring jobs, starting with when `salt-minion` starts up and continuing every `10` minutes thereafter. This time period was chosen only because it's the default for `sysstat`. Other monitoring software uses other intervals, such as every `15` minutes. Before deciding on a time period based on what you are used to in other software, decide whether or not this is the most appropriate interval for your needs.

Deciding on a returner

While only a selected set of returners can be used to manage the external job cache, any returner can be used to store the job return data. However, not all external storage mechanisms are created equally. While the job return data will always come from Salt in exactly the same format, it frequently needs to be massaged into something different in order to meet the requirements of the other API.

NoSQL style databases are the most natural choice because they generally store data in exactly the same format as Salt. However, not everybody uses this type of database, and in fact, some organizations avoid them entirely.

MySQL may feel like a natural choice because it is one of the world's most popular database servers, especially for beginners. However, its internal data format doesn't support Salt's data structures. In order to accommodate the requirements of SQL, most SQL returners convert the job return data to a JSON BLOB and store it in a single field. Other fields will also be used to store metadata, but searching through data structures inside the return is likely to be cumbersome at best.

Then, there are these special-case returners. Some, such as `hipchat`, `slack`, and `xmpp`, are designed to drop return data in a chat room. The `smtp` returner will send one e-mail per job per minion with the return data. Separate integrations could be written, which make use of these platforms, but it's definitely not a natural fit.

Lastly, there are returners designed to dump data directly to a database. This is designed specifically for monitoring purposes. One such returner is for a piece of software called **Carbon**. This is a component of the **Graphite** tool, which in turn can be used to generate graphs from data such as the one that is returned from Salt.

Using monitoring states

Monitoring states are one of the less commonly known pieces of functionality inside Salt, and that's a shame. While execution modules are superb for building and maintaining a baseline of information about a machine, monitoring states are designed to raise a notification when a metric falls out of the desired range.

 The notification in this case is not the same as an alert. It can be used to raise alerts, but it is an independent action.

As you may recall, there are four pieces of information that will always be returned from each individual state:

- Name
- Result
- Changes
- Comment

Monitoring states differ from standard states in three ways. First of all, they are not allowed to make changes to the system. Their job is to observe and report. Secondly, they return a fifth piece of information:

- Data

This contains a dictionary of data that was retrieved by the monitoring state. This could be a metric involving disk usage, a particular CPU load average, or even the contents of a web page that is being monitored.

The last difference is that when a monitoring state is called, it can be given parameters that define what is considered acceptable for the data field. If the data falls within these parameters or no parameters are given, the result of this state will be True. However, if parameters are given and they fall outside what is defined to be acceptable, the result of this state will be False.

As monitoring states are handled during a state run, they can be used to trigger other states to run. The triggered states may attempt to perform auto-healing or raise an alert. We'll talk about alerts later on in the chapter; first, let's talk about how to define a monitoring state.

Defining a monitoring state

Let's take a look at a very simple monitoring state: disk.status. The purpose of this state is to monitor usage on a specific filesystem. The default outputter does not show the data output, so let's use the nested outputter instead:

```
[root@dufresne ~]# salt myminion state.single disk.status / --out nested
myminion:
    ----------
    disk_|-/_|-/_|-status:
        ----------
        __run_num__:
            0
        changes:
            ----------
        comment:
            Disk in acceptable range
        data:
            ----------
            1K-blocks:
                414569456
            available:
                270866984
            capacity:
```

```
                    32%
              filesystem:
                    /dev/sda4
              used:
                    122636848
        duration:
              8.604
        name:
              /
        result:
              True
        start_time:
              04:06:56.587517
```

If a minimum or maximum is defined as a percentage, Salt will check to see whether the disk usage is inside this range. If it is not, it will return `False`. Otherwise, it will return `True`:

```
[root@dufresne ~]# salt myminion state.single disk.status / minimum=50
maximum=90 --out nested
myminion:
    ----------
    disk_|-/_|-/_|-status:
        ----------
        __run_num__:
            0
        changes:
            ----------
        comment:
            Disk is below minimum of 50 at 32
        data:
            ----------
            1K-blocks:
                414569456
            available:
                270866960
            capacity:
                32%
            filesystem:
                /dev/sda4
            used:
                122636872
        duration:
            8.96
        name:
            /
        result:
            False
```

```
start_time:
    04:11:45.476257
```

Monitoring with web calls

The most unique of the monitoring states is probably `http.query`. Rather than checking the local system, it makes a web call and then analyzes the return from it.

There are two items that can be checked with the `http.query` state. A match pattern may be specified either as a block of plain text or as a regular expression. Here's an example:

```
http://example.com/page1.html:
   http.query:
     - match: 'This is page 1'
http://example.com/page2.html:
   http.query:
      - match: 'This is page [two|2]'
      - match_type: pcre
```

It is also possible to specify a status code. This is expected to be returned from the page. Normally, this will be `200`, but there are reasons to check for others. For instance, if a page is supposed to be missing, then it is reasonable to check for a 404 page not found error. The code for it is as follows:

```
http://example.com/not_found.html
   http.query:
      - status: 404
```

It is also possible to check for a match pattern and a status code in the same state, as shown in the following code:

```
http://example.com/jungle.html:
   http.query:
      - match: 'Welcome to the Jungle'
      - match_type: string
      - status: 200
```

Any argument that can be used with the `http.query` execution and runner modules can also be declared here, with two exceptions: the `text` and `status` arguments will always be set to `True` because these are the items that are being checked, and the `status` argument behaves differently in the `http.query` state.

In order to run a web query (which posts actual data), you would run this:

```
http://example.com/orderpizza.py:
  http.query:
    - text: success
    - status: 200
    - method: POST
    - params:
        toppings: pepperoni
        crust: pan
```

This is a good time to put in a warning about the `http.query` state. As it has no way to check whether the parameters that are given to it are read only on the target server, it is possible for a bad set of parameters to make changes to the target URL. It is entirely up to the user to ensure that the parameters given are safe.

However, it is possible to run the `http.query` state in test mode. This is another thing that is unique about this monitoring state. Normally, monitoring states do not need to check to see whether they are being run in test mode because they are not making any changes. However, the `http.query` state will allow an alternate URL to be specified, which it will use instead if it detects that it is running in test mode.

This URL is specified as `test_url`:

```
http://prod.example.com/orderpizza.py:
  http.query:
    - text: success
    - status: 200
    - test_url: http://dev.example.com/orderpizza.py
    - method: POST
    - params:
        toppings: pepperoni
        crust: pan
```

Working with beacons

Beacons are a very new feature in Salt, but they've already gained quite a following. In past versions of Salt, if a third-party process needed to raise an event inside Salt, it would have to explicitly make a call to Salt to do so. Beacons overcome this by allowing events to be triggered by third-party processes without having to perform any work inside that process itself.

As you can imagine, beacons were designed for monitoring and, specifically, alerting purposes. While monitoring states are fairly passive, in which they only run when called explicitly or via the scheduler, beacons are very proactive, in which they are constantly watching for changes.

Monitoring file changes

Beacons are run on a regular basis on the target minion. When they pick up important changes, they will fire an event that describes these changes.

The first beacon that was ever added was for the `inotify` system. This is built in the Linux kernel, starting with version 2.6.13. The `inotify` system can perform an operation when certain activity happens to a file or directory. For instance, some organizations use it to track changes to files across a set of directories and then use these change notifications to perform incremental backups.

To use this beacon, the `python-pyinotify` package must be installed on the target minion. Once it is installed, let's go ahead and watch a file called `services` in the `/tmp/` directory. Add this block to the minion configuration:

```
beacons:
  inotify:
    /tmp/services:
      mask:
        - modify
        - delete_self
```

This will watch for `/tmp/services` to be modified or deleted. This file doesn't exist yet, but that's okay. We can still set up notifications on it. Go ahead and restart the minion, and then start up the event listener on the master. Run the following command to put the file in place:

```
# cp /etc/services /tmp
```

You won't see any events just yet because `inotify` does not track the creation of a single file that is being monitored. It can track the creation of a file in a directory that is being watched, but let's stay focused on just one file at a time.

If you issue the preceding command again, it will register a change in `inotify`:

```
# cp /etc/services /tmp
```

Go ahead and look at the event listener. You should see an event that looks similar to the following code:

```
Event fired at Sat Jun 13 23:02:57 2015
*************************
Tag: salt/beacon/myminion/inotify//tmp/services
Data:
{'_stamp': '2015-06-14T05:02:57.257879',
 'data': {'change': 'IN_MODIFY', 'id': 'myminion', 'path':
'/tmp/services'},
 'tag': 'salt/beacon/myminion/inotify//tmp/services'}
```

You can see a namespacing in the tag: beacon tags start with `salt/beacon/`, followed by the minion ID, then the name of the beacon module, and the item that is being watched.

Go ahead and delete the file with the following code:

```
# rm /tmp/services
```

Then, look at the following event listener:

```
Event fired at Sat Jun 13 23:09:45 2015
*************************
Tag: salt/beacon/myminion/inotify//tmp/services
Data:
{'_stamp': '2015-06-14T05:09:45.257790',
 'data': {'change': 'IN_DELETE_SELF',
          'id': 'myminion',
          'path': '/tmp/services'},
 'tag': 'salt/beacon/myminion/inotify//tmp/services'}
```

The tag hasn't changed, but the data has. In the case of this beacon, we're interested in what the change item in the data dictionary contains.

Beacon intervals

By default, beacons are run once every second. As a result, they need to be quite light, and they perform their work as quickly as possible. However, you may not want the beacons to run this often. Say you're using the load beacon to keep an eye on the load average for a system. You've decided that you don't need a check every second, but that every 30 seconds is reasonable.

You can change the beacon interval with the `interval` argument. For our example, you can configure the load beacon with the following code:

```
beacons:
  load:
    1m:
      - 0.0
      - 2.0
    - interval: 30
```

This beacon will fire an event if the 1-minute load average ever drops below zero or goes above `2.0`.

Setting up alerts

Now that you've seen various ways to monitor minions, let's go ahead and set up some alerts.

Alerting in state files

In `Chapter 5`, *Managing Tasks Asynchronously*, we discussed how to use the reactor system to file incidents in the `PagerDuty` service in response to events. Our example also made use of the `disk.status` monitoring state.

 Keep in mind that any state inside an SLS file can raise an alert; monitoring states are not alone here.

Alerting from beacons

As beacons are designed to do nothing more than send an event when a certain threshold is reached, they are perfect for alerting purposes! Let's go ahead and set up a couple of examples.

Watching file changes

Let's go back to `inotify` for a moment. Say that you're using the `/etc/hosts` file to manage local DNS lookups. You may have some software that manages this file for you, perhaps automatically adding entries as necessary; you want to be notified via e-mail when this happens.

First off, the minion needs to be properly configured to send e-mails. The minion ID in this example is called `smtpminion`. Add the appropriate values to your minion configuration:

```
my-smtp-login:
  smtp.server: smtp.example.com
  smtp.tls: True
  smtp.sender: larry@example.com
  smtp.username: larry
  smtp.password: 123pass
```

Then, add a beacon to keep an eye on this file:

```
beacons:
  inotify:
    /etc/hosts:
      mask:
        - modify
```

Go ahead and restart the `salt-minion` process. Then, we'll need to set up a reactor on the master. Go ahead and add the reactor mapping with the following code:

```
reactor:
  - salt/beacon/dufresne/inotify/etc/hosts:
    - /srv/reactor/hosts_changes.sls
```

Finally, create the `/srv/reactor/hosts_changes.sls` file with the following content:

```
hosts_changed:
  cmd.smtp.send_msg:
    - tgt: smtpminion
    - kwarg:
        recipient: larry@example.com
        message: Hosts File Changed on {{data['id']}}
        subject: Hosts File Changed on {{data['id']}}
        profile: my-smtp-login
```

Restart the `salt-master` process. Go ahead and add an entry to your `/etc/hosts` file on this minion, and check your e-mail.

Monitoring bad logins

Most Linux users don't keep a watchful eye on the `btmp` file, which is unfortunate. This file keeps track of failed login attempts on the system. On a public-facing system, this can mean serious trouble. However, in recent years, it has become common practice for attackers to make several dozen, or even several hundred, attempts to log in to a system at once. Using SMTP for alerts is probably a bad idea because your inbox may get flooded from a single attack run.

So, let's go ahead and set up our alert system to send a webhook that reports on bad logins instead.

If you were to fire up the event listener and then attempt a bad login to the system, you would see something similar to the following code:

```
Event fired at Sun Jun 14 00:46:46 2015
*************************
Tag: salt/beacon/dufresne/btmp/
Data:
{'_stamp': '2015-06-14T06:46:46.609763',
 'data': {'PID': 1492058112,
          'addr': -971811459,
          'exit_status': 0,
          'hostname': '',
          'id': 'dufresne',
          'inittab': '10',
          'line': 'pts/10',
          'session': 0,
          'time': 592838656,
          'type': 6,
          'user': 'curly'},
 'tag': 'salt/beacon/myminion/btmp/'}
```

Now that we know what the event looks like, we can set up an alert for it. First, we'll set up the beacon in the minion configuration:

```
beacons:
  btmp: {}
```

The configuration for this beacon is very simple; as it requires no arguments to tell it to look at the `btmp` file, an empty configuration block is used. Go ahead and restart the `salt-minion` process.

Then, we will set up the reactor mapping on the master, as follows:

```
reactor:
  - salt/beacon/dufresne/btmp/
    - /srv/reactor/btmp.sls
```

Finally, we will create `/srv/reactor/btmp.sls` with the following content:

```
btmp_alert:
  runner.http.query:
    - kwarg:
      url: 'http://example.com/alerts.py'
      method: POST
      params:
        id: {{data['id']}}
        user: {{data['user']}}
```

Using aggregate data with Thorium

Because Thorium can store data in its register, you can keep track of a certain amount of aggregate data and perform operations based on it. Let's take a look at a classic example: load average. We'll use the `load` beacon to keep track of load on a minion and fire events when it falls outside the bounds configured for it. Then we'll have Thorium perform calculations and react when another threshold is reached.

First, we need to set up the `load` beacon. Let's go ahead and use the configuration that we looked at earlier in the chapter, with one addition. Add the following configuration to your `minion` file:

```
beacons:
  load:
    - 1m:
      - 0.0
      - 2.0
    - interval: 30
    - onchangeonly: True
```

Setting `onchangeonly` to `True` will tell the beacon not to fire any events unless the thresholds that we have configured have been passed. This will cut down on the amount of traffic that is sent to the master.

Then we'll set up a Thorium SLS file to take a look at those beacons as they come in. Go ahead and create `/srv/thorium/load.sls` with the following content:

```
loadavg:
  reg:
    - list
    - add: 1m
    - match: 'salt/beacon/*/load/'
    - prune: 10
  file:
    - save
```

This will store 1-minute load averages in a register called `loadavg`. Because this register uses a list, we can tell Thorium to keep it pruned to only save the last 10 entries. As before, `file.save` is only there so that we can watch what's happening.

This takes care of populating the register, but now we need to do something with it. There is a Thorium module called `calc` that can perform statistical calculations on a list of data in a register. It supports the following functions:

- `add`: Add the last *x* values together
- `mul`: Multiply the last *x* values together
- `mean`: Calculate the mean of the last *x* values
- `median`: Calculate the median of the last *x* values
- `median_low`: Calculate the low median of the last *x* values
- `median_high`: Calculate the high median of the last *x* values
- `median_grouped`: Calculate the grouped median of the last *x* values
- `mode`: Calculate the mode of the last *x* values

For now, we'll just look at the mean (or average) of the last 5 values in the register:

```
average:
  calc.mean:
    - name: loadavg
    - num: 5
    - maximum: 5
    - ref: 1m
```

The `num` value is the number of entries to look at, and `maximum` is the maximum of the mean. Because the `load` beacon can return `1m`, `5m`, and `15m`, we have directed Thorium to reference (`ref`) only the `1m` value.

This will perform the calculations that we need, but we still need to actually do something when the `mean` exceeds the threshold we have set. If you specify a `minimum` or `maximum` value for any of the `calc` functions and that value is exceeded, then the code block will return `False`.

Because Thorium supports state file logic, we can add one more code block to perform an operation when that threshold is exceeded:

```
alert:
  runner.cmd:
    - fun: pagerduty.create_event
    - onfail_in:
      - calc: average
    - kwargs:
      description: High Load Average
      details: Salt Has Detected High Load Average
      service_key: 01234567890ABCDEF0123456789abcde
      profile: my-pagerduty-account
```

You may recall our discussion of PagerDuty from Chapter 5, *Managing Tasks Asynchronously*. The call really isn't much different inside of Thorium: we use `runner.cmd` and `fun: pagerduty.create_event` instead of `runner.pagerduty.create_event`, and we specify `kwargs` instead of `kwarg`.

Of course, if you're going to use PagerDuty, make sure to configure it in your master file:

```
my-pagerduty-account:
  pagerduty.subdomain: mysubdomain
  pagerduty.api_key: 1234567890ABCDEF1234
```

Summary

Establishing a historical baseline of data is critical to monitoring systems, and Salt has been using returners to do this since the beginning. You can also use monitoring states and beacons to collect data and perform actions based on it.

Salt has a very powerful set of tools to monitor systems in order to establish a baseline of information and raise alerts when something goes awry.

Thorium can be used to collect aggregate data and perform operations based on statistical analysis of it.

In the next chapter, we'll take a look at some of the best and worst practices in Salt.

12
Exploring Best Practices

Like all tools, Salt is easier to use and gives more consistent results when you use it right. Referring to a piece of equipment in his kitchen, a chef once told me, "I've seen a number of really ingenious ways to use this tool wrong". This chapter aims to give guidance to help you use Salt in the best way possible. We'll cover the following topics:

- Future-proofing your infrastructure
- Establishing a proper directory structure
- Creating efficient SLS files
- Using intuitive naming conventions
- Using effective variables with templates

Future-proofing your infrastructure

One of the most aggravating things about technology is its ability to change before you can adapt, and in some cases, before you even finish implementing what was considered new when you started. Future-proofing refers to planning things out as far in advance as possible. It also refers to working in a way that minimizes the amount of work that will have to be done in the future to make the current technology still work.

One of the most famous examples of code that was not future-proofed was the Year 2000 or the Y2K bug. For those who missed it, here's what happened. Developers needed to store dates. It was already common usage outside computers to store two-digit years. For example, January 1, 1970 may be stored as 1/1/70. Using a two-digit year saved space, which was at a premium at the time.

Unfortunately, far more of the code that used this strategy survived into the future than was expected. Even worse, even some code written in the 1990s was still designed to store two-digit years instead of four-digit years.

It would have been far better to store four-digit years in the first place. In fact, a date stored as YYYYMMDD (including zero-padded two-digit months and days, such as 01) can be considered future-proof for a very long time; it has the added bonus of being easier to sort chronologically. Storing timestamps in a 24-hour mode (13:00 instead of 1:00 PM) is a similar strategy.

We will come back to future-proofing regularly in this chapter. It's something that should always be in the back of your mind when you work on any technology.

Setting up your directories

A good directory structure is important in any platform, and Salt is no different. The default placement of directories inside Salt was very carefully considered in order to maintain the best balance between the **Filesystem Hierarchy Standard (FHS)**, **Linux Standard Base (LSB)**, and various nuances between different Linux distributions.

As a user, you have a number of directories to contend with yourself, especially when planning both your state files and your pillar files. There's no official standard inside these directories, but there are some things that you can do to keep your directory trees in good order.

Standard directory locations

Most Linux distributions place files directly in their appropriate directories. Configuration files and directories live in /etc/ files, whose content is variable (logs, caches, and so on) and belong directly in /var/, and site-specific files that belong to a network server often go in /srv/ (although this can change depending on your environment). However, many Unix and some Linux distributions prefer to extend this structure by adding a local/ directory. If you are currently using one of these operating systems, you're probably already used to its conventions.

One of the design decisions behind Salt was to use as few directories as possible. It's not reasonable to force users to look all over their system for files, and Salt strives to be reasonable. Again, some of these locations will differ depending on your platform, but the locations that Salt normally uses are:

- `/usr/bin/` : This specifies executables
- `/usr/lib/python<version>/site-packages/salt/`: This denotes the bulk of Salt code
- `/etc/salt/`: This specifies the configuration and key files
- `/var/log/salt/`: This denotes log files
- `/var/cache/salt/`: This specifies the cache data
- `/var/run/salt/`: This denotes socket files
- `/srv/salt/`: This specifies state files
- `/srv/pillar/`: This specifies pillar files
- `/srv/reactor/`: This denotes reactor files

Most of these directories will never even be seen by the average user. They keep themselves in check when necessary and require no maintenance or modifications by most administrators.

The files in the `/srv/` directories are what most Salt users will look at and modify on a regular basis. It is possible to change any one of these directories both in and out of the `/srv/` directories, but resist the temptation. Users are used to finding these files here. Also, moving to a nonstandard location adds an unnecessary layer of confusion to new hires and consultants working with you.

.sls versus init.sls

Both the `/srv/salt/` and `/srv/pillar/` directories may include a `top.sls` file, any number of other SLS files, directories that contain an `init.sls` file, and optionally, other SLS files and directories. Both of these files will refer to a state called `Apache`:

- `/srv/salt/apache.sls`
- `/srv/salt/apache/init.sls`

While it is perfectly acceptable to use either, consider what may happen further down the road. Apache is the sort of service that doesn't just get installed and started; chances are you will be modifying at least one configuration file. Therefore, it makes more sense to create a directory called `apache/` with its own `init.sls` file and keep Apache-related files in there.

But what about other services? NTP is often the sort of thing that comes with perfectly good configuration out of the box. It does not often need modification. However, it can be modified, and the more mature your infrastructure becomes, the more likely it is that you will need to customize something.

When that time comes, changing `ntp.sls` to `ntp/init.sls` may only take a couple of extra steps. However, these are steps that can be saved up front. Also, certain other procedures in your organization may necessitate even more work. For instance, do you have other software, such as backup or security solutions, which is expecting files to be in a specific place? Skip `<module>.sls` and maintain a policy of segregating states and pillars into their own directories up front.

Shallow versus deep

A number of different organization mindsets can be found in the modern world of system administration. Some people like to be very specific when they organize data, creating kingdoms, classes, and phylums, as if they were keeping track of plant and animal species.

For example, the three most popular text editors in the Linux world are arguably vim, emacs, and nano. Two popular graphics editors in the open source world are GIMP and Inkscape. When you manage an infrastructure that includes all of these programs, it may be tempting to start classifying like a scientist, but this can quickly get out of hand.

Take a look at this directory structure:

```
/srv/salt/
├── editors
│   ├── graphics
│   │   ├── gimp
│   │   │   └── init.sls
│   │   └── inkscape
│   │       └── init.sls
│   └── text
│       ├── emacs
│       │   └── init.sls
│       ├── nano
│       │   └── init.sls
│       └── vim
│           └── init.sls
└── top.sls
```

This is somewhat of a deep directory structure. This kind of structure may be aesthetically pleasing to the obsessively organized, but it adds extra complexity for others to have to deal with. Finding in which directories files live in takes extra steps, whereas the classification of some software can be ambiguous. Did the original maintainer put `vim` in `core_tools/` or `dev_tools/`?

Let's take a look at a different directory structure:

```
/srv/salt/
├── emacs
│   └── init.sls
├── gimp
│   └── init.sls
├── inkscape
│   └── init.sls
├── nano
│   └── init.sls
├── top.sls
└── vim
    └── init.sls
```

This is a more shallow directory structure. It's not so shallow that we would resort to `vim.sls`, `emacs.sls`, and so on, but it is shallow enough that states can easily be found just by looking in the `/srv/salt/` directory.

Subdividing further

Descending further into these directories, you will find a number of different techniques to organize files specific to one package. Some prefer to use a `files/` directory, while others just dump all the files for an SLS in one directory.

In most cases, putting all of your files in one directory will be the easiest to work with. The shallow structure will make them easy to find and modify.

However, if a full directory structure is to be copied to a minion, it makes absolutely no sense to remain completely shallow. Move those files to their own directory and use the `file.recurse` state to provision them on the minion. The shallow structure is only a guideline; it is up to you to decide what makes the most sense for your situation.

The SLS efficiency

When building an SLS tree, the directory structure is only part of the equation. There are a number of strategies that can be employed in the SLS files, which will increase their ease of use and maintainability.

Includes and extends

Like a number of modern languages and file formats, SLS files were designed to take advantage of code reuse. Rather than creating large, monolithic files, states can be broken down into smaller files, which can be combined together across multiple environments.

Consider the following partial SLS file:

```
iptables:
  service:
    - dead
httpd:
  pkg:
    - installed
  service:
    - running
/opt/codebase:
  file.recurse:
    - source: salt://codebase/files
```

Obviously, a production version of this would be far longer, but this short version fits our needs.

There are three distinct components of this SLS: the firewall, the web server, and the code base. There is an implied order here: the web server can't serve pages if the firewall is blocking it, and the code base is useless without the web server to connect it to users.

The first problem with this SLS is that each component should be broken down into individual files. This state tree is likely to grow, and other components may be added, which takes advantage of the firewall configuration or the web server.

The second problem is that managing the firewall by flat out disabling it is neither extensible nor future-proof. However, we'll talk about that in a moment.

Using includes

Let's go ahead and break this SLS into three separate files:

```
# cat /srv/salt/firewall/init.sls
iptables:
  service:
    - dead
# cat /srv/salt/webserver/init.sls
httpd:
  pkg:
    - installed
  service:
    - running
# cat /srv/salt/codebase/init.sls
include
  - firewall
  - httpd
/opt/codebase:
  file.recurse:
    - source: salt://codebase/files
```

See the names that we have used for our SLS files. It may be natural for Linux users to refer to the firewall configuration as `iptables`, but it's not future-proof. A number of users have found themselves in situations where they suddenly need to support new platforms that they did not originally plan for. Mergers or partnerships between companies and directives from upper levels of management may dictate the use of other firewalls, such as the `pf` firewall program in BSD or the Windows firewall system. Referring to this SLS as firewall will help simplify these changes when necessary.

The same goes for the web server, which is currently set to use httpd: the package and service name for Apache on certain Linux platforms. But what happens if the infrastructure switches from a Red Hat-based platform to one based on Debian? Or if a change is made from Apache to Nginx?

In such cases, using more generic names will simplify further changes to the infrastructure. Detailed configuration is still possible of course, but it can be localized to the individual SLS files that it pertains to, instead of affecting the set of files as a whole.

You may also have noticed that the code base SLS file includes the firewall and the web server SLS files. Why not have the web server include the firewall and the code base only include the web server? To answer this, let's expand our code base SLS file:

```
# cat /srv/salt/codebase/init.sls
include
  - firewall
  - httpd
installed_codebase:
  file.recurse:
    - source: salt://codebase/files
    - name: /opt/codebase
codebase-web-config:
  file.managed:
    - source: salt://codebase/apache.conf
    - name: /etc/httpd/conf.d/codebase.conf
```

Remember that other components may be added later, which make use of the web server, but which include their own configuration files that are specific to that web server.

In this case, it's okay that we put Apache in the name of the configuration file. In fact, it's preferable so that we know that we're not dealing with an Nginx configuration file. We've referred to the block of code that handles the web server configuration generically so that if we need to change to Nginx later, we only need to change it inside this block, and not inside the references to this block.

Speaking of generic names, we've also changed the state that handles the code base itself to have a more generic name; just in case /opt/codebase/ is changed at a later point to /srv/codebase/ for example.

Using extends

There's a little more work that we can do in the code base SLS file. Our current example assumes that no changes need to be made to the default Apache configuration file; the file that appears in the conf.d/ directory should be enough.

However, this may not in fact be the case. In fact, Apache is historically handled very differently across various platforms. While Red Hat's Apache automatically includes /etc/httpd/conf.d/*.conf by default, Arch Linux does not; the httpd.conf file in that platform does not include a number of the conf files that ship with it by default. It will need to be updated. Also, with Debian-based Apache installations, the entire directory structure is different.

We will go ahead and make changes to the SLS files for both the webserver and the codebase:

```
# cat /srv/salt/webserver/init.sls
httpd:
  pkg:
    - installed
  service:
    - running
  file.managed:
    - source: salt://webserver/httpd.conf
    - name: /etc/httpd/conf/httpd.conf
# cat /srv/salt/codebase/init.sls
include
  - firewall
  - httpd
extend:
  httpd:
    file:
      - source: salt://codebase/httpd.conf
installed_codebase:
  file.recurse:
    - source: salt://codebase/files
    - name: /opt/codebase
codebase-web-config:
  file.managed:
    - source: salt://codebase/codebase-apache-vhost.conf
    - name: /etc/httpd/conf.d/codebase.conf
```

We've added a generic configuration file to the web server configuration, which will automatically be included along with all the other Apache code blocks in the web server SLS file. However, we are then modifying the source of this file so that it points to a specific httpd.conf file in the codebase directory.

Using `httpd.conf` as the filename makes more sense because it's the upstream name for that file. It is also the name that is used on pretty much every non-Debian distribution.

However, having both an `httpd.conf` and an `apache.conf` file in the same directory can be confusing. The `apache.conf` file is likely to contain little more than a `<VirtualHost>` directive that is specific to the codebase. We can see now that while `Apache` should probably still be in the filename, it would have been more future-proof to give more information in the filename on the server. Fortunately, as we've already used generic names for the block that controls this file, we only need to make two changes: one to the SLS file and one to rename the file itself.

Using templates to simplify SLS files

Using the built-in `include` and `extend` blocks is helpful to tie files together, but it doesn't help much in the files. This is where templates can really shine. We can take advantage of them to shorten some code blocks or decide whether or not the state compiler will actually see them in the first place.

Working with loops

There are times when using a loop inside a template can seem helpful. For instance, managing a group of users, all of which have identical settings and permissions:

```
{% for user in ('larry', 'curly', 'moe') %}
{{ user }}:
  user.present
{% endfor %}
```

This Jinja code block will effectively create the following SLS to be sent through the state compiler:

```
larry:
  user.present
curly:
  user.present
moe:
  user.present
```

However, while using template loops can save a lot of time and tedium in some places, there are other places where it's just not appropriate. For instance, take the following SLS snippet to install CloudStack:

```
{% for pkg in ('cloudstack-agent', 'cloudstack-management') %}
{{ pkg }}:
  pkg.installed
{% endfor %}
```

It may look like a quick way to install packages without creating a single block per package, but Salt already has its own ways to handle this. As each package (presumably) has identical settings, we can create a single block to include them all:

```
cloudstack-pkgs:
  pkg.installed:
    - names:
      - cloudstack-agent
      - cloudstack-management
```

However, the `pkg` state is special because it supports the state aggregation. With either of the preceding code blocks, the minion's package manager will be called once per declaration. With a large list of packages, this can quickly grow to be much too long of a list.

Using `pkgs` instead of `names` will cause Salt to aggregate these package names together and call the minion's package manager only once to deal with all the declared packages.

The user state doesn't support this kind of aggregation, but it does support using the `names` argument. The following code is a much simpler version of the preceding SLS for users:

```
my-users:
  user.present:
    - names:
      - larry
      - curly
      - moe
```

It may be starting to look like loops have no place inside the SLS files. That's not true. While the names and pkgs arguments alleviate the need for loops inside a single state, it may be helpful to use loops to handle repetitive code across multiple states. Let's modify our user SLS to include a sandbox for each user:

```
{% for user in ('larry', 'curly', 'moe') %}
{{ user }}:
  user.present
/srv/sandbox/{{ user }}:
  file.directory:
    - require:
      - user: {{ user }}
{% endfor %}
```

This block goes beyond just managing users. It creates a directory for each user, but not until making sure that the user exists first.

There is no functional difference between using names and using a loop to add users; unlike with packages, the useradd command will be called once per user. However, without using a template, there is no way to create the kind of dependency between the two states that we have used before.

Decisions, decisions

There are times when we need our SLS files to make decisions based on certain aspects of the minion. In the programming terminology, this is often called *branching*.

Let's go back to our code base example. At the moment, we are just killing the firewall in order to open up the web port or ports that we need. However, this is sloppy at best. It is far better to maintain a firewall with all the ports closed, except for the ones that are needed.

We'll assume for now that we're working with Red Hat-based minions, which store their firewall configuration in the /etc/sysconfig/iptables file. Rather than shutting down the firewall, we'll take a look at the role of the minion, as declared in a grain, and lay down the appropriate file:

```
# cat /etc/salt/grains
role: webserver
# cat /srv/salt/firewall/init.sls
firewall-configuration:
  file.managed:
{% if grains['role'] == 'webserver' %}
    - source: salt://firewall/webserver-iptables
{% else %}
```

```
    - source: salt://firewall/webserver-default
{% endif %}
    - name: /etc/sysconfig/iptables
```

Looking at this example, you may be considering that an `if`/`endif` block is perhaps unnecessary; after all, since the value of the `role` grain is also used in the filename, we could perhaps just refer to the variable name there instead:

```
# cat /srv/salt/firewall/init.sls
firewall-configuration:
  file.managed:
    - source: salt://firewall/{{ grains['role'] }}-iptables
    - name: /etc/sysconfig/iptables
```

However, this is not a future-proof solution. What happens if a minion does not have an associated firewall file on the server? Also, what if the `role` grain has not been defined yet for this minion? Either will cause errors to appear in the state runs on these minions.

Rather than ignoring all but those who are explicitly set up, it is better to define what we can and set defaults for everybody else:

```
# cat /srv/salt/firewall/init.sls
firewall-configuration:
  file.managed:
{% if grains.get('role') == 'webserver' %}
    - source: salt://firewall/webserver-iptables
{% else %}
    - source: salt://firewall/default-iptables
{% endif %}
    - name: /etc/sysconfig/iptables
```

We can take this one step further and ensure that this state is only executed on minions that are actually running Linux and therefore have `iptables` available:

```
# cat /srv/salt/firewall/init.sls
{% if grains['oscodename'] == 'Linux' %}
firewall-configuration:
  file.managed:
{% if grains.get('role') == 'webserver' %}
    - source: salt://firewall/webserver-iptables
{% else %}
    - source: salt://firewall/default-iptables
{% endif %}
    - name: /etc/sysconfig/iptables
{% endif %}
```

Using the built-in states

In the previous example, we manually laid down files for the `iptables` configuration. In order to see what's going on, we'll actually have to view the files directly. This also makes the files somewhat rigid.

There are a number of configuration file formats that are natively supported in Salt. When this is the case, it is often easier to manage components of those files directly in states, rather than create large, monolithic files with less visibility.

`iptables` is a great example too because like packages, the `iptables` state supports aggregation. This means that a number of components throughout the SLS tree can define their own `iptables` rules, and when a high state is run, they will all be aggregated together into a single `iptables` configuration file.

Let's switch our firewall SLS from laying down monolithic configuration files to generating the framework of a stateful set of firewall rules, as shown in the following code:

```
# cat /srv/salt/firewall/init.sls
INPUT:
  iptables.chain_present:
    - table: filter
    - family: ipv4
input_policy:
  iptables.set_policy:
    - chain: INPUT
    - policy: DROP
    - require:
      - iptables: INPUT
icmp_accept:
  iptables.insert:
    - table: filter
    - chain: INPUT
    - jump: ACCEPT
    - proto: icmp
    - position: 1
    - require:
      - iptables: INPUT
lo_accept:
  iptables.insert:
    - table: filter
    - chain: INPUT
    - jump: ACCEPT
    - if: lo
    - position: 2
    - require:
```

```
        - iptables: icmp_accept
state_tracking:
  iptables.insert:
    - table: filter
    - chain: INPUT
    - jump: ACCEPT
    - match: conntrack
    - ctstate RELATED,ESTABLISHED
    - position: 3
    - require:
      - iptables: lo_accept
default_rule:
  iptables.append:
    - table: filter
    - chain: INPUT
    - jump: REJECT
    - reject-with: icmp-proto-unreachable
    - require:
      - iptables: state_tracking
```

This is too much to handle, so let's break it down.

As `iptables` is based on chains, we start off by making sure that the chain that we need is present. The `INPUT` chain in the filter table is normally built-in, but it doesn't hurt to be explicit. The default policy for this chain is `ACCEPT`, and for our purposes, we will change it to `DROP`, meaning that if a network packet does not match any of the rules, it will simply be ignored.

Then, we will set up a series of rules that make `iptables` behave in a stateful manner, which, in this case, is not a Salt term; it refers to the ability of `iptables` to track the connection state. The rules that we have set up allow all traffic that originates from the minion's local network interface and all traffic that uses the ICMP network protocol.

The next rule checks the network packet to see whether it belongs to a connection that has already been established, or is related to a connection that has already been established. In either case, it is assumed that the connection has already been validated and no further checking is required.

The last rule tells `iptables` to reject any network traffic that has not matched any rules in the chain. With this current definition, no outside traffic will be allowed to this minion.

The first three rules need to exist in a specific order, so their position has been explicitly declared using the `iptables.insert` state. The last rule needs to appear at the end of the chain. Since `iptables.append` does just this, it's perfect here.

However, we still need to open up the firewall ports for the web server. We'll go ahead and add these rules to the code base SLS because other components in the state tree, which use the web server, may require different ports:

```
# cat /srv/salt/codebase/init.sls
include
  - firewall
  - httpd
extend:
  httpd:
    file:
      - source: salt://codebase/httpd.conf
installed_codebase:
  file.recurse:
    - source: salt://codebase/files
    - name: /opt/codebase
codebase-web-config:
  file.managed:
    - source: salt://codebase/codebase-apache-vhost.conf
    - name: /etc/httpd/conf.d/codebase.conf
port-80-firewall:
  iptables.insert:
    - table: filter
    - chain: INPUT
    - jump: ACCEPT
    - match: state
    - connstate: NEW
    - dport: 80
    - proto: tcp
    - save: True
    - position: -1
    - require:
      - iptables: default_rule
```

As before, the codebase SLS requires the firewall state. However, it now explicitly requires the last rule (the one that rejects unidentified traffic) to be run before it applies its own rule. This is because of the position that has been specified.

Salt's `iptables.insert` state allows a negative position to be declared. This is not a feature that has been built-in `iptables` itself; it's a convenience feature that Salt added for this exact use case. When a negative number is declared, Salt will start at the end of the chain and start counting backwards. The last rule is position `0` (which should be declared with `iptables.append`, not `iptables.insert`). The rule before it is position `-1`, the rule before that is `-2`, and so on.

This allows a default rule to be set at the very end of a chain and other rules to be set before it. The advantage is that users don't need to manually track all of their rules in their SLS tree and then set the final rules to explicitly happen last.

There is one more trick that the `iptables` state module has up its sleeve. Recent versions of `iptables` are able to check to see whether a rule already exists in a chain, and if so, do not try to add it again. This allows states to declare `iptables` rules, which are both stateful to `iptables` and stateful in terms of Salt.

Naming conventions

An important aspect of the SLS organization is a sensible naming structure. As we have seen, when components are named generically, it is less likely that they will need to be renamed at a later point. However, when a component is named explicitly, it is more likely that a user who is unfamiliar with the SLS tree will understand what it is trying to accomplish.

A good naming convention strives to strike a balance between the oil and water of generic versus explicit. To borrow from the food and chemistry worlds, a good naming convention is the emulsifier that binds everything in a recipe or formula together.

Generic names

Before starting out with an SLS tree, let's try to plan out as many of the primal components as possible. As an example, a modern infrastructure may reasonably include the following components:

- A load balancer
- A database server
- A web server
- A firewall
- An application code base
- An e-mail server

We will start with names that reflect these primal components before moving on to sub primal components. The code for the same is as follows:

```
/srv/salt/
├── codebase
│   └── init.sls
├── database
│   └── init.sls
├── email
│   └── init.sls
├── firewall
│   └── init.sls
├── load_balancer
│   └── init.sls
└── webserver
    └── init.sls
```

Some of these primal components may be broken down into smaller components. For instance, an organization may include both a web application server and a static content web server, as shown in the following code:

```
/srv/salt/
├── app_webserver
│   └── init.sls
├── static_webserver
│   └── init.sls
└── webserver
    └── init.sls
```

Each of the `app_webserver` and `static_webserver` SLS files will include the web server SLS and make their own additions and modifications to it. You can also make use of premade formulas on the `saltstack-formulas` repository on GitHub, as shown in the following URL: `https://github.com/saltstack-formulas/`

If this is the case, then you probably have the web server SLS, which includes one or more of these as well:

```
/tmp/salt/
├── apache-formula
│   └── init.sls
├── app_webserver
│   └── init.sls
├── static_webserver
│   └── init.sls
└── webserver
    └── init.sls
```

Explicit names

With generically named directories, it is important that the files in these directories are as explicit as possible, but not to the point of being unusable. The following filename is probably okay:

```
apache-acorn-vhost.conf
```

However, this filename is just too much:

```
apache-project_acorn_codebase-virtualhosts-non_ssl.conf
```

When naming files like this, try to be reasonably lazy. If a file is in a directory that implies its purpose, then perhaps this directory name doesn't need to appear again in the file, unless doing so would add needed clarity. However, if making a filename slightly more explicit avoids confusion down the road, then it's worth being explicit now.

Templates and variables

When we're talking about the balance between generic and explicit, we'd better talk about variable names. A good variable name will also strike this balance and become an emulsifier between the minion and the state tree.

Nested variables

Salt allows hierarchical data structures to be used in order to define variables. In a way, this allows variables to behave like directories, in which these structures may be either shallow or deep.

However, unlike directory structures, searching through deep variable structures is not necessarily as painful. When you use flat files to define a structure, it may actually be easier to read a structure that is deeply nested. Let's turn the ingredients for a chocolate chip cookie recipe into a set of Salt grains, as follows:

```
cookies:
  fats:
    - butter
  sugars:
    - granulated sugar
    - light brown sugar
  wet_ingredients:
    - eggs
    - vanilla extract
  dry_ingredients:
    - flour
    - baking soda
    - baking powder
    - salt
  garnish:
    - chocolate chips
```

Now, imagine these variables as a shallow data structure:

```
cookies_fats:
  - butter
cookies_sugars:
  - granulated sugar
  - light brown sugar
cookies_wet_ingredients:
  - eggs
  - vanilla extract
cookies_dry_ingredients:
  - flour
  - baking soda
  - baking powder
  - salt (non-iodized)
cookies_garnish:
  - chocolate chips
```

A data structure that contains even more components can quickly get out of hand and become cumbersome to declare inside multiple SLS files.

Referring to variables in templates

There are a number of ways to refer to variables in templates, in part because there are multiple ways to store variables in the first place. In a default installation of Salt, a minion may pull variables from:

- The minion configuration
- Grains
- Pillars
- The master configuration

Old-school Salt users could have stored all of their variables in grains. Early adopters of Salt could have started stored variables in grains before migrating to pillars. Also, there are a number of use cases where it is more appropriate to store a variable in either the master or minion configuration.

If you want to ensure that you are looking explicitly for a grain, it's easy enough to look in the grains dictionary in a template:

```
{{ grains['foo'] }}
```

Using grains.item, you could also make a cross call to the grains execution module in a template:

```
{{ salt['grains.item']('foo') }}
```

However, it's more reliable to use grains.get, which has the added advantage of allowing you to supply a default when necessary:

```
{{ salt['grains.get']('foo', 'bar') }}
```

The pillar data may also be called the same way:

```
{{ salt['pillar.get']('foo', 'bar') }}
```

The most versatile call to use here is `config.get`, which will look through each area where a variable may possibly be stored in this order:

1. The minion configuration
2. Grains
3. Pillars
4. The master configuration

The call, of course, looks like this:

```
{{ salt['config.get']('foo', 'bar') }}
```

It's important to note that `grains.get`, `pillar.get`, and `config.get` are the only calls that allow retrieval of a specific item in a nested dictionary. To get a list of the wet ingredients from our preceding cookie recipe, we will call:

```
{{ salt['config.get']('cookies:wet_ingredients', []) }}
```

The colon (`:`) is what delimits the layers of the nested dictionary.

Summary

It is important to consider the potential future for your infrastructure. Saving time by cutting corners can have disastrous consequences. Try to keep your directory structure simple and easy to browse. Consider how deep your code tree really needs to be, and design it accordingly.

Efficient SLS files makes for simpler and easier maintenance in the future. Using descriptive variable names will help you and others keep track of what data each variable represents.

There are two recurring themes that you will find when you explore the best practices of any project: making future-proof decisions and giving things names that are as descriptive as they need to be (no more, no less). When these practices are followed, the results will be easy to read and easy to maintain.

Following best practices is important in creating an environment that is easy to maintain. In the next chapter, we'll finish up by looking at various techniques to troubleshoot our Salt infrastructure.

13
Troubleshooting Problems

It doesn't matter what software you use, or how useful it is to you, sooner or later there will be problems. Some of these arise from a simple misunderstanding of the software, but sooner or later, there will be a problem with the software itself. In this chapter, we'll talk about some of the tools that are available to users, and discuss the following:

- Properly identifying problems
- Using Salt in debug/trace mode
- Using salt-call locally
- Dealing with YAML idiosyncrasies
- Using Salt's mailing list and issue tracker

What the…?

Things go wrong. And you don't always notice when they do, at least not at first. And when you do, your first response is likely to sound like, *"Hey, that's weird!"*

Before you can really start troubleshooting a problem, it always helps to build some context around it, so that you know where to look for the solution. It has been said that *real programmers cook popcorn on the heat of their CPU. They can tell which jobs are running based on the rate of the popping.* You don't need to get so involved as that to work around problems in Salt, but a little knowledge will go a long way.

Addressing the problem source

A common mistake in any troubleshooting situation is to address the symptoms when they occur, with little regard to what's actually causing the problem. For example, if a roof is leaking during a rainstorm, the only step that some people will take is to leave out containers under the leak to catch the water, and empty them when they get full. When the sun comes out, far too many people won't bother to venture up onto the roof, or call a roofing professional, to locate and fix the source of the leak.

When troubleshooting, addressing symptoms is usually also appropriate, but unless you're also trying to figure out what is generating the symptoms, they are likely to keep appearing. Be wary of problems that seem to fix themselves; oftentimes, they are only lying in wait to spring on you again.

Where is the trouble?

A lot of systems are somewhat easier to troubleshoot because their complexity does not extend beyond a single computer. Any networked system immediately suffers from the complexity of troubleshooting multiple machines.

In its original default operation, Salt always consisted of at least two components: the master and a minion. In the years since its introduction, this is no longer always the case. A handful of master-side operations can be performed in the absence of minions, and a number of minion-side operations can be performed without a master. In fact, several organizations don't even employ a master in their infrastructure; all activities are performed locally by the minions, orchestrated by third-party elements.

When a problem occurs in Salt, the first step is often to determine the component in which the root of that problem lies. Let's take a look at a few examples.

Master-to-minion communication

Let's say that a job is sent from the master to a minion, and the minion doesn't respond. There are at least two potential places that the problem could be occurring, starting with the master and the minion.

The first thing that many users would do is to send a very simple job to the minion and see if it responds. The most simple of jobs is a `test.ping`, which when functioning correctly, will return `True`.

If sending a `test.ping` does indeed return `True`, then we know several pieces of information already:

- The master is running
- The minion is running
- A network connection exists between the master and the minion
- The master is able to communicate with the minion
- The minion is able to communicate with the master

This implies that Salt itself, and all its basic components, are functioning properly. In fact, it strongly implies that the master itself is functioning normally, and that the problem likely resides with the minion.

Network and CPU congestion

Perhaps a `test.ping` only returns `True` intermittently. The fact that it does return `True` in the first place strongly implies that:

- There is a valid connection between the master and the minion
- Any gateways, firewalls, and switches between the master and the minion are appropriately configured

One or more of the network segments between the master and the minion may be experiencing congestion. This is even more likely if one or more network segments are across the Internet.

It is also possible that either the master or the minion, or both, are experiencing a high amount of CPU load. Checking the `uptime` command on the master will show its load average across a time lapse of 1 minute, 5 minutes, and 15 minutes. Checking `status.loadavg` on a Unix or a Linux minion will show the same kind of information.

Interpreting load average can be tricky, since it doesn't reflect the percentage of CPU use. What's more, interpreting it on a multi-processor system can be deceiving to the uninitiated, so let's take a quick moment to explain.

The system load average is the average number of processes that are either in a runnable, or uninterruptable state. A runnable process is one that is either currently using CPU cycles, or is waiting to do so. An uninterruptable process is one which is waiting for some sort of I/O access to happen (usually the disk).

On a single processor system, a load average of 1 means that the CPU on that system is busy 100% of the time. Less than 1 means that the CPU has had some idle time, and more than 1 means that one or more processes are waiting to use the CPU.

On a multi-core or multi-processor system, increment that number for each core or processor. For instance, on a 2-core system, a value of 2 means that both the CPUs are busy 100% of the time. On a 4-core system, a value of 4 means that all 4 CPUs are busy 100% of the time.

Because this load average is reported in increments of 1, 5, and 15 minutes, we have a tiny amount of historical data which can be used to tell us whether or not the system was likely to be busy when the messages were not properly seen by the master, so long as we check as quickly as possible.

Checking `status.cpuload` on a Windows minion will show a CPU load as a percentage. This is different from a load average, and should be interpreted differently. The CPU load in Windows refers to the amount of time that the processor(s) spends doing work, as opposed to the amount of time that it is idle.

For instance, on a single 2 GHz processor, a CPU load of 50% means that the processor is performing one billion cycles of work per second. As with Unix and Linux, adding in multiple cores and processors will affect this percentage, in part because switching tasks between cores and processors will add to the percentage.

Checking minion load

If a minion is only responding intermittently, it may be more reliable to log into the minion manually and troubleshoot. How you log in and check the load depends on whether you're troubleshooting a Unix, Linux, or a Windows minion.

In Linux, we'll assume that you're logging in via SSH and issuing commands via a command shell. The standard tool for checking the minion load is `top`, which shows which processes are consuming the most resources. By default, it refreshes every 2 seconds, but it can be manually refreshed by hitting the space bar. However, auto-refreshing can get in the way, and you may want a report that can be analyzed for longer than 2 seconds, or you may want to save that report. Try this command:

```
# top -b -n1
```

The -b in this command starts up top in batch mode, which will perform a certain number of iterations before exiting. The -n1 will set that iteration count to 1, meaning that a single report will be generated, and then `top` will exit.

The report will look exactly like the standard output from `top`, except that all processes will be displayed, since it doesn't have to worry about the screen real estate.

```
top - 15:25:08 up 16 days, 15 min, 25 users,   load average: 0.15, 0.40,
0.52
Tasks: 273 total,   1 running, 272 sleeping,   0 stopped,   0 zombie
%Cpu(s):  9.2 us,  7.6 sy, 24.1 ni, 58.6 id,  0.6 wa,  0.0 hi,  0.0 si,
0.0 st
GiB Mem :   15.367 total,    2.421 free,    6.789 used,    6.157 buff/cache
GiB Swap:    8.000 total,    8.000 free,    0.000 used.    6.774 avail Mem

  PID USER       PR  NI    VIRT    RES  %CPU %MEM     TIME+ S COMMAND
  368 larry      19  -1  339.3m  73.2m   6.7  0.5 145:04.32 S Xorg
  433 larry      20   0 1692.4m 488.3m   6.7  3.1 486:44.41 S chromium
  531 larry       9 -11  668.9m  15.0m   6.7  0.1  1609:12 S pulseaudio
  563 larry      20   0 3157.3m 695.4m   6.7  4.4 193:55.73 S chromium
 4846 larry      20   0 1585.1m 296.7m   6.7  1.9 361:15.15 S chromium
11791 root       20   0 1011.9m  30.7m   6.7  0.2 166:36.88 S salt-master
30205 larry      20   0  925.7m 130.9m   6.7  0.8  73:21.05 S chromium
    1 root       20   0   33.7m   4.8m   0.0  0.0   0:20.06 S systemd
    2 root       20   0    0.0m   0.0m   0.0  0.0   0:00.25 S kthreadd
    3 root       20   0    0.0m   0.0m   0.0  0.0   0:39.95 S ksoftirqd/0
    5 root        0 -20    0.0m   0.0m   0.0  0.0   0:00.00 S kworker/0:0H
    7 root       20   0    0.0m   0.0m   0.0  0.0   3:41.63 S rcu_preempt
    8 root       20   0    0.0m   0.0m   0.0  0.0   0:00.10 S rcu_sched
    9 root       20   0    0.0m   0.0m   0.0  0.0   0:00.00 S rcu_bh
   10 root       rt   0    0.0m   0.0m   0.0  0.0   0:00.72 S migration/0
...etc...
```

Because `top` performs calculations across all processes, it is able to generate percentages, as seen in the preceding code. This information can be invaluable in troubleshooting the load.

In Windows, there are similar tools for troubleshooting the CPU load, though they are graphical, and therefore do not output text reports like `top` can in Linux. The **Task Manager** can be reached by pressing the *Ctrl+Alt+Del* key sequence and clicking **Task Manager**:

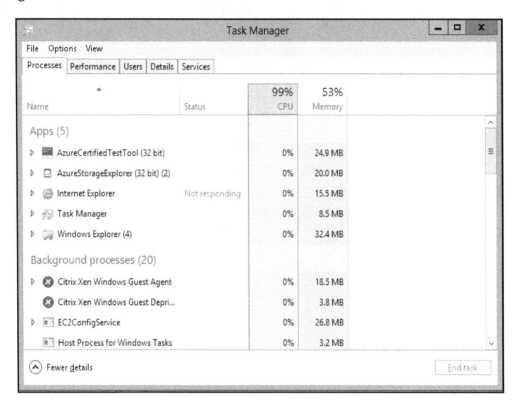

Unlike `top` in Unix and Linux, the **Task Manager** will not auto-refresh, so there's no need to generate a report for longer viewing. The **Task Manager** will show the CPU percentage, just like with `status.cpuload`. However, it will also show application percentages, like top will.

Querying the Salt job data

Some jobs take longer to complete than others. Assuming that there are no issues with network and CPU congestion, and that Salt itself is functioning properly, a `test.ping` should return immediately, with at least one minion.

With hundreds or thousands of minions, it may take a little longer to receive the return from every minion. Keep in mind that Salt is an asynchronous architecture, and that when commands are published to minions, the minion will always return when their job finishes, so long as the minion is functioning properly. The salt command does listen to the return bus for a few seconds (10 by default), but if any commands take longer than the timeout, they won't show.

The Salt job system will cache the return data as soon as it receives it, and it is still be able to receive queries later. To see this in action, run the following from the master:

```
# salt --async myminion test.sleep 60
Executed command with job ID: 20150704100203488893
# salt-run jobs.active
20150704100203488893:
    ----------
    Arguments:
        - 60
    Function:
        test.sleep
    Returned:
    Running:
        |_
          ----------
          myminion:
              18788
    StartTime:
        2015, Jul 04 10:02:03.488893
    Target:
        myminion
    Target-type:
        glob
    User:
        sudo_larry
# salt myminion saltutil.running
myminion:
    |_
      ----------
      arg:
          - 60
      fun:
          test.sleep
      jid:
          20150704100203488893
      pid:
          19094
      ret:
      tgt:
```

```
                   myminion
         tgt_type:
              glob
         user:
              sudo_larry
# salt myminion saltutil.find_job 20150704100203488893
myminion:
    ----------
    arg:
         - 60
    fun:
         test.sleep
    jid:
         20150704100203488893
    pid:
         19014
    ret:
    tgt:
         myminion
    tgt_type:
         glob
    user:
         sudo_larry
```

Once the job has finished running, you can look at the return data with:

```
# salt-un jobs.lookup_jid  20150704100203488893
myminion:
    True
```

Using debug and trace modes

Every Salt command has the ability to change the amount of information displayed to the user by changing the log level. The following log levels, and an explanation of each, are the most commonly used in Salt:

info

This is the default log level in every Salt command. It shows information that is considered helpful to any user, but not part of the return output of the actual Salt command.

warn

This is the level used when something has gone wrong, but not so horribly wrong that it causes Salt to die. Often, this level is used to inform users when they are using Salt in a way that has been deprecated. When this happens, the message will give you information on the updated usage.

error

In a case where something has gone wrong and Salt is unable to recover from it, Salt will usually exit without completing the task it is working on, and give you any information that it has.

debug/trace

These modes are normally reserved for administrators and developers to give information that is only useful when writing code or troubleshooting problems. Both modes are extremely verbose, but the trace level is the noisiest.

The debug mode may have some information that is useful to end-users, such as status codes from HTTP calls, or the name of a shell command that was executed.

The trace mode should generally be avoided, unless you are writing code. It contains information such as full HTTP responses, and the output from shell commands.

To change the log level for the information that is printed to the screen, use -l, or --log-level:

```
# salt -l debug myminion test.ping
[DEBUG   ] Reading configuration from /etc/salt/master
[DEBUG   ] Using cached minion ID from /etc/salt/minion_id:  myminion
[DEBUG   ] Missing configuration file: /root/.saltrc
[DEBUG   ] Configuration file path: /etc/salt/master
[DEBUG   ] Reading configuration from /etc/salt/master
[DEBUG   ] Using cached minion ID from /etc/salt/minion_id:  myminion
[DEBUG   ] Missing configuration file: /root/.saltrc
[DEBUG   ] MasterEvent PUB socket URI:
ipc:///var/run/salt/master/master_event_pub.ipc
[DEBUG   ] MasterEvent PULL socket URI:
ipc:///var/run/salt/master/master_event_pull.ipc
[DEBUG   ] Initializing new AsyncZeroMQReqChannel for
('/etc/salt/pki/master', 'dufresne_master', 'tcp://127.0.0.1:4506',
'clear')
```

```
[DEBUG   ] LazyLoaded local_cache.get_load
[DEBUG   ] get_iter_returns for jid 20150704104519952743 sent to
set(['myminion']) will timeout at 10:45:24.975093
[DEBUG   ] jid 20150704104519952743 return from  myminion
[DEBUG   ] LazyLoaded nested.output
myminion:
    True
[DEBUG   ] jid 20150704104519952743 found all minions set(['myminion'])
```

To change the log level for information that is sent to the log file, use `--log-file-level`.

```
# salt --log-file-level debug myminion test.ping
```

To change the path to the log file to be used, use `--log-file`:

```
# salt --log-file /tmp/salt.log myminion test.ping
```

Running services in debug mode

When troubleshooting issues between master and minion, it is often helpful to run both services in the foreground using the `debug` log level.

Log into the master, and shut down the `salt-master` service:

```
# service salt-master stop
```

Then, start it up in `debug` mode:

```
# salt-master -l debug
```

A slew of information will fly past, but eventually you will see a series of lines interpolated in the output that signify that the master has its queues up and listening:

```
[INFO    ] Worker binding to socket ipc:///var/run/salt/master/workers.ipc
[DEBUG   ] MasterEvent PUB socket URI:
ipc:///var/run/salt/master/master_event_pub.ipc
[DEBUG   ] MasterEvent PULL socket URI:
ipc:///var/run/salt/master/master_event_pull.ipc
```

Once these messages appear, the master is ready to start receiving data from its minions. Log into the problem minion and shut down the `salt-minion` service:

```
# service salt-minion stop
```

Then, start up the minion in `debug` mode:

```
# salt-minion -l debug
```

Again, a slew of information (though not much) will fly past, eventually ending with the establishment of the minion's socket files:

```
[DEBUG    ] MinionEvent PUB socket URI:
ipc:///var/run/salt/minion/minion_event_0348bb4768_pub.ipc
[DEBUG    ] MinionEvent PULL socket URI:
ipc:///var/run/salt/minion/minion_event_0348bb4768_pull.ipc
```

This signifies that the minion is now connected to the master, and is watching its queues for messages for it.

Open up another shell on the master, and issue a command to the minion:

```
# salt myminion test.ping
```

Switch over to the shell running the `salt-master` process in `debug` mode, and you will see another information dump:

```
[DEBUG    ] Sending event - data = {'_stamp': '2015-07-04T17:40:14.817522',
'minions': ['myminion']}
[DEBUG    ] Sending event - data = {'tgt_type': 'glob', 'jid':
'20150704114014817167', 'tgt': 'myminion', '_stamp':
'2015-07-04T17:40:14.817831', 'user': 'sudo_larry', 'arg': [], 'fun':
'test.ping', 'minions': ['myminion']}
[DEBUG    ] Could not LazyLoad local.save_load
[INFO     ] User sudo_larry Published command test.ping with jid
20150704114014817167
[DEBUG    ] Published command details {'tgt_type': 'glob', 'jid':
'20150704114014817167', 'tgt': 'myminion', 'ret': 'local', 'user':
'sudo_larry', 'arg': [], 'fun': 'test.ping'}
[DEBUG    ] LazyLoaded local_cache.prep_jid
[INFO     ] Got return from myminion for job 20150704114014817167
[DEBUG    ] Sending event - data = {'fun_args': [], 'jid':
'20150704114014817167', 'return': True, 'retcode': 0, 'success': True,
'cmd': '_return', '_stamp': '2015-07-04T17:40:14.893997', 'fun':
'test.ping', 'id': 'myminion'}
```

If you switch over to the window running the `salt-minion` process in `debug` mode, you will also see some information about the job:

```
[INFO     ] User sudo_larry Executing command test.ping with jid
20150704114014817167
[DEBUG    ] Command details {'tgt_type': 'glob', 'jid':
'20150704114014817167', 'tgt': 'myminion', 'ret': 'local', 'user':
'sudo_larry', 'arg': [], 'fun': 'test.ping'}
[INFO     ] Starting a new job with PID 22092
[DEBUG    ] LazyLoaded test.ping
[INFO     ] Returning information for job: 20150704114014817167
```

```
[DEBUG    ] Initializing new AsyncZeroMQReqChannel for
('/etc/salt/pki/minion', 'myminion', 'tcp://127.0.0.1:4506', 'aes')
[DEBUG    ] Initializing new SAuth for ('/etc/salt/pki/minion', 'myminion',
'tcp://127.0.0.1:4506')
[DEBUG    ] LazyLoaded local.returner
{'fun_args': [], 'jid': '20150704114014817167', 'return': True, 'retcode':
0, 'success': True, 'fun': 'test.ping', 'id': 'myminion'}
```

If a process on the minion that is related to this job has issues, then helpful information is likely to be shown here. To test this, go ahead and create an execution module on the minion with intentionally bad code:

```
# cat /usr/lib/python2.7/site-packages/salt/modules/mytest.py
def badcode():
    die()
```

Stop the `salt-minion` process with a *Ctrl+C*, and start it up again:

```
# salt-minion -l debug
```

Switch over to the master shell and run a command that executes the bad code:

```
# salt myminion mytest.badcode
```

In that shell window, you may see an error message about the bad code:

```
myminion:
    The minion function caused an exception: Traceback (most recent call
last):
      File "/usr/lib/python2.7/site-packages/salt/minion.py", line 1037, in
_thread_return
        return_data = func(*args, **kwargs)
      File "/usr/lib/python2.7/site-packages/salt/modules/mytest.py", line
2, in badcode
        die()
    NameError: global name 'die' is not defined
```

If you switch over to the `salt-minion` process, you will see the `traceback` again:

```
[INFO    ] User sudo_larry Executing command mytest.badcode with jid
20150704115054076084
[DEBUG    ] Command details {'tgt_type': 'glob', 'jid':
'20150704115054076084', 'tgt': 'myminion', 'ret': 'local', 'user':
'sudo_larry', 'arg': [], 'fun': 'mytest.badcode'}
[INFO    ] Starting a new job with PID 22669
[DEBUG    ] LazyLoaded mytest.badcode
[WARNING ] The minion function caused an exception
Traceback (most recent call last):
```

```
  File "/usr/lib/python2.7/site-packages/salt/minion.py", line 1037, in
_thread_return
    return_data = func(*args, **kwargs)
  File "/usr/lib/python2.7/site-packages/salt/modules/mytest.py", line 2,
in badcode
    die()
NameError: global name 'die' is not defined
[DEBUG   ] SaltEvent PUB socket URI:
ipc:///var/run/salt/minion/minion_event_0348bb4768_pub.ipc
[DEBUG   ] SaltEvent PULL socket URI:
ipc:///var/run/salt/minion/minion_event_0348bb4768_pull.ipc
[DEBUG   ] Sending event - data = {'message': u'The minion function caused
an exception', 'args': ('The minion function caused an exception',),
'_stamp': '2015-07-04T17:50:54.114916'}
[DEBUG   ] Handling event "_salt_error\n\n\x83\xa7message\xda\x00'The
minion function caused an exception\xa4args\x91\xda\x00'The minion function
caused an exception\xa6_stamp\xba2015-07-04T17:50:54.114916"
[DEBUG   ] Forwarding salt error event tag=_salt_error
[DEBUG   ] Initializing new AsyncZeroMQReqChannel for
('/etc/salt/pki/minion', 'myminion', 'tcp://127.0.0.1:4506', 'aes')
[DEBUG   ] Initializing new SAuth for ('/etc/salt/pki/minion', 'dufresne',
'tcp://127.0.0.1:4506')
[INFO    ] Returning information for job: 20150704115054076084
[DEBUG   ] Initializing new AsyncZeroMQReqChannel for
('/etc/salt/pki/minion', 'myminion', 'tcp://127.0.0.1:4506', 'aes')
[DEBUG   ] Initializing new SAuth for ('/etc/salt/pki/minion', 'myminion',
'tcp://127.0.0.1:4506')
[DEBUG   ] LazyLoaded local.returner
{'fun_args': [], 'jid': '20150704115054076084', 'return': 'The minion
function caused an exception: Traceback (most recent call last):\n  File
"/usr/lib/python2.7/site-packages/salt/minion.py", line 1037, in
_thread_return\n    return_data = func(*args, **kwargs)\n  File
"/usr/lib/python2.7/site-packages/salt/modules/mytest.py", line 2, in
badcode\n    die()\nNameError: global name 'die' is not defined\n',
'success': False, 'fun': 'mytest.badcode', 'id': 'myminion', 'out':
'nested'}
```

Using salt-call locally

Very often, it is helpful to issue commands directly on the minion without involving the master, or at least minimizing communication with the master. The salt-call command can be used with or without the local mode:

```
# salt-call test.ping
# salt-call --local test.ping
```

The difference between these two commands is that the first will still contact the master to ask for data such as pillar data, files from the master file server (if needed), and so on. The second will tell the minion to behave as if it has no master, and look for that information locally. If data has been set up in `file_roots` or `pillar_roots` directly on the minion, it will be used instead of contacting the master:

```
# salt-call mytest.badcode
[ERROR   ] An un-handled exception was caught by salt's global exception
handler:
NameError: global name 'die' is not defined
Traceback (most recent call last):
  File "/usr/bin/salt-call", line 11, in <module>
    salt_call()
  File "/usr/lib/python2.7/site-packages/salt/scripts.py", line 224, in
salt_call
    client.run()
  File "/usr/lib/python2.7/site-packages/salt/cli/call.py", line 50, in run
    caller.run()
  File "/usr/lib/python2.7/site-packages/salt/cli/caller.py", line 133, in
run
    ret = self.call()
  File "/usr/lib/python2.7/site-packages/salt/cli/caller.py", line 196, in
call
    ret['return'] = func(*args, **kwargs)
  File "/usr/lib/python2.7/site-packages/salt/modules/mytest.py", line 2,
in badcode
    die()
NameError: global name 'die' is not defined
```

If you issue a command using `salt-call` on the minion while running the `salt-minion` process in the foreground, you will notice that the foreground window will not respond to your command.

This is because the `salt-call` command will fire up its own, single-use `salt-minion` process, perform the requested task, and then exit. It will not interact with any other `salt-minion` processes that are running.

Working with YAML

YAML is a very easy language to work with. It is very easy for humans to read, and in most cases, it is easy for computers to parse. However, there are little things inside YAML that can cause pain to even the most experienced users.

YAML basics

Before we get into troubleshooting YAML, let's go over the basic functionality that you are likely to use in Salt.

YAML is based on a key/value model that is very common in a number of programming languages. In Perl and Ruby it's called a *hash*, in Python it's called a *dictionary* (or *dict*, for short), and in other languages it has other names. Because Salt is written in Python, we'll henceforth refer to it as a dict.

dict

A **dict** is a set of keys, each of which has a value. This value may be a number of things, including a string, a number, a list (or array), another dict, and so on. The following is a very basic dict, in YAML format:

```
larry: cheesecake
shemp: chocolate cake
moe: apple pie
```

The order of the items in a dict is not normally important, and in most cases will be ignored. Salt is different in that some of its code uses what's called an *OrderedDict*, which maintains the order of the keys and their associated values. One of the places where this is used is in the state compiler, which is designed to evaluate SLS data in the order in which it appears.

list

A list is just that: a group of items in a specific order. The order will always be preserved, at least during the phases which read in and parse the data. In YAML, items in a list are preceded by a dash:

```
- apples
- oranges
- bananas
```

In Salt, you will usually not find lists by themselves in YAML. They are usually the value of a key in a dict. However, a list item may in turn contain a dict, or even another list:

```
favorite_desserts:
  larry: cheesecake
  shemp: chocolate cake
  moe: apple pie
fruits:
  - apples
  - oranges
  - bananas
  - berries:
    - nightshade:
      - tomato
      - chile
```

There are a number of ways to organize these dicts and lists in YAML. The most common in Salt is to use whitespace, as with the preceding data structure. However, YAML also supports using braces and brackets to organize data:

```
favorite_desserts: {larry: cheesecake, shemp: chocolate cake, moe: apple
pie}
fruits: [apples, oranges, bananas, berries: {nightshade: [tomato, chile]}]
```

Items in YAML may also be quoted, which makes them easier for the compiler to parse, and in many cases, easier for humans to read:

```
'favorite_desserts': {'larry': 'cheesecake', 'shemp': 'chocolate cake',
'moe': 'apple pie'}
'fruits': ['apples', 'oranges', 'bananas', 'berries': {'nightshade':
['tomato', 'chile']}]
```

Either single quotes (') or double quotes (") may be used. It is often better to use double quotes, for two reasons. First, it avoids having to escape apostrophes which are likely to occur in sentences meant for humans. Second, if double quotes are used, and the entire structure is set up as a properly-formed dict or list, the YAML can also be read by a JSON intepreter:

```
{"favorite_desserts": {"shemp": "chocolate cake", "larry": "cheesecake",
"moe": "apple pie"}, "fruits": ["apples", "oranges", "bananas", {"berries":
[{"nightshade": ["tomato", "chile"]}]}]}
```

This is why all JSON is syntactically-correct YAML; YAML is actually a superset of JSON.

YAML idiosyncrasies

If you decide to store all your YAML data in proper JSON format, then it will always be correctly parsed by the computer. However, it will be more difficult for humans to read and modify. This is one reason why YAML is generally preferred for Salt states.

However, there are some nuances in YAML that can trip up even the most experienced user, especially if they aren't paying enough attention.

Spacing

Without braces and brackets, YAML uses whitespace to determine where blocks of text begin and end. If a dict contains another dict, then that second dict will contain spaces at the beginning of each line. Technically, a single space is enough, but Salt has standardized on two spaces. This is enough to determine where the lines start, without going overboard.

```
mydict:
  item1: value1
  item2: value2
```

If you spend a lot of time writing code, you may have your own preference for spacing. Some coders use three or four spaces, and some even use as much as eight.

When working with YAML that is meant for Salt, avoid the temptation to use anything other than two spaces. First, longer pieces of YAML start to look weird with too many spaces – spend enough time writing YAML and you'll see what I mean. Second, the Salt community at large tends to follow Salt's two-space model. Asking others for help, or hiring experienced Salt users, will become that much more painful if they have to re-adjust themselves to your style.

Technically, list items belonging to a dict do not generally need to be spaced out:

```
mylist:
  - one
  - two
  - three
```

But it is still a better practice to space them anyway. Not only is it easier for humans to read, but in some situations, it is actually easier for Salt to read as well.

Numbers

YAML is usually able to distinguish between text and numbers. However, there are some situations where it needs to be forced to do the right thing.

A very common example is file modes in Unix and Linux. For example, a directory might have a mode of 775, meaning the user and the group which own it have full (read, write, execute) permissions, while other users have only read and execute permissions.

This number is in fact a bit-mapped set of digits, stored in an octal (base-8). It can also contain more fields than just the User, Group, and Other fields that were shown previously. For instance, another bit can be added to the beginning, which specifies special attributes (SUID, SGID, and Sticky). A mode of 0775 may look identical to 775, but it will enforce that the special bits are not set.

When digits appear in YAML, it is assumed that they are base-10, and that any leading zeroes are to be stripped. If you need to explicitly set a directory's permissions to 0775, this will be a problem. In order for Salt to see the correct value, it must be converted to a string by placing it in quotes ('0775'). The following SLS data shows an example of this:

```
/srv/mydata/:
  file.directory:
    - mode: '0775'
```

Booleans

Boolean values refer to things that are True or False (or None, in Python). These data are very commonly used throughout Salt, including YAML files. If you are used to quoting all your values in your YAML, this is likely to trip you up. The following two keys do not have the same value:

```
key1: True
key2: 'True'
```

YAML will convert the second line to a string, which will not evaluate to a Boolean data type like the first one will.

JSON adds an extra element of confusion because it does not support Booleans, and is more strict when it finds unquoted data. The following line is a valid JSON:

```
{"key": "True"}
```

While this is not:

```
{"key": True}
```

Salt will generally try to do the most appropriate thing based on the information that it receives. For instance, the state compiler will attempt to properly read Booleans as Booleans, even if they are quoted in a way that is inconsistent with what is expected.

List items

A very common mistake in YAML involves spacing with list items. Because each list item resembles a bullet point, and because word processors don't require spaces after bullet points, many users often forget to add the required space after a dash for a list item. The following list is valid YAML:

```
- one
- two
- three
```

While this list will not read properly:

```
-one
-two
-three
```

Troubleshooting YAML

Writing YAML may seem easy to the experienced user, but it is very easy to trip it up. Very often, mistakes are easy to see when we are able to see what our YAML will look like once it is parsed.

An excellent tool that is available is the Online YAML Parser: http://yaml-online-parser.appspot.com/
This tool will take YAML input from the user, and translate it to either JSON, Python's *pretty print* format, or to canonical YAML. If there are errors in YAML, an error will instantly be thrown which attempts to inform where the problem lies.
However, this is of no use if you are in an environment that is restricted in its Internet access such that this site is unavailable. Fortunately, it is possible to perform a similar test from the command line on a machine with Python installed (such as any master or minion).

Create a file called `/tmp/yaml.yml` with the following content:

```
mylist:
  - one
  - two
  - three
```

Then, use the following one-line command to parse it:

```
# python -c 'import yaml; fh = open("/tmp/yaml.yml",
"r"); print(yaml.safe_load(fh.read()))'
```

Okay, so there's a fair amount of typing involved. Fortunately, if you are using a command shell (like `bash` or `zsh`) which supports command history, you can just use your Up arrow key to navigate to the command and issue it again.

Go ahead and modify `/tmp/yaml.yml`, and remove the leading spaces from one of the list items:

```
mylist:
  - one
  - two
- three
```

Then, issue the Python command again:

```
# python2 -c 'import yaml; fh = open("/tmp/yaml.yml", "r");
print(yaml.safe_load(fh.read()))'
Traceback (most recent call last):
  File "<string>", line 1, in <module>
  File "/usr/lib/python2.7/site-packages/yaml/__init__.py", line 93, in
safe_load
    return load(stream, SafeLoader)
  File "/usr/lib/python2.7/site-packages/yaml/__init__.py", line 71, in
load
    return loader.get_single_data()
  File "/usr/lib/python2.7/site-packages/yaml/constructor.py", line 37, in
get_single_data
    node = self.get_single_node()
  File "/usr/lib/python2.7/site-packages/yaml/composer.py", line 36, in
get_single_node
    document = self.compose_document()
  File "/usr/lib/python2.7/site-packages/yaml/composer.py", line 55, in
compose_document
    node = self.compose_node(None, None)
  File "/usr/lib/python2.7/site-packages/yaml/composer.py", line 84, in
compose_node
    node = self.compose_mapping_node(anchor)
```

```
  File "/usr/lib/python2.7/site-packages/yaml/composer.py", line 127, in
compose_mapping_node
    while not self.check_event(MappingEndEvent):
  File "/usr/lib/python2.7/site-packages/yaml/parser.py", line 98, in
check_event
    self.current_event = self.state()
  File "/usr/lib/python2.7/site-packages/yaml/parser.py", line 439, in
parse_block_mapping_key
    "expected <block end>, but found %r" % token.id, token.start_mark)
yaml.parser.ParserError: while parsing a block mapping
  in "<string>", line 1, column 1:
    mylist:
    ^
expected <block end>, but found '-'
  in "<string>", line 4, column 1:
    - three
    ^
```

The last couple of lines give some information about where the YAML parser thinks that the problem might be. It may not be the easiest message in the world to interpret, but it will tell you if you have poorly-formatted YAML, and where to look for the problem.

You may be interested to know that JSON content can be parsed using a similar command:

```
# python2 -c 'import json; fh = open("/tmp/json.json",
"r"); print(json.loads(fh.read()))'
```

Asking the community for help

Salt boasts of a very large community of very friendly and helpful users. When you're unable to figure out a problem by yourself, you can try turning to the community for help.

The salt-users mailing list

There is a very active mailing list for Salt users, hosted on Google Groups. A Google account is not required to participate in the mailing list itself, but it is required to participate in the web version.

The web version of the list can be found at:
https://groups.google.com/forum/#!forum/salt-users
If you do not have a Google account and you still wish to subscribe to the list, visit:
https://groups.google.com/forum/#!forum/salt-users/join

Fill out the required fields, and a confirmation e-mail will be sent to you. Click the **Join This Group** link and you will be subscribed.

 If you ever decide to unsubscribe, you can do so from
`https://groups.google.com/forum/#!forum/salt-users/unsubscribe`.

Asking questions

When you have a question about Salt usage, or you're attempting to troubleshoot a problem, the mailing list is an excellent place to ask. When posting a message, it is best to be as informative and helpful as possible with your question, without going overboard.

It will be helpful to know which Salt version you are using, both on your master and on any affected minions (if they differ). This can be obtained from Salt using the `--versions-report` flag:

```
# salt --versions-report
Salt Version:
          Salt: 2016.3.2

Dependency Versions:
        Jinja2: 2.7.3
      M2Crypto: 0.22
          Mako: Not Installed
        PyYAML: 3.11
         PyZMQ: 14.6.0
        Python: 2.7.10 (default, May 26 2015, 04:16:29)
          RAET: 0.6.3
       Tornado: 4.2
           ZMQ: 4.1.2
         ioflo: 1.2.1
       libnacl: 1.4.0
   msgpack-pure: Not Installed
 msgpack-python: 0.4.6
      pycrypto: 2.6.1

System Versions:
          dist:
       machine: x86_64
       release: 4.0.5-1-ARCH
```

If you are asking a question concerning Salt Cloud, be sure to get the `--versions-report` from it instead, as it contains additional information that is specific to Salt Cloud:

```
# salt-cloud --versions-report
Salt Version:
          Salt: 2016.3.2

Dependency Versions:
  Apache Libcloud: 1.0.0
...etc...
```

Other users will frequently ask for this information if you don't provide it, so it's best to post it with your initial question to save a little time.

When asking your question, try to explain the situation as clearly and simply as possible. It is extremely common for other users to experience the same sorts of issues, especially within the same release versions, and there's a good chance that somebody has already seen your issue, and either has a solution, or is able to collaborate to find a solution.

Do not be discouraged if you don't receive a response right away. Salt has a very international user base, and the person who is willing to help you may not live within your time zone. Weekends and holidays will also play a part in the amount of time it takes to answer your message.

If you do not hear from anybody for a few days, it is not unreasonable to ask again. Perhaps somebody saw your message and intended to respond, but got distracted. It's also possible that the person who can help you didn't see the message the first time.

I have seen a number of messages over the years from users, followed an hour or two later by an impatient, "*Is anybody there?*" e-mail. This will not expedite your message at all, and in fact may keep somebody from answering who otherwise would have. Be friendly and patient, and you will have much better luck.

The Salt issue tracker

When you encounter a problem that you believe to be an issue with Salt itself, the issue tracker is the place to go to.

 The Salt issue tracker can be found at https://github.com/saltstack/salt/issues.

The occasional user does post questions in the issue tracker, and they will receive the same sort of attention that other issues get, but the mailing list is usually the more appropriate place.

When deciding whether a problem is an issue or not, ask yourself if it may be a problem with your understanding of the usage of Salt, or if it is inconsistent with how you have been led to believe that Salt should behave. A `traceback` is almost always appropriate for the issue tracker. Some examples of tracebacks appear earlier in this chapter, and here's one again for reference:

```
Traceback (most recent call last):
  File "/usr/bin/salt-call", line 11, in <module>
    salt_call()
  File "/usr/lib/python2.7/site-packages/salt/scripts.py", line 224, in
salt_call
    client.run()
  File "/usr/lib/python2.7/site-packages/salt/cli/call.py", line 50, in run
    caller.run()
  File "/usr/lib/python2.7/site-packages/salt/cli/caller.py", line 133, in
run
    ret = self.call()
  File "/usr/lib/python2.7/site-packages/salt/cli/caller.py", line 196, in
call
    ret['return'] = func(*args, **kwargs)
  File "/usr/lib/python2.7/site-packages/salt/modules/mytest.py", line 2,
in badcode
    die()
NameError: global name 'die' is not defined
```

> Note that tracebacks do start with the word `traceback`, and show a trail of the pieces of code that were accessed before finding the line of code which actually raised the error.

Researching before posting

Before posting an issue, it is important to perform a little research first. Duplicate issues are surprisingly uncommon on Salt's issue tracker, at least in comparison to others, but they do happen. Use the search button in the issue tracker to see if your particular issue has already been reported.

GitHub allows you to apply filters to your searches, and knowing how to use them is also important. They will show up in the issue search box. The default filters are **is:open** and **is:issue**, which means that only issues that are open, and not pull requests, will be searched.

If searching with the defaults yields no suitable results, try changing **is:open** to **is:closed**, or removing it altogether. There are thousands of closed issues in GitHub, and your particular issue may already be resolved.

If you are unable to find the issue, try putting together a list of steps which can be used to reproduce the problem, as simply and quickly as possible. If you have access to virtual machines that can be used to reproduce the issue with a stock version of Salt, other users will also be much more likely to reproduce the problem.

Formatting your issues

When posting an issue to the issue tracker, it is very helpful to be able to format certain data in a way that makes it easy to read. GitHub supports a markdown language which makes it possible to format code appropriately.

 You can find documentation on their markdown format at
`https://help.github.com/articles/github-flavored-markdown/`.

By far, the most useful formatting trick involves the grave symbol (`` ` ``), also known as backticks. On modern US keyboards, this usually shares a key with the tilde (~), located in the top-left corner of the keyboard.

Placing one or more words between backticks will cause them to be formatted as code. If you have multiple lines that all need to be formatted as code, you can place them between two lines, each of which contains three backticks together (` ``` `):

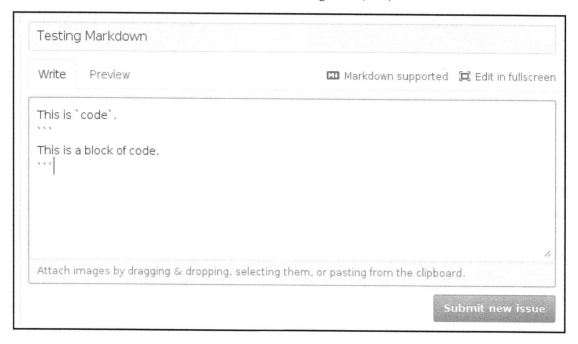

GitHub contains a **Preview** mode, which can be used to test your formatting before submitting it to ensure that it looks the way you want it to:

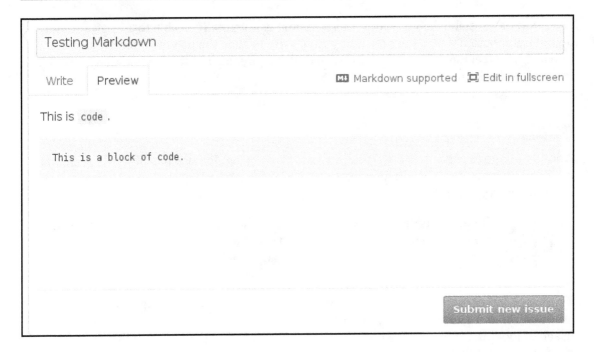

Requesting features

It may be that what you need is not an actual issue, but in fact a piece of functionality that is not yet supported in Salt. One of the most powerful aspects of Salt is the willingness of the developers to consider new ideas for adding functionality.

Before requesting a new feature, please do take a moment to think about that feature in a way that extends beyond your own reach. Are you looking for a feature that is only useful to you, or is it something that you feel that others can also benefit from? If its scope is very limited, is it possible to approach it from a more generic point of view?

Once you have established a feature in a way that is potentially usable to a large audience, do not hesitate to file an issue requesting it. Be sure to state the use case clearly, and the way in which you feel that it should be addressed. If you are unsure, it is appropriate to state the use case and ask for ideas.

#salt on IRC

Another venue to check is the *#salt* channel in (**IRC**Internet Relay Chat (IRC). This channel is hosted by a service called Freenode. If you already have an IRC client and know how to configure it, connect it to the `irc.freenode.net` server, and join the #salt chatroom.

 If you are unfamiliar with IRC, or don't have a standalone client, you can try out the chatroom using the web client at `http://webchat.freenode.net/?channels=salt`.

The `#salt` chatroom has several hundred users at any given time, though fortunately they are not all chatting at once. Many are users such as yourself, asking questions about Salt usage or looking for help with specific issues. Others are Salt enthusiasts who periodically check in to see if there is anything that they can help with.

It is useful to know about the netiquette that goes along with IRC rooms. A common phrase is, *"Don't ask to ask; just ask"*. This means that if you have a question, don't start by saying, *"Can I ask a question?"* The answer is yes. Just ask the question, and you'll be fine.

When you do ask a question, don't be alarmed or impatient if it is not answered immediately. Most users are not keeping a constant eye on the chatroom, but many do check in on a fairly regular basis.

Do not log into the chatroom, ask a question, and then log out a minute or two later. Generally, that is not enough time for your question to be appropriately answered. If you have waited several minutes and seem to be ignored, it may be that nobody who is able to help is online at the moment. Give it some time. If you are unable to find the help you need, consider using the mailing list.

Final community thoughts

Remember that whichever avenue you decide to turn to, some SaltStack employees may respond, but most of the people you talk to are members of the community, just like you. They have full-time jobs at other companies, and any time they spend helping is, essentially, volunteer time. When they help out, they do so out of the kindness of their hearts and not out of any sort of obligation.

With that in mind, please be friendly and helpful as you speak with them. There are some brilliant minds in the world who have discovered Salt, and who enjoy working with others on this tool. As you foster relationships with them, do not be surprised if some of those relationships grow into life-long friendships. And remember that if you are unfriendly and demanding, you may miss out on those opportunities.

Summary

There are a number of tools available, both inside Salt and from external sources, which can be used when troubleshooting problems. Clearly identifying the problems, tracking down their source, and asking for help when necessary are all important when trying to work through difficulties inside of Salt.

Congratulations, you made it to the end! We're very thankful that you have decided to use this book to help guide you in your journey to master SaltStack, and hope that it was everything you needed and more.

Index

load balancing, IP-based 245
multiple masters 243
round-robin DNS 245
high data 47
high states 47, 48
host-based security 219
HTTP library
about 191
http.query function, using 193, 194
http.query state, using 197
Salt-specific library 192, 193
http.query function
GET, versus POST 194, 195, 196
return data, decoding 196
using 193, 194
http.query state
using, with reactors 199, 201, 204
HTTP
considerations 224, 225

I

idempotency 43
imperative
versus declarative 45
include blocks
using 18
infrastructure
load, testing in 270
planning 295, 296
init.sls file
versus .sls file 297, 298
Internet Relay Chat (IRC)
about 344
URL 344
issue tracker, Salt
features, requesting 343, 344
issues, formatting 341, 342
posting, research 340, 341
reference link 339
issue
addressing 318
CPU congestion 319, 320
identifying 318
master-to-minion communication 318, 319
minion load, checking 320, 321, 322

network conjestion 319
Salt job data, querying 322, 323

J

Jinja 28, 29, 30, 40
JSON file 40

L

lazy loader 43
legacy deploy scripts 171
Linux Standard Base (LSB) 296
load
minionswarm.py script, using 270
testing, in infrastructure 270
loader
about 42
cloud modules 44
dynamic modules 42, 43
execution modules 43, 44
low chunk 51
low data 47
low state 51
low states 50, 51
LWP (lib-www-perl) 194

M

Mako 40
markdown format
reference link 341
master 8
master API
configuration 268
file_roots 268
pillar_roots 268
Salt keys 267
using 267
wheel reactor, using 268, 269
master configuration 32
master tops 60, 61
Mercurial (HG) 258
minion configuration 32
minions
about 8
compound 11
glob 8

www.ingramcontent.com/pod-product-compliance
Lightning Source LLC
Chambersburg PA
CBHW062048050326
40690CB00016B/3021